Avant-Gardes in Crisis

Avant-Gardes in Crisis

Art and Politics in the Long 1970s

Edited by

Jean-Thomas Tremblay

and

Andrew Strombeck

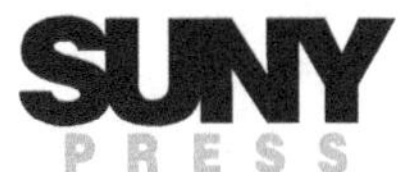

Cover image: Theresa Hak Kyung Cha: Untitled (Glass Jar), 1980, glass jar with lid containing paper with type-written text, black string; University of California, Berkeley Art Museum and Pacific Film Archive, gift of the Theresa Hak Kyung Cha Memorial Foundation, 1992.4.31

Published by State University of New York Press, Albany

Printed in the United States of America

For information, contact State University of New York Press, Albany, NY
www.sunypress.edu

Library of Congress Cataloging-in-Publication Data

Names: Tremblay, Jean-Thomas, editor. | Strombeck, Andrew, editor.
Title: Avant-gardes in crisis : art and politics in the long 1970s / Jean-Thomas Tremblay and Andrew Strombeck.
Description: Albany : State University of New York Press, [2021] | Includes bibliographical references and index.
Identifiers: ISBN 9781438485157 (hardcover : alk. paper) | ISBN 9781438485171 (ebook)
Further information is available at the Library of Congress.

10 9 8 7 6 5 4 3 2 1

Contents

II. Infrastructures

III. Commitments

Illustrations

Acknowledgments

We wish to thank the scholars and artists who participated in the seminar "The Avant-Garde and the Crisis of the Long 1970s" held at the 2019 meeting of the American Comparative Literature Association. We are grateful to the ACLA for making possible the gathering during which the idea for this book took shape. We also thank our extraordinary editor, Rebecca Colesworthy, who shepherded this project with vision and conviction. Thanks, as well, to State University of New York Press's editorial, production, and marketing teams.

Jean-Thomas Tremblay wishes to thank Jules Gill-Peterson, Dan Guadagnolo, Chase Joynt, and, especially, Sam Creely for their support and insight.

Andrew Strombeck wishes to thank Crystal Lake for, well, most things, but here, the many conversations about both editing and the avant-garde.

Introduction

Avant-Gardes in Crisis

Jean-Thomas Tremblay and Andrew Strombeck

"To encounter the history of avant-garde poetry," begins Cathy Park Hong's 2014 polemic, "is to encounter a racist tradition."[1] What Hong calls the avant-gardists' "delusion of whiteness" is a belief, propagated by artists and critics alike, that aesthetic experimentation flourishes only when it is shielded from matters of racial identity.[2] "The avant-garde has become petrified, enamored by its own past, and therefore forever insular and forever looking backwards," Hong concludes; "Fuck the avant-garde. We must hew our own path."[3] Surveying high-profile accounts of the avant-garde, from Peter Bürger's classic *Theory of the Avant-Garde* to Marjorie Perloff's canonization of white experimental poetry, we find ourselves agreeing with Hong.[4] All too often, *avant-garde* has served as shorthand for a certain dogma around experimental work—a dogma that, at its worst, disguises whiteness as post-identity. Although Hong urges us to give up the avant-garde label altogether, we would be better off refusing the constrained definitions promoted by Perloff, Bürger, and likeminded critics. Rather than bury the avant-garde as a concept, we argue that we cannot speak of it without engaging the genealogies that these critics deem disposable. In the period covered in this collection, spanning the late twentieth and early twenty-first centuries, avant-garde radicalism, we contend, is inextricable from minoritarian aesthetics and politics.

Avant-Gardes in Crisis: Art and Politics in the Long 1970s seeks to restore the historical and political contexts for the questions raised about the avant-garde since the 1970s. As such, this collection casts the avant-gardes of the late twentieth and early twenty-first centuries as responses to a crisis in the reproduction of life. This is in part a crisis of resource distribution, one that pertains to the exacerbation of economic inequality and the coeval dissolution of social services, destruction of unions, and mass incarceration. Such policies have come to be grouped under the catchall term *neoliberalism*. Although neoliberalism, as a school of thought and a set of recommendations made by a transatlantic network of economists, dates back to the 1930s, the crisis of the 1970s issued from, and in turn justified, the widespread implementation of neoliberal policies, with deleterious effects for marginalized populations.[5] This crisis in resource distribution was accompanied by a crisis in resource depletion. The oil crises of 1973 and 1979 marked bottlenecks in the supply of energy to the Western economy. The political and economic conflicts labeled "oil crises" hide a more colossal disaster: a climate crisis precipitated by such factors as an overreliance on fossil fuel. Theorists of precarization observe that the collapse of unemployment services, the rising cost of health care, the toxification of environments, and other threats to survival amount to a historical transformation whose metrics include the wearing out of populations.[6] This wearing out is uneven: in the long fallout from the 1970s, vitality is managed along axes of race, gender, sexual orientation, class, citizenship status, disability, and age. Together, the contributors to this collection argue that an avant-garde concept attuned to patterns of resource concentration and attrition clarifies the contemporary interplay between art and politics.

In framing the long 1970s as a crisis in the reproduction of life, we combine the codes of political economy, specifically its Marxist tradition, with those of biopolitics, generally attributed to Michel Foucault. These critical idioms have not always cohabited harmoniously. Recent Marxist theories of aesthetics pin the evacuation of labor from critical debates on, among other factors, the widespread adoption of biopolitics as a paradigm for understanding the subjugation of bodies and control of populations.[7] According to this logic, discourses of biopolitics, in trading labor for "biopower" and "human capital" as categories of analysis, have been complicit with "the rise of neoliberalism as an antilabor discourse."[8] While we devote much attention to artistic labor, we maintain that questions of political economy are not incompatible with questions of biopolitics, especially when the latter have to do with a management of resources that invigorates privileged populations and exhausts marginalized ones. As Melinda Cooper has demonstrated, the political-economic crisis of the 1970s amplified conservative ideologies and practices of exclusion and exploitation that both preceded and exceeded it.[9] Approaching the crisis of the long 1970s on political-economic *and* biopolitical terms allows us to chart with specificity the conditions in which minoritarian artists have labored.

The term *long 1970s* has been used to designate a variety of economic and political transformations, both global and domestic. For Poul Villaume, Rasmus Mariager, and Helle Porsdam, the long 1970s encompass a series of shifts in the world order that foreshadowed the end of the Cold War, from the first international economic crisis since World War II, to the liberalization of capitalist markets, to United States–Soviet nuclear parity, to the East–West détente process.[10] The US historian Judith Stein argues that in the 1970s, the Age of Compression, driven by the assumption that capital and labor should prosper together, gave way to the Age of Inequality, driven by an ethics claiming that the promotion of capital would eventually benefit labor.[11] In *Avant-Gardes in Crisis*, we use the term *long 1970s* to suggest, as Jefferson Cowie has done before us, that "within the gloomy seventies we can find the roots of our own time."[12] We, in the twenty-first century, are still dealing with the unfinished business of the 1970s. Art is still grappling with the economic and political aftershocks of that "pivotal decade."[13] Throughout a collection whose archive spans the 1960s to the 2010s, the seventies perform a metonymic function. The decade stands in for the historical process through which minoritarian art has become an index of, and a tactic or strategy for moving through, an accelerated crisis in the reproduction of life.

Hong was not the first to pronounce the avant-garde dead. As Paul Mann demonstrates in *The Theory-Death of the Avant-Garde*, declaring the avant-garde dead is endemic to avant-garde criticism in the long 1970s; Bürger himself, as we will see, has made a similar argument. From its origins, the avant-garde was bound to notions of progress.[14] The 1970s mark a moment when the very notion of historical progression is thrown into disarray as the economy stagnates and resource extraction reaches its limits.[15] In the 1970s, it is not just one form or another of the old order that refuses to hold. Instead, the entire system undergirding oppositions between new and old orders is no longer operative. The longer this crisis unfolds, the more obsolete appears Bürger's version of avant-garde radicalism, inherited from early twentieth-century movements like surrealism, constructivism, and futurism. Everything ends in the 1970s: the institutions against which Bürger's avant-garde struggled and, more importantly, the material conditions under which such oppositions could register as historically significant.

From our contemporary standpoint, the avant-garde is a problem of the 1970s. Art criticism devoted to avant-garde anti-institutionality proliferated in that decade; meanwhile, the institutional grounds of art and criticism were dramatically shifting. Yet, debates about the avant-garde have seldom considered how the larger crisis initiated in the 1970s enabled, forced, constrained, or provided a framework for experimentation in the literary, visual, and performed arts. The economic shocks of the 1970s and concurrent attacks on the welfare state constricted the institutions of artistic production and circulation. As Leigh Claire La Berge explains, labor's declining share of social wealth has been felt acutely in the arts. While schemes of professionalization like the MFA have enabled artists to conceive of themselves as individuals with artistic labor to sell, this labor has been "decommodified," meaning that it is less and less compensated by a wage.[16] It is also the case, however, that the economic shocks of the 1970s ignited new possibilities for aesthetic production, particularly as cheap rents provided an informal supplement to artists' income and as rising austerity provoked vibrant debates among activist-inclined artists like the Nuyorican poets. Paradoxically, then, crisis imperils artists but prompts new avant-gardes. "A crisis," Mike Sell notes, "is an imminent movement that marks, after the requisite unsettling and reconfiguring of social institutions, language, aesthetics, and so forth, the birth of new criteria."[17] No recent decade is more synonymous with crisis than the 1970s. After fifty or so years of unsettling, we search here for new criteria.

Our search takes us not only to the gallery, museum, and classroom but to a variety of public and private sites where artists have reacted to crisis by improvising new parameters for living and working. Within those sites, we find, in Mann's words, "earthworks that do not trail lifelines to the gallery, clandestine associations of writers, correspondence networks that conceal themselves from the economy at all costs."[18] Following Mann's lead, John Roberts and Gregory Sholette point to the existence of a vast realm of aesthetic production in the shadow of the official institutions of the academy and the artworld. Roberts calls this realm a "second economy."[19] Borrowing a term from physics, Sholette calls it "dark matter": a space for artists who reject artworld demands of visibility or have no choice but to be invisible.[20] Roberts and Sholette agree that it is within this avant-garde realm, however supplementary or invisible it may be, that genuine innovation and even, in Roberts's ambitious terms, revolution can be brought about. "The avant-garde does not exist as a given thing," Roberts writes, "but rather as a set of unnamed possibilities."[21] We understand Roberts and Sholette's notions of second economy and dark matter to be gesturing to *minoritarian* aesthetic production: artistic production by subjects whose life and work take place on the fringes of legitimizing institutions, or whose inclusion within such institutions remains provisional.

The concept of the avant-garde, Marc James Léger argues, has a particular purchase on our thinking in times of crisis because it explicitly asks whether it is possible to be radical or to disturb the established order.[22] Ben Hickman goes further: it might be in the avant-gardists' best interest to label the late twentieth and early twenty-first centuries a crisis, insofar as the term opens the period up to critique.[23] While recognizing that crises can be manufactured to justify extralegal acts and further disenfranchise oppressed populations, we assert that crisis, by destabilizing or defamiliarizing normative ways of living, prompts artists and critics to demand alternatives to unlivable conditions.[24] Such alternatives emerge with particular force in the work of artists working in minoritarian spaces. They also emerge from the work of artists working across national borders. James M. Harding has suggested that the avant-garde is a transnational phenomenon, where *transnational* means "both the processes of global hegemony and the practice of counterhegemonic resistance."[25] Even though many of the figures whose work is analyzed in this collection have transited through the US at one point or another, the following chapters underscore the transnational constitution of the avant-garde. The essays retrace avant-gardes and crises across the US, Central America, Germany, Japan, Belgium, and France, in addition to exposing the colonial apparatus supporting what are widely accepted as national traditions.

Institutionality and Anti-Institutionality amid Institutional Collapse

In troubling the whiteness of the avant-garde, Hong takes up the terms of a long debate with origins in the social struggles of the late 1960s and 1970s, when writers, artists, and activists developed innovative rebukes to the institutions of literature, visual art, and theater that had flourished during the economic expansion of the immediate postwar era.[26] In this context, the term *avant-garde* became a charged site for interrogating the legacy of modernist experimentation in terms of its political valence and its relation to the institutions it sought to critique. Debates on the avant-garde took shape across venues, including the journal *October*, which printed many a polemic on anti-institutional art.[27] Such debates have lived on in retorts to Kenneth Goldsmith and Vanessa Place's conceptual poetry—retorts whose proliferation in the mid-2010s more or less coincided with the publication of Hong's essay in the journal *Lana Turner*. The now-defunct Mongrel Coalition Against Gringpo, for example, used the humorous argot of the internet age to denounce white male hegemony within US poetry as well as the importation of US cultural models into Mexican poetry—two phenomena encapsulated by the portmanteau *gringpo*, for *gringo poetics*.[28]

Recent debates around the avant-garde have generally been cast as offshoots of the canon wars, or the struggle between defenders of a white, male canon of so-called "great books" and critics who have asserted that this canon marginalizes nonwhite and nonmale authors. The critic Dorothy Wang laments that the canon wars led to "the firm clicking into place of the terms 'identity,' 'identitarian,' and, most overtly, 'identity politics' as the antithesis of . . . literary value and critical rigor."[29] For Wang, the problem of the avant-garde is, in the end, a problem of literary institutions:

> Poetry by racialized persons, no matter the aesthetic style, is almost always read as secondary to the larger (and more "primary") fields and forms of English-language poetry and poetics—whether the lyric, prosody, rhetorical tropes, the notion of "avant-garde"—categories all too often presumed to be universal, overarching, and implicitly "racially unmarked."[30]

Wang paints an illuminating portrait of the disciplinary siloing whereby minority poetry appears supplementary to literary studies' "proper" objects. But the university is not the only institution that has shaped avant-garde production, circulation, and reception in the late twentieth and early twenty-first centuries. The university has enjoyed a slightly longer half-life than other institutions that fell into crisis in the 1970s—a fact admittedly hard to discern from the contemporary vantage point of the humanities' decimation, amid which the labor of some of this collection's contributors is not even indirectly compensated through the structures of tenure and promotion. As the canon wars raged in the last decades of the twentieth century, life outside the university was becoming untenable.

The crisis of the 1970s and its attendant disruptions across institutions, modes of living, and particularly the social movements of the 1960s have remained hidden in plain sight in discourses of the avant-garde. As Wang observes, the fact of a writer's close association with a social movement often obscures their commitments to experimental aesthetics. Wang offers, as a premier example, the writer Amiri Baraka, whose work has been "endlessly inventive," but who has been typecast as "stuck in the 1960s."[31] It is also true, though, that Baraka's innovations were enabled by the fiscal crises of the long 1970s. Baraka's revolutionary arts center Spirit House took shape as Newark lost 24 percent of its manufacturing jobs between 1958 and 1970.[32]

A similar case can be made for Theresa Hak Kyung Cha's *Dictee*. "While [*Dictee*] is considered as seminal as *Tender Buttons* among Asian American circles," Hong notes, "it's still treated like a fringe classic in the avant-garde canon."[33] Hong draws attention to *Dictee*'s status as a text that refracts an attention to Asian American—specifically Korean American—identity through the avant-garde's formal innovation. And yet, Cha's work is seldom, if ever, understood in terms of the crisis-driven downtown New York scene from which it emerged. As rents dropped because of the ongoing fiscal crisis, artists moved to the city in droves, developing enclaves, first in SoHo and then in the Lower East Side, in which experiments in literary, visual, and performed arts proliferated. The multimedia form of *Dictee* reflects Cha's immersion in these cultures. At the least, as Sue J. Kim has demonstrated in her reading of Cha's edited anthology *Apparatus*, Cha engaged the cutting-edge aesthetic theories of her moment—theories that were circulating in New York.[34] Moreover, Tanam Press, which published *Dictee* alongside a range of innovative books, was enabled, as founder Reese Williams has reflected, by the economic freedom tied to the crisis of the 1970s.[35] *Dictee*, then, brings Cha's concerns as a Korean American female artist to "debates on the politics of avant-garde art forms" that took place among a diverse group of artists initially drawn to the city by cheap rents.[36] Tracking the impact of the crisis of the 1970s on the avant-garde reveals the artificiality of the dichotomy, cultivated by disciplinary divisions, between avant-garde and "identity" art.

Questions of institutionality have long been at the heart of debates on the avant-garde. While they have taken place in a range of sites, both central and peripheral to the artworld, these debates have, to an impressive extent, coalesced around Bürger's keystone *Theory of the Avant-Garde*. Bürger argues that the historical avant-gardes of the 1910s and 1920s criticized, rather than prior artistic movements and schools, art as an institution and its development in bourgeois society.[37] For Bürger, the historical avant-gardes aimed, but failed, to merge art with the praxis of life. Yet, this failure fulfilled a pedagogical function: it made visible the normative frame of art as an institution and its influence on the social import of artworks. As Bürger puts it in a 2010 essay, "The failure of the avant-garde utopia of the unification of art and life coincides with the avant-garde's overwhelming success within the art institution. One could almost say: in their very failure, the avant-gardes conquer the institution."[38] In the 1950s and 1960s, the artists of the "neo-avant-gardes," no longer in a position to assert art's autonomy from its institutions, turned the historical avant-gardes' chief techniques (collage and assemblage, the readymade and the grid, monochrome painting and constructed sculpture) into "internal aesthetic procedures."[39] The avant-gardes, it seemed, had run out of steam.[40] For Bürger, once the revolutionary moment of the early twentieth century had passed, the avant-garde could only repeat its earlier moves as it ran in circles. Bürger's account, like others of its ilk, tends, as Harding observes, to privilege "artistic innovation over and above political struggle," locking the avant-garde into doomed repetitions of politically neutralized artistic gestures.[41]

Bürger does not provide any evidence of crisis's alleged irrelevance at midcentury. More troubling still, in his late-career writing, Bürger reduces the period since the 1970s to an extended artistic and political status quo.[42] In light of the frequent use of the term *crisis* in relation to the 1970s, how could Bürger contend, either in 1974 or in 2010, that the context for the avant-garde was no longer one of crisis? Bürger, we offer, was looking in the wrong places. The reason Bürger cannot decipher an avant-garde in the 1970s onward is intimately linked to Hong's critique. Bürger believes that it is possible to determine whether an artistic movement is *either* a success *or* a failure because he holds a narrow view of what a crisis is, of who counts as a subject of crisis, and of what it looks like to mediate a crisis.[43] A crisis in the reproduction of life that penalizes marginalized people simply does not fit Bürger's paradigm, calibrated as it is for the white male artist imbued with revolutionary fervor. What is more, Bürger's conflation of crisis aesthetics with anti-institutionality is ill-fitted to a historical period during which some institutions are crumbling faster than they may be opposed. Bürger's analysis builds toward a "gotcha" moment when the use of institutional criteria to evaluate a work of art invalidates its claim to autonomy. But what happens when there are fewer and fewer institutions to sell out to?

This is not to say that Bürger's claims—or the claims of critics, like Hal Foster, who followed his lead—were unfounded.[44] Channeled through the narrow corridors of success and failure, the avant-garde did appear corralled within institutions in the immediate postwar moment, as the economy expanded the markets and institutions for art, such that avant-garde work of modernist orientation became a part of a certain artworld firmament. However, just as women, minorities, and radicals were either dismissed or attacked in the US of the postwar boom, artists who fell under one or more of these rubrics mostly struggled *outside* artistic institutions.[45] For Bürger, the avant-garde is, as Roberts puts it, a "placeholder for art's autonomy."[46] Autonomous art, according to Juliana Spahr's pithy definition, "is free from outside interference, from the market, from the government."[47] The view that autonomy decreased in the 1950s and 1960s is parochial. When we pay attention to the art made amid the struggles for *political* autonomy of minority groups, for instance, we realize that institutional exclusion rushed some avant-gardes into partial aesthetic autonomy—a tendency intensified by the institutional bust that succeeded the postwar boom.[48] Our claim is not, of course, that in the 1970s art became outright autonomous; for one, blockbuster exhibitions of contemporary art in corporate-sponsored museums prove that the institutional extraction of value from the avant-gardes is ongoing. Instead, the polarity of autonomy-versus-institutionality, wherein standing outside of institutions registers as deliberate and freeing, strikes us as anachronistic amid the crisis in the reproduction of life catalyzed by the 1970s. While notions of plural avant-gardes, as Harding notes, have become commonplace, much remains to be said—and much is said in our collection—about the economic and political circumstances that disrupted the institutionalization of the avant-garde bemoaned by Bürger.[49] Taking Bürger's historical materialism seriously, we call for a mapping of the contemporary avant-gardes that better reflects their conditions of emergence. This mapping promises to show that the 1970s inaugurated, rather than a post-avant-garde status quo, a moment when, as Sell puts it, "the avant-garde has achieved ubiquity."[50]

Minoritarian and Radical Avant-Gardes

If we are to counter the logic of exclusion that Hong denounces, how are we to define the avant-garde? Sell's solution is to tie the avant-garde not to a specific genealogy but more flexibly to a commitment to political resistance. "The avant-garde," Sell writes, "is a minority formation that challenges power in subversive, illegal, or alternative ways; in particular, by challenging the routines, assumptions, hierarchies, and/or legitimacy of cultural institutions."[51] Elisabeth A. Frost submits a similarly open definition, whereby the avant-garde comprises "any artistic practice that combines radical new forms with radical politics or utopian vision."[52] Following these critics, *Avant-Gardes in*

Crisis: Art and Politics in the Long 1970s places the adjectives *minoritarian* and *radical* at the heart of a consideration of the contemporary avant-gardes.

Radical art advocates thorough social and political reform or revolution. By labeling the contemporary avant-gardes *minoritarian*, we seek to center the contributions of artists from historically subordinated groups. A minoritarian concept of the avant-garde upends the epistemologies that have ratified a white male canon. The term *minoritarian* also refers to art that exceeds prestigious or permanent media. The contemporary avant-gardes go beyond painting, sculpture, film, and poetry and include theater, dance, performance art, fiction and nonfiction prose, and ephemeral interventions.[53] As Gabriele Schor reminds us, the two definitions of *minoritarian*—as identity and medium—often prove inextricable; in the 1970s, feminists turned to photography, film, and video to "make their mark in the art world outside the male-dominated medium of painting."[54] By dwelling on the convergences and divergences between the two meanings of *minoritarian*, the contributors to this collection outline the imbrication of art and politics in the long 1970s. Our motivation in generating concepts fit for the contemporary avant-gardes is not presentist. In fact, a focus on the political interventions of the late twentieth- and early twenty-first-century avant-gardes helps to clarify retroactively the politics of the so-called historical avant-gardes.[55]

To underscore the importance of a study of the avant-garde that treats radicalism and minoritarianism as bound but not isometric, we now turn to "Fuck the Avant-Garde," a 2019 essay by Rachel Greenwald Smith. Smith reads Hong's pronouncement as the avant-garde gesture par excellence. In their illiberalism, manifestos that say "fuck the avant-garde" are, in Smith's view, more avant-gardist than the self-proclaimed avant-garde artists who hold on to liberal myths of "recognition, justice, and equality" and, in doing so, prove "complicit with the most egregious injustices of the dominant culture throughout the postwar period."[56] We agree with Smith that Left critics who condemn the avant-gardes on the basis of their failure to live up to their radical ambitions implicitly suggest that more committed avant-garde praxes would be desirable. But by equating critique with manifesto, and manifesto with avant-garde, Smith ends up emptying Hong's argument of its content. Indeed, if we reduce all Left criticism of the avant-garde, including Hong's essay, to an illiberal "fuck the avant-garde," then we fail to be accountable to the differently situated individuals and groups behind this criticism, and thereby lose track of the avant-garde's relation to minoritarian perspectives.

Likewise, boiling down the Mongrel Coalition Against Gringpo's intervention to a stauncher avant-gardism than the one exhibited by its targets would erase the specificity of the collective's critique of white supremacy and patriarchy. It would also ignore the coalition's attacks on nonwhite and nonmale poets. In Trisha Low's estimation, the coalition attacked "more people of color and queer women than straight white men."[57] Low expresses anger at Kenneth Goldsmith for appropriating Michael Brown's autopsy report, and at Vanessa Place for tweeting Margaret Mitchell's novel *Gone with the Wind*: "I'm mad at Kenny and Vanessa for making some racist poems that aren't even good art, I'm even madder that they don't understand that they have to be accountable for the hurt they've caused and that sometimes, you just have to say you're wrong."[58] Yet, Low, a Chinese writer who has lived in Singapore, London, Philadelphia, New York City, and the San Francisco Bay Area, refuses to disavow her ties with conceptualism and its white leaders. Low maintains that it is not because an artistic family is chosen that it can be unchosen, and so she decides to grapple with her position *within* conceptualism's legacy. "I feel implicated, complicit," she admits; "I don't just get to walk away from that guilt. I won't let myself."[59] In no way a straightforward defense of conceptualism, Low's rejoinder to the Mongrel Coalition hints at a racial, gender, and sexual geography of the avant-gardes whose complexity exceeds a critical paradigm wherein the loudest voices of dissent qualify as the most avant-gardist. Instead of folding *minoritarian* into *radical*, this collection examines the interplay between the two qualifiers amid a crisis whose impact is unevenly distributed.

We contend that the avant-gardes of the late twentieth and early twenty-first centuries are *in crisis*, in that artmaking both responds to political, economic, social, and environmental crises and reveals a crisis of confidence regarding aesthetic resistance's very possibility. Experimental writing, Tyler Bradway argues, "actively [rethinks] the chiasmus of politics and poetics through their formal experimentation."[60] A focus on the avant-gardes allows us to map out how experimentation reconfigures the relation between poetics and politics *across media*. Influential views of the avant-garde in such disparate domains as poetry studies and art history are united by their shortcomings, which is to say their insistence that radical subjects should be able to relinquish their identity. Accordingly, we situate our counterargument—that the contemporary avant-garde is a minoritarian formation—in the movement across established medium and media boundaries.

Becoming Minor in the Long 1970s

One response to the uncertainty of the 1970s—a response offered by critics like Perloff and the October Group—was to hold on to, and extend, the lineage celebrated by Bürger. Surveying the art of the decade, Rosalind Krauss, in the 1979 essay "Sculpture in the Expanded Field," worries that the category of sculpture has become "infinitely malleable."[61] "The category," Krauss continues, "has now been forced to cover such a heterogeneity that it is, itself, in danger of collapsing. And so we stare at the pit in the earth and think we both do and don't know what sculpture is."[62] That loss of bearings drives the remainder of Krauss's piece, in which she ponders how the viewer can live with the uncertainty prompted by the dislocations of nonsculpture. Krauss's solution, one that her students Craig Owens and Foster later take up, is to rescue formlessness by recourse to semiotics: "The expanded field," she concludes," is "generated by problematizing [a] set of oppositions" between marked sites and axiomatic structures, sculpture and site construction.[63] Hereafter, the avant-garde will consist of a movement between oppositional poles, enabling aesthetic production to become, once again, "rigorously logical."[64] What seemed malleable or squishy finds its structure. It is no accident that most of Krauss's examples involve large-scale interventions: Richard Serra's plates of lead, Robert Smithson's mounds of slag, Alice Aycock's tremendous *Maze*. One may be forgiven for reading "Sculpture in the Expanded Field" as a meditation on the category of bigness.

The works discussed in *Avant-Gardes in Crisis* operate in a more minor mode and on the scales of the small and the quotidian. Contributors center short poems, ephemeral exhibitions, repressed or outright censored works, and minor works by major artists. Sianne Ngai lays a foundation for a study of minor-key avant-gardes in her theory of the cute. Ngai describes the "cuteness" of the avant-garde as, paradoxically, that which meditates on art's powerlessness while retaining "aesthetic power" by resisting a complete reabsorption into commodity culture.[65] Cuteness, that is, displays "aesthetic power *made available* by art's social ineffectuality."[66] For Ngai, it is by acknowledging its own ineffectuality that the cute maintains a longer shelf life than harder-edged versions of the avant-garde. Sophie Seita takes the little literary magazine to be exemplary of Ngai's avant-garde cute. Cherished by the Dadaists and ubiquitous in today's literary communities, the little literary magazine is the rare artifact to travel across the avant-gardes of the twentieth and twenty-first centuries. As a cute object, the avant-garde magazine, Seita argues, invites the mix of care and sadism charted by Ngai: "The avant-garde little magazine demands we pay attention, with care; it is an object that we might wish to be politically stronger at the same time as we believe we can no longer reject it because it is too intimately ours."[67] Cuteness clears room for a set of inquiries about the avant-garde that allow it to recede from Bürger's stringent requirements and from the heroism often attributed to avant-garde interventions. Cuteness, whose gendered and raced manifestations Ngai tracks from Yayoi Kusama's polka-dotted phallus pillows to Harryette Mullen's homage to Gertrude Stein's own examination of lesbian domesticity in *Tender Buttons*, is not only a minor but a *minoritarian* formation of the avant-garde.

According to Ngai, cuteness comes to dominate a set of aesthetic practices that respond to a rough moment in the late twentieth and early twenty-first centuries when "artfully designed, packaged, and advertised merchandise . . . surrounds us in our homes, in our workplaces, and on the street," and subjects are surrounded by "an age of high-tech simulacra and media spectacles."[68] But when Ngai announces that the cute avant-garde is an aesthetic of powerlessness, we hear the creaky uncertainty of the 1970s lumber into earshot. The crisis of the 1970s at once denied agency to a large portion of the population and made clear that the distributed power of the welfare state and consensus politics of the Fordist/Keynesian era had been a lie all along. Ngai's formulation of the cute as a "*minor* commodity aesthetic" that calls "up a range of *minor* negative affects [like] helplessness, pitifulness, and even despondency" hence constitutes a platform from which to launch our investigation of the avant-gardes in the long 1970s.[69] Pushing a limit established by Bürger, Ngai contends that through cuteness, the avant-garde contemplates the problem of its own limited effect: "art has the capacity not only to reflect and mystify power but also to reflect on and make use of powerlessness."[70] Likewise, the insurgent texts and objects taken up in this collection "reflect on and make use of" accelerated powerlessness in the long 1970s.

Genealogies of Crisis

This collection comprises two primary sections, followed by a shorter section that functions as something of a rejoinder. Sections on enclosures and infrastructures construct distinct genealogies of the crisis of the long 1970s, while the last section outlines varyingly upheld commitments to a revolutionary transition out of imperialism and capitalism.

Two pairs of essays—one on property, one on censorship—compose the first section, on enclosures. The authors featured in this section adopt an anticolonial and anti-imperial approach to increased privatization in the long 1970s. The first two chapters, specifically, decode the late twentieth- and early twenty-first-century poetics and discourses of "nonpossession" and their ties to long histories of dispossession, including settler colonialism, slavery, and segregation. In the first chapter, the quiet polemic "Against Possession," Sarah Dowling reads Lorine Niedecker's compact poem "Foreclosure," written sometime during the 1960s, as both proleptic and recapitulative, speaking to a post-2008 moment while considering the dispossessions of Indigenous peoples in what is currently Wisconsin alongside settlers' land losses during the Great Depression. "Foreclosure," Dowling argues, calls for an end to property as a system and imagines, in its ruins, a white selfhood detached from territorial possession and bourgeois liberal humanism. In "The Poetics of Drift: Coloniality, Place, and Environmental Racialization," Samia Rahimtoola contends that African American poetry's formal engagement with place-based liberation paves a way through and beyond the colonial binary of possession and dispossession. Rahimtoola follows Dawn Lundy Martin and Ed Roberson's "drift" through landscapes of urban destitution. At once a decolonial practice of reinhabiting place and an ecological practice of staying with the damage, drift contests the narratives of economic overcoming and environmental repair that seek to redeem Black suffering.

RL Goldberg begins our next dyad, on censorship and the administration of publics, with "*Pansexual Public Porn*: Trans Gender Docu-Porn in the Long 1970s." In this chapter, Goldberg examines transness in the context of the sanitization of pornography that resulted from the rise of the VHS and the criminalization of public sex. Del LaGrace Volcano's 1998 avant-garde film *Pansexual Public Porn aka The Adventures of Hans and Del*, Goldberg notes, accentuates the slippage between gender identity and sexual practice found in censorship rhetoric. In doing so, *Pansexual Public Porn* predicates structures of care and recognition on a refusal to separate *public* from *sex*. To end the section on enclosures, Priscilla Layne, in "The Ethics of Provocation: Censoring the Past in German Cold War Punk," reflects on the illegibility of anti-state art to Germany's Federal Department of Media Harmful to Young Persons. In 1987, the department indexed the band OHL's album *Heimatfront* because of its use of Nazi imagery, thus restricting the album's advertising and sales via child protection laws. Yet, OHL, Layne argues, used such imagery to confront West Germany with the persistence of fascist and authoritarian tendencies. Layne ultimately debunks Bürger's assertion that the neo-avant-garde cannot be as transgressive as the historical avant-garde: OHL's punk resists institutionalization by eluding the moral codes of left- *and* right-wing state politics.

The collection's second section frames the long 1970s as an infrastructural crisis. In the late twentieth and early twenty-first centuries, public infrastructures that had carried some of the burden of the reproduction of life collapsed: social services shrunk, and so did public housing. Meanwhile, corporate-owned infrastructures, such as satellite-based global communication networks, reshaped everyday life. The first two essays included in this section tell a pair of stories about a crisis of medium precipitated by installation art's uneasy ontological proximity to infrastructure within shaky institutions. Andrew Strombeck's "Indexing Post-Fordism at P.S. 1" revisits the 1975 exhibit *Rooms*, held at P.S. 1, in Queens, New York, and hailed as a defining moment of the site-specific art of that decade. Site-specific art has been celebrated for what Krauss calls its "indexicality": an unmediated access to natural and built environments that, for Krauss and others, achieves the rebuke of the institutions of art dreamed up by the historical avant-garde. *Rooms*' coincidence with the New York fiscal crisis, Strombeck contends, highlights a troubling aspect of this rebuke: it occurred at the very post-Fordist moment when life-supporting infrastructures of care, such as public education, were being destroyed by the state. By reading avant-garde discourses through the lens of the economic fluctuations of the 1970s, Strombeck de-idealizes Krauss's criterion of indexicality, proposing that another index—the Consumer Price Index—might better account for the status of art amid the fear of inflation. The next chapter, Jennifer Wild's "Under the Figure of the Palm Tree," turns to the site-specific art of Marcel Broodthaers and Jean-Luc Godard, wherein the palm tree registers the instability of medium specificity and of the institutional structures upholding the idealist functions and historical fictions of art. Whereas Godard's use of the palm betrays an attachment to a Romantic, ahistorical concept of art, Broodthaers's animates an ethics of historical recognition, or an encounter with the museum's function in monetizing and displaying colonial spoils. Wild claims the very desire for such an ethics as an artifact of the 1970s, one that manifests in disparate works by the decade's most influential theorists, from Julia Kristeva to Peter Brooks.

The last two essays on infrastructures zoom in on influential feminist artists who have raised the question of how to relate to one's own body in and beyond the corporatized museum. In "I Felt Like a Machine: Martha Rosler's Aesthetics of Survival," Matt Tierney surveys Martha Rosler's critical and creative writing from the last third of the twentieth century. Tierney reads Rosler's mail art project, *Service: A Trilogy on Colonization*, as an exemplar of what Rosler calls "person-centered counter practices" and what George Rochberg terms an "aesthetics of survival." By trading speed and conquest for slowness and play, Rosler develops humane tactics for opposing the mechanization of laboring bodies promoted by a certain avant-garde's uncritical embrace of science as well as the techno-fascism of "state art." The systematization of embodiment is also a concern in the section's last chapter, Shannon Finck's "Yayoi Kusama's Immaterial Drive." In a retrospective essay that spans Kusama's entire career, Finck refutes the common narrative that posits the end of the artist's Happenings period, in the 1970s, as a turn away from embodiment, offering instead that Kusama's more recent work nostalgically holds the memory of her early work's tactility. The Infinity Mirror Rooms, emblems of Kusama's late career, offer infrastructures of mourning, in which spectators living in the age of digital reproduction can remember the body as a seat of experience and a medium for protest in the years leading up to the crisis of the 1970s.

Whereas the collection's first two sections narrate the crisis of the long 1970s as a series of limits that avant-garde artists have inventively reframed, the last section considers the avant-garde commitments that have emerged in spite, or in full dismissal, of such limits. In "*Sandinista!* The US Avant-Garde's Response to Central American Upheavals in the Long 1970s," Javier Padilla studies Language poetry's relation to the *poesía comprometida* or "poetics of commitment," which became the hallmark of Central American poets' response to regional upheavals, specifically the failed Salvadorian rebellion of the 1970s and the successful 1979 Sandinista revolution in Nicaragua. Hannah Weiner, Carolyn Forché, and Lawrence Ferlinghetti, Padilla argues, developed a tactical poetics of "political tourism" that, in imposing some distance between the poet and the subject of Central America's revolutions, accurately describes the US poet's relation to the outside world. In the collection's final chapter, "The Making of New Narrative: Gay Liberation and the Poetics of Revolutionary Agency," David W. Pritchard, too, relays a poetics of commitment. Pritchard's is located in the origins of the experimental writing movement known as New Narrative. Positioning New Narrative as an extension of both Gay Liberation and the New Left's project of revolutionary transition out of capitalism, Pritchard deciphers in Bruce Boone's poem "Karate Flower" an "oppositional language" that structures revolutionary agency amid global economic crisis.

An ekphrastic afterword by Jean-Thomas Tremblay closes the collection. Methodologically, the afterword takes inspiration from Brian Glavey's insight that "hyper-mimetic ekphrasis," a certain "minoritizing" avant-gardism that runs from modernist literature to queer theory, "blurs the line that separates description from narration" and "stresses the rewards of forming extremely close attachments to aesthetic objects without abdicating strategies of contextualization and critique."[71] Weaving the prior chapters' themes into a close description of Theresa Hak Kyung Cha's *Untitled*, a tiny sculpture produced in 1980, Tremblay sketches an avant-garde aesthetics of commitment that refuses to disentangle a critique of resource concentration and attrition from a critique of attendant systems of domination.

We hope that our collective commitments, as editors and authors, resonate loudly and clearly across this collection's pages. *Avant-Gardes in Crisis* refutes the notion that experimentalism grants artists and critics an exemption from political considerations. If we seek to develop a minoritarian and radical concept of the avant-garde, it is because, as the crisis of the long 1970s rages on, this concept—indeed even an antagonistic relation to this concept—continues to magnetize the utopian fantasy of an alignment between political, intellectual, and aesthetic revolutions.

Notes

1. Cathy Park Hong, "Delusions of Whiteness in the Avant-Garde," *Arcade* 7 (2014): https://arcade.stanford.edu/content/delusions-whiteness-avant-garde.

2. Hong, "Delusions of Whiteness in the Avant-Garde."

3. Hong, "Delusions of Whiteness in the Avant-Garde."

4. Peter Bürger, *Theory of the Avant-Garde*, trans. Michael Shaw (Minneapolis: University of Minnesota Press, 1984); Peter Bürger, "Avant-Garde and Neo-Avant-Garde: An Attempt to Answer Certain Critics of 'Theory of the Avant-Garde,'" trans. Bettina Brandt and Daniel Purdy, *New Literary History* 41, no. 4 (2010): 704; Marjorie Perloff, "Avant-Garde Poetics," in *The Princeton Encyclopedia of Poetry and Poetics*, 4th ed., ed. Roland Greene (Princeton, NJ: Princeton University Press, 2013), 110–113; Kent Johnson, "Marjorie Perloff, Avant-Garde Poetics, and 'The Princeton Encyclopedia of Poetry and Poetics,'" *Chicago Review* 57, nos. 3–4 (2013): 209–215. Other works that discuss the avant-garde in terms of a largely white, European tradition include Renato Poggioli, *The Theory of the Avant-Garde*, 2nd ed. (Cambridge, MA: Belknap Press of Harvard University Press, 1981); Matei Călinescu, *Faces of Modernity: Avant-Garde, Decadence, Kitsch* (Bloomington: Indiana University Press, 1977).

5. Relaying the views of the George Jackson Brigade, an underground group of working-class former prisoners, Stephen Dillon remarks that the 1970s heralded

new forms of racialized and gendered value and disposability within a neoliberal-*carceral* state. Stephen Dillon, *Fugitive Life: The Queer Politics of the Prison State* (Durham, NC: Duke University Press, 2018), 10, 13.

6. Lauren Berlant, Judith Butler, Bojana Cvejić, Isabell Lorey, Jasbir Puar, and Ana Vujanović, "Precarity Talk: A Virtual Roundtable," *TDR: The Drama Review* 56, no. 4 (2012): 166.

7. See Leigh Claire La Berge, *Wages Against Artwork: Decommodified Labor and the Claims of Socially Engaged Art* (Durham, NC: Duke University Press, 2019), 20–21. Sianne Ngai rehearses La Berge's argument in *Theory of the Gimmick: Aesthetic Judgment and Capitalist Form* (Cambridge, MA: Belknap Press of Harvard University Press, 2020), 34–35.

8. Ngai, *Theory of the Gimmick*, 35; La Berge, *Wages Against Artwork*, 21.

9. Melinda Cooper, *Family Values: Between Neoliberalism and the New Social Conservatism* (Brooklyn, NY: Zone Books, 2019).

10. Poul Villaume, Rasmus Mariager, and Helle Porsdam, "Introduction: The 'Long 1970s': New Perspectives on an Epoch-Making Decade," in *The "Long 1970s": Human Rights, East-West Détente, and Transnational Relations*, ed. Poul Villaume, Rasmus Mariager, and Helle Porsdam (New York: Routledge, 2016), 1.

11. Judith Stein, *Pivotal Decade: How the United States Traded Factories for Finance in the Seventies* (New Haven, CT: Yale University Press, 2010), xii.

12. Jefferson Cowie, *Stayin' Alive: The 1970s and the Last Days of the Working Class* (New York: New Press, 2010), 11.

13. We borrow this phrasing from Stein, *Pivotal Decade*.

14. Paul Mann, *The Theory-Death of the Avant-Garde* (Bloomington: Indiana University Press, 1991), 70–71.

15. We find Mann's language in *The Theory-Death of the Avant-Garde* telling in the context of environmental crisis: "The rhetoric of the new in which the avant-garde is so deeply implicated has also been polluted by this progress" (70–71).

16. La Berge, *Wages Against Artwork*, 4, 16.

17. Mike Sell, *Avant-Garde Performance and the Limits of Criticism: Approaching the Living Theatre, Happenings/Fluxus, and the Black Arts Movement* (Ann Arbor: University of Michigan Press, 2005), 46. John Roberts, in *Revolutionary Time and the Avant-Garde* (New York: Verso, 2015), similarly observes that "the experience and mediation of crisis and decline is indivisible from the judgements of value and critical materials that art is able to bring to bear on its own traditions and representation of the world, what we have so far called realized reflexivity" (53). On the avant-garde's entanglement with crisis, see also James Martin Harding, *The Ghosts of the Avant-Garde(s): Exorcising Experimental Theater and Performance* (Ann Arbor: University of Michigan Press, 2013); Ben Hickman, *Crisis and the US Avant-Garde: Poetry and Real Politics* (Edinburgh: Edinburgh University Press, 2015).

18. Mann, *Theory-Death of the Avant-Garde*, 142–143.

19. Roberts, *Revolutionary Time and the Avant-Garde*, 10.

20. Gregory Sholette, *Dark Matter: Art and Politics in the Age of Enterprise Culture* (London: Pluto Press, 2010), 1.

21. Roberts, *Revolutionary Time and the Avant-Garde*, 260.

22. Marc James Léger, "This Is Not an Introduction," in *The Idea of the Avant-Garde, and What It Means Today*, ed. Marc James Léger (Manchester: Manchester University Press, 2014), 1.

23. Hickman, *Crisis and the US Avant-Garde*, 2–3. On the relation between critique and crisis, see Seyla Benhabib, *Critique, Norm, Utopia: A Study of the Foundations of Critical Theory* (New York: Columbia University Press), 19.

24. Jordy Rosenberg and Amy Villarejo dwell on this tension in "Queerness, Norms, Utopia," *GLQ* 18, no. 1 (2012): 1–18.

25. James M. Harding, "From Cutting Edge to Rough Edges: On the Transnational Foundations of Avant-Garde Performance," in *Not the Other Avant-Garde: The Transnational Foundations of Avant-Garde Performance*, ed. James Martin Harding and John Rouse (Ann Arbor: University of Michigan Press, 2006), 20.

26. See La Berge, *Wages Against Artwork*, 4; Sharon Zukin, *Loft Living: Culture and Capital in Urban Change* (New Brunswick, NJ: Rutgers University Press, 1986).

27. See Alexander Alberro and Blake Stimson, eds., *Institutional Critique: An Anthology of Artists' Writings* (Cambridge, MA: MIT Press, 2009).

28. Carmen Giménez Smith, "Make America Mongrel Again," *Poetry Foundation*, April 19, 2018, https://www.poetryfoundation.org/harriet/2018/04/make-america-mongrel-again; Tim MacGabhann, Mariana Rodríguez, and John Z. Komurki, "Goldsmith, Place and What Gringpo Means for Your Reading," *The Quietus*, May 24, 2015, https://thequietus.com/articles/17912-kenneth-goldsmith-vanessa-place-michael-brown-appropriation-gringpo-mongrel-coalition.

29. Dorothy Wang, *Thinking Its Presence: Form, Race, and Subjectivity in Contemporary Asian American Poetry* (Stanford, CA: Stanford University Press, 2013), 12.

30. Wang, *Thinking Its Presence*, xix–xx.

31. Wang, *Thinking Its Presence*, 21–22.

32. See Komozi Woodard, *A Nation Within a Nation: Amiri Baraka (LeRoi Jones) and Black Power Politics* (Chapel Hill: University of North Carolina Press, 1999), 74–78.

33. Hong, "Delusions of Whiteness in the Avant-Garde."

34. Sue J. Kim, "Apparatus: Theresa Hak Kyung and the Politics of Form," *Journal of Asian American Studies* 8, no. 2 (2005): 143–169.

35. Williams recounts, "It was possible to move to New York and rent a large, spacious loft, and pay $250 a month. What that meant is that there were just hundreds of creative types living there, being able to have kind of an unusual life that they could afford. If you wanted to publish books, then you had space to put all the boxes in. There was kind of a freedom because of the economic situation." Reese Williams, Interview with Peter d'Agostino, "Library Lecture: Reese Williams," *TUTV*, February 6, 2015, https://vimeo.com/118927793.

36. Kim, "Apparatus," 163.

37. Bürger, *Theory of the Avant-Garde*, 22.

38. Bürger, "Avant-Garde and Neo-Avant-Garde," 705.

39. Bürger, "Avant-Garde and Neo-Avant-Garde," 707.

40. In "Avant-Garde and Neo-Avant-Garde," Bürger sums up, "While the historical avant-gardes could rightly consider the social context of their actions to be one of crisis, if not revolution, and could draw from this realization the energy to design the utopian project of sublating the institution of art, this no longer applied to the neo-avant-gardes of the 1950s and 1960s" (712).

41. Harding, *Ghosts of the Avant-Garde(s)*, 165.

42. Harding, *Ghosts of the Avant-Garde(s)*, 706–707.

43. Richard Schechner, too, relies on criteria of success and failure in a simplistic and positivist account of the avant-garde: "Innovation and excellence are in an inverse relationship to each other. When innovation is high, excellence is low; and vice versa. This is not always true, but it operates as an overall tendency. It makes sense because when people experiment, most of what they try fails." Richard Schechner, "The Conservative Avant-Garde," *New Literary History* 41, no. 4 (2010): 899.

44. Hal Foster, "What's Neo about the Neo-Avant-Gardes?," *October* 70 (1994): 5–32; Sell, *Avant-Garde Performance and the Limits of Criticism*, 43.

45. Sell, *Avant-Garde Performance and the Limits of Criticism*, 43.

46. Roberts, *Revolutionary Time and the Avant-Garde*, 56.

47. Juliana Spahr, *Du Bois's Telegram: Literary Resistance and State Containment* (Cambridge, MA: Harvard University Press, 2018), 16.

48. Williams, Interview with Peter d'Agostino. Blake Stimpson and Gregory Sholette argue that the social upheavals of second half of the twentieth century and the beginning of the twenty-first century have kept alive, while transforming, the collectivism dreamed up by modernism: "It is nothing other than this old dream of actually existing autonomy, of autonomy realized, of autonomy institutionalized, that haunts now with new vigor as a ghost from the past, but it does so not on the basis of the sheer strength of principle but instead by drawing its renewal and revitalization, by drawing replenishment of its lifeblood, from those strike forces of collectivization that are peculiar to our moment now." Blake Stimpson and Gregory Sholette, "Introduction: Periodizing Collectivism," in *Collectivism after Modernism: The Art of Social Imagination after 1945*, ed. Blake Stimpson and Gregory Sholette (Minneapolis: University of Minnesota Press, 2007), 4.

49. Harding, *Ghosts of the Avant-Garde(s)*, 9. Harding's point is specifically about performance art, but the term *avant-gardes*, in the plural, also appears in the introduction to a special issue of *New Literary History* edited by Jonathan P. Eburne and Rita Felski. See Jonathan P. Eburne and Rita Felski, introduction to *New Literary History* 41, no. 4 (2010): v–xv.

50. Mike Sell, "Resisting the Question, 'What Is an Avant-Garde?,'" *New Literary History* 41, no. 4 (2010): 754.

51. Sell, "Resisting the Question, 'What Is an Avant-Garde?,' " 770, emphasis removed.

52. Elisabeth A. Frost, *The Feminist Avant-Garde in American Poetry* (Iowa City: University of Iowa Press, 2003), xiv.

53. Sell, "Resisting the Question, 'What Is an Avant-Garde?,' " 757.

54. Gabriele Schor, "The Feminist Avant-Garde: A Radical Revaluation of Values," in *Feminist Avant-Garde: Arts of the 1970s*, ed. Gabriele Schor (New York: Prestel, 2016), 31.

55. On this note, Griselda Pollock argues that the attention to the maternal-feminine in the feminist avant-garde of the 1970s marked a return of the repressed of sorts: it unearthed "the maternal as body or ground for the autogenetic fantasy of masculine creativity" that had fueled the early twentieth-century avant-gardes. Griselda Pollock, "Moments and Temporalities of the Avant-Garde 'in, of, and from the feminine,' " *New Literary History* 41, no. 4 (2010): 816.

56. Rachel Greenwald Smith, "Fuck the Avant-Garde," *Post45* 2 (2019): http://post45.research.yale.edu/2019/05/fuck-the-avant-garde/.

57. Trisha Low, "On Being-Hated: Conceptualism, the Mongrel Coalition, the House That Built Me," *Open Space*, May 20, 2015, https://openspace.sfmoma.org/2015/05/on-being-hated-conceptualism-the-mongrel-coalition-the-house-that-built-me/.

58. Low, "On Being-Hated."

59. Low, "On Being-Hated."

60. Tyler Bradway, "Introduction: The Promise of Experimental Writing," *College Literature* 46, no. 1 (2019): 1–31.

61. Rosalind Krauss, "Sculpture in the Expanded Field," *October* 8 (1979): 30.

62. Krauss, "Sculpture in the Expanded Field," 33.

63. Krauss, "Sculpture in the Expanded Field," 38. For examples of important art critical texts by Krauss's students that take up semiotics as *the* framework for 1980s art, see Craig Owens, "The Allegorical Impulse: Toward a Theory of Postmodernism," *October* 12 (1980): 67–86; Hal Foster, "The Passion of the Sign," in *The Return of the Real: The Avant-Garde at the End of the Century* (Cambridge, MA: MIT Press, 1996), 71–96. Both Owens and Foster studied with Krauss at the City University of New York.

64. Krauss, "Sculpture in the Expanded Field," 42.

65. Sianne Ngai, *Our Aesthetic Categories: Zany, Cute, Interesting* (Cambridge, MA: Harvard University Press, 2012), 107.

66. Ngai, *Our Aesthetic Categories*, 103.

67. Sophie Seita, *Provisional Avant-Gardes: Little Magazine Communities from Dada to Digital* (Stanford, CA: Stanford University Press, 2019), 191–192.

68. Ngai, *Our Aesthetic Categories*, 58, 59.

69. Ngai, *Our Aesthetic Categories*, 101, 65, emphasis added.

70. Ngai, *Our Aesthetic Categories*, 109. For Ngai, the cute enacts a "meditation on the social status of the avant-garde and the criticisms its ambitions have

received from the Left" (97). Alongside Bürger, Ngai identifies this Left with Theodor Adorno, *Aesthetic Theory*, trans. Robert Hullot-Kentor (Minneapolis: University of Minnesota Press, 1998); Pierre Bourdieu, *The Rules of Art: Genesis and Structure of the Literary Field*, trans. Susan Emanuel (Stanford, CA: Stanford University Press, 1996); Raymond Williams, *The Politics of Modernism: Against the New Conformists* (New York: Verso, 2007); and Mann, *Theory-Death of the Avant-Garde*.

71. Brian Glavey, *The Wallflower Avant-Garde: Modernism, Sexuality, and Queer Ekphrasis* (New York: Oxford University Press, 2016), 4, 7, 15.

PART I

ENCLOSURES

Chapter 1

Against Possession

Sarah Dowling

If we are going to discuss the relationship between experimental aesthetic production and accelerating fiscal crisis, we could do worse than to consider a poem titled "Foreclosure." Such a poem would seem to speak directly to the twenty-first century's signature cruelties, evoking the transformations in the global economy that have taken place since the 1970s. We might expect a poem titled "Foreclosure" to make reference to the fact that some six million American homes have been foreclosed on—they've been seized back from their owners by banks and mortgage lenders—over the past decade. We might expect a poem by this title to situate the US crisis in home ownership within a broader, worldwide phenomenon, the financialization of housing, which has transformed rental and real estate markets by treating housing as a vehicle for wealth and investment rather than as a social good. Maybe we'd want a poem called "Foreclosure" to comment on the mass evictions, vacant properties, and displacement of residents and communities that have resulted, in the US and around the world. Perhaps we'd hope that this hypothetical poem, "Foreclosure," would offer perspective on the transformations in capitalism that have taken place over the past four or five decades, and that it would criticize the prioritization of wealth and investment over practical necessity and human need. At any rate, it's easy to imagine that these are some of the expectations that readers might bring to a poem titled "Foreclosure," particularly those readers who are interested in the ways in which experimental writers have responded to the accelerating crises in the reproduction of life that have unfolded under neoliberalism.

But poems, especially experimental ones, rarely do exactly what we want them to. I'm going to describe a real poem titled "Foreclosure," which offers something different—I'll suggest that it offers something more. Despite the sharp immediacy of its title, the real poem called "Foreclosure" is neither about the 2008 financial crisis, nor about the ways it has impacted individuals' and communities' rights to be housed. In fact, it's not about any aspect of the time period identified with neoliberalism. Written by Lorine Niedecker sometime during the 1960s—the last decade of her life and the one generally considered as immediately preceding the multifaceted crises we are now living through—this poem speaks instead to the never-ending series of dispossessions that its author suffered before, during, and after the Great Depression. Niedecker's small, fractured lyrics document the life she spent as a low-wage, often underemployed worker in rural Wisconsin; her poems track various forms of powerlessness, both artistic and social. Describing layered and interrelated forms of enclosure, Niedecker intimately links the lyric's tight smallness with the constrained circumstances of poor women and working people.

In these and other respects, Niedecker "could not have been further removed from the avant-garde poetry scene," although she did participate in lively and intense epistolary exchanges with Louis Zukofsky, Cid Corman, Ian Hamilton Finlay, and other midcentury experimentalists.[1] This social location, along with her reception as an objectivist poet—that is, as a "persistently under-known and under-valued" late modernist for whom "the praxis of the poem [was] a mode of thought, cognition, investigation," and for whom investment in the real and the material was paramount—marks her as a writer and thinker who stood outside of, and creatively challenged, the institutions of her day.[2] In keeping with this volume's project of contesting the model of the avant-garde offered by Peter Bürger, "calibrated as it is for the white male artist imbued with revolutionary fervor," to quote the introduction to this volume, Niedecker's poetry exemplifies a minoritarian mode and accordingly offers a different approach to the periodization of crisis, one that is counterintuitively expansive.

"Foreclosure" evokes that treasured American fantasy: ownership of one's own home, and of a parcel of territory—perhaps one marked with a white picket fence. The poem shows what happens when the fantasy implodes, presenting dispossession as an undoing of the self. Compressed, grief-stricken, and exhausted, this little poem does not valorize the right to property; it doesn't discuss loss through the lens of nostalgia or suggest restitution. Instead, it impugns possessive individualism and the legal system that enshrines and supports it, calling for a new relationship to land and, by implication, a new and nonpossessive structure of selfhood. In its entirety, the poem reads:

> Tell em to take my bare walls down
> my cement abutments
> their parties thereof
> and clause of claws
>
> Leave me the land
> Scratch out: the land
>
> May prose and property both die out
> and leave me peace.

That's it: one quatrain, two couplets; eight lines offering more resignation than revolution. The reading of this poem that I'll offer is that it shows what happens when the thief who steals your home and tosses you off your land is the state, an entity well beyond legal reproach—particularly in this period, when the US state had positioned itself as the benevolent provider and protector of private property.[3] "Foreclosure" anticipates how, in the long 1970s, the worst nightmare of the anti-state critique of sixties radicalism would come true—but it also insists that the capacity to project dispossession into the future is a privilege, given the operations of settler colonialism and segregation. Small as it is, this poem offers a radical analysis of the relationships between the individual, the state, and the institution of property: in mourning the loss of a home and a severed relationship to land, "Foreclosure" suggests that dispossession is a foundational, if too-often obscured, American experience. It locates the losses suffered by its speaker within a longer series of dispossessions affecting the territory where Niedecker lived, describing relationships to land as fundamentally characterized by dispossession and displacement. As a solution, and as a source of "peace," this poem calls for an end to property and to the cruel legal "prose" in which its rules are enforced.

Even though Niedecker's poem falls slightly outside of the temporal frame suggested in this collection, having been composed some five to ten years prior to the period under consideration, it nonetheless offers a useful perspective on the relationship of experimental aesthetics to the periodization of crisis. "Foreclosure" places dispossession at the heart of liberal democracy in the US and hints at the ways in which dispossession must be considered structural, rather than appearing as an exceptional and discrete historical event. This poem calls for a reformulation of selfhood and of human relationships to land as the foundations of a way that we might live differently—as the foundations for "peace." I take Niedecker's poem as one example of the processes through which experimental art and literature in the later twentieth century detach themselves from the ideologies and logics of liberalism in order to document the tangled ways that people are impoverished and worlds are ended. "Foreclosure" tracks a deformation of subjectivity: as its speaker is dispossessed of her home and her land, so too does she lose legibility as an expressive, humanistic subject. I contend that this poem's discussion of property marks it as proleptically contemporary and as historically sedimented: the poem seems to speak directly to a post-2008 moment, but it also evokes a long history of settler-colonial dispossessions. Like much of Niedecker's work, "Foreclosure" creates echoes between the dispossessions of Indigenous peoples in what is currently Wisconsin, settlers' own land losses during the Great Depression, and the ravages of rural poverty—which are discussed as though they existed endlessly and constantly, transcending time. These repeating losses press Niedecker's "I" into a new intimacy with the earth, one that exceeds the severance of legal possession effected by the foreclosure process. This new, nonpossessive relationship is expressed through evocations of physical proximity, images of abandonment, and suggestions of persistence beyond death. Reading this poem in relationship to new analyses of the racialization of property emerging from Indigenous and settler-colonial studies, and to Kandice Chuh's recent theorization of "illiberal humanisms," I argue that Niedecker's short piece can be understood as offering a necessary—and necessarily minoritarian—vision of white selfhood: one that is severed from territorial possession and thus is also divested from bourgeois liberal humanism.[4]

Property

Theoretical discussions of property tend to emphasize its abstract nature, describing the processes by which intangible entities such as rights or ideas have come to be understood as ownable, how the capacity to make a claim to these abstract bundles of rights shapes subjectivation, or how property is fundamentally a relationship.[5] A foundational critique of classical liberal and commonsense notions of property is C. B. MacPherson's *The Political*

Theory of Possessive Individualism: Hobbes to Locke, which outlines the view that individuals are not only the sole proprietors of their skills, which can be bought and sold on the open market, they are the sole proprietors of *themselves*.[6] MacPherson argues that within liberal thought the individual is "nothing more than an owner of himself" and that society consists of nothing more than "a free exchange between proprietors," a view that some prominent political theorists have argued lay at the root of the 2007–2008 financial crisis.[7] Building on MacPherson's reevaluation of classical liberal political theory, Cheryl I. Harris argues that whiteness is not just a racial identity but has become a form of property acknowledged and protected in American law; the conceptual clarity of her argument has been borne out by the recent spate of racist murders wherein the citation of defense of property has proved exculpatory for white killers of African American and Indigenous men.[8] MacPherson's and Harris's foundational works reveal that the critique of abstractions such as recognition, justice, equality, and even personhood itself must be brought into conversation with the material forms of dispossession that remain resolutely unabstractable.[9] Thus, as Niedecker's poetry shows, it is necessary to ground discussions of property and possession in considerations of real property—of land—whose possession remains fundamental, particularly in the US, Canada, and other settler colonies.

The risk here is that abstract forms of possession come to obscure lived realities of dispossession in ways that are continuous with settler-colonial forms of erasure. Amy Carillo Rowe and Eve Tuck (Unangax̂), among other critics, argue that what distinguishes settler colonialism from other historical and contemporary forms of colonization is the pursuit of land.[10] In conceiving of land exclusively as property or as resource, they explain, settlers make their appropriations seem "natural, logical, or invisible."[11] The logic of appropriation itself evacuates any prior claims of their validity—it insists that claimed territory was simply unowned prior to its settler-colonial appropriation—and thereby confers righteous possession upon the person who, or the nation that, appropriates it. Importantly, the settler-colonial reconception of land as property negates any prior or ongoing claim that does not conform to the legal framework by which private property is recognized. This naturalization of territorial possession can be viewed as a component or perhaps as an example of what Aileen Moreton-Robinson (Goenpul) calls "white possessive logics."[12] Drawing attention to the conditions of Indigenous existence and to the regimes of common sense and disciplinary knowledges that shape and produce indigeneity, Moreton-Robinson frames white possessive logics as modes of rationalization that reproduce and reaffirm the nation-state's ownership, control, and domination in ways that make it seem natural and inevitable.[13] These possessive logics are specifically white because they "circulate sets of meanings about ownership of the nation," decision making therein, and other social conventions that systematically identify whiteness with possession of land and of the settler nation-state.[14] Building upon Harris's influential theorization of whiteness itself as a type of property, Moreton-Robinson argues that "whiteness accumulates capital and social appreciation as white people are recognized within the law primarily as property-owning subjects."[15] While white possessive logics operate at all levels of discourse, Moreton-Robinson repeatedly emphasizes that their foundation is the appropriation of Indigenous lands, which serves to naturalize subsequent forms of taking and possession.[16]

Much as Moreton-Robinson demonstrates the identification of whiteness with property ownership, legal scholar Brenna Bhandar's groundbreaking study *Colonial Lives of Property: Law, Land, and Racial Regimes of Ownership* also builds on Harris's work in order to argue that "the commodity logic of abstraction that underlies modern forms of private property shares conceptual similarities with the taxonomization and deracination of human life based in racial categorizations."[17] Bhandar examines the development of property law in settler colonies, arguing that property law—an amalgam of diverse legal strategies and techniques—is one of the most significant means through which the colonial appropriation of land and the fashioning of modern racial subjectivities take place and are secured.[18] She traces property's relationship to social and cultural norms and examines the role that property relations play in the distribution of social goods, arguing that modern concepts of race and modern laws of property share conceptual logics and are articulated in conjunction with one another. In particular, she explains:

> Those communities who lived as rational, productive economic actors, evidenced by particular forms of cultivation, were deemed to be proper subjects of law and history; those who did not were deemed to be in need of improvement as much as their lands were. Prevailing ideas about racial superiority were forged through nascent capitalist ideologies that rendered race contingent on specific forms of labor and property relations. Property ownership was not just contingent on race and notions of white supremacy; race, too, in the settler colonial context, was and remains subtended by property logics that cast certain groups of

> people, ways of living, producing, and relating to land as having value worthy of legal protection and force.[19]

Bhandar demonstrates that all modern racial categories—not just whiteness—are entwined with property logics: not only is the appropriation of Indigenous lands contingent upon notions of European racial superiority; the law also racializes those who do not relate to land through property ownership or who are prevented from relating to land in this way. Reading between her work and Moreton-Robinson's, we see how settler-colonial property relations are naturalized, and how white people come to be identified with property ownership. The right to appropriate, then, emerges as a facet of the racial superiority that white people impute to ourselves. Correspondingly, Indigenous people and people of color are identified with dispossession and with ineligibility for property ownership precisely as evidence of the racial inferiority that white people in turn impute to them. While Moreton-Robinson's and Bhandar's work takes shape within a broader and more complex debate about settler-colonial racialization, one of the few points of commonality across the many perspectives comprising this debate is the identification of whiteness with property ownership.[20] Moreover, the racial coding of the sovereign right to appropriate as distinctively and definitionally white operates well beyond the realm of law. White people's status as property-owning subjects, or as subjects identified with property ownership, shapes cultural conceptions of personhood and thingness, relationships to land and to the nation, and other destructive binaries.

I hope I can be forgiven for being this direct: "Foreclosure" is a poem about property. But more importantly, it is a poem about what happens to an individual who possesses property when that individual is dispossessed. Rather than lamenting that dispossession or seeking to reverse or correct it, "Foreclosure" interrogates the system of property ownership as it is constituted, demanding something more, something different. The poem begins by contrasting a specifically legal and contractual idiom with the speaker's own vernacular. The title, of course, comes from mortgage law; the phrase "parties thereof" is recognizable as legalese; the term "abutments" is highly technical; and the unpoetic echo between the words "their" and "thereof" replicates the awkward repetitions of a legal document. Placed into collision with this technical language is the speaker's opening plea, "Tell em to take my bare walls down." Whom does the speaker address in this clear and unrefined appeal—the banks? The lenders? The reader? Calling out to a nebulous no one, in an idiom less Latinate than the contractual language she references, the speaker conveys frustration. The riffing, quotational quality of her reaction to the law's predation lends the poem an element of humor, but Niedecker is vivid and specific in describing how the law operates. Rather than showing two equal "parties" to this contract, the image that concludes the first stanza, the "clause of claws," asks readers to imagine the law, or a legal document, as a bird of prey. The law swoops in, snatching the "bare walls" and "cement abutments" from the speaker, their former owner. We are asked to imagine the speaker's "bare" vulnerability before these clawed clauses, which "scratch out," or erase, the shape of her dwelling, as well as her relationship to the land. The law struggles fiercely to get possession of—it *scratches for*—the one thing from which the speaker could "scratch out" a living. Following this attack, the speaker is left pleading for respite, for mercy, for "peace."

I also read the speaker's opening address, "Tell em to take my bare walls down / my cement abutments," as describing a fundamental transformation in her selfhood. The speaker asks that the addressee "tell em" to complete this act of destruction as part of the process of foreclosure. It isn't enough that the speaker is dispossessed, then: some further transformation, she argues, will or ought to take place. She is dispossessed of her property, and so her land, her fundamental structure—her bare walls and cement abutments—should also be destroyed. The framework undergirding the speaking "I" will come apart, its structural supports sacrificed and sundered. If we read the first stanza of the poem as a list, we can see this plea for destruction as extending beyond the speaker's own self, however. Her "bare walls" and "cement abutments," which seem to identify her bodily and fully with the parcel of land that she is losing, will be taken down, but in addition to that, "their parties thereof / and clause of claws" should also be demolished. What are we to make of that? Walls and abutments are structural supports. Abutments are structures that join things, whether bits of property that cross from one parcel of land over to another or the masonry offering structural support to a bridge, arch, vault, or dam. Although this use is relatively rare, the word is also used figuratively to describe forms of support that are more properly social.[21] If we understand the word "parties" to refer to "an individual concerned in a proceeding," then we might conclude that it refers to those who have entered into the legal contract that is at the heart of the poem.[22] We can also consider that the word "parties" refers to constituted groups, to "sides" in a proceeding, and even to factions. In other words, in addition to the projected destruction of the speaker's selfhood, there is some broader form of destruction projected here: entailed in the foreclosure process is a destruction of the speaker's self, and of the forms of relationship in which she is embedded, whether positively or negatively conceived. What the "clause of claws" tears apart is not just the speaker's ownership of her property but her selfhood and her relationship to others. Indeed, we might suggest that the speaker, weakened and denuded by the foreclosure process, is egging on and goading a more powerful entity to enact a fuller and more complete destruction, tearing the property relation from its fundamental position in order to enable the possibility of some other structure to be built. I know we're supposed to avoid the heresy of paraphrase, but what I take from the first stanza is a sentiment something like this: *Tell em that if they're going to destroy this, me, us, they might as well go all the way—they might as well destroy everything.*

Personhood

In its refusal to toe the line of a fundamental fairness, to honor some foundational notion that the state safeguards individual rights and fosters the individual's capacity to mature, progress, and develop, "Foreclosure" aligns with the model of "illiberal humanisms" Kandice Chuh calls for in her recent book, *The Difference Aesthetics Makes: On the Humanities "After Man."* Chuh defines illiberal humanisms as offering alternate sensibilities that "differ and dissent from liberal common sense" as it exists today in the United States.[23] Illiberal humanisms, she explains, bring forward "an understanding of human beingness . . . defined not by discrete and self-possessed individuality but instead by constitutive relationality."[24] Chuh argues that illiberal humanisms "afford the emergence of a critical taxonomy that features encounter without conquest and entanglement in lieu of terms and concepts inhering in knowledge paradigms that hold the political and cultural, and economic and artistic as discretely bounded realms," and that they also "facilitate the articulation and elaboration of epistemes thoroughly incommensurate with the developmental geographies and temporalities of bourgeois liberal humanism."[25] Most crucially, illiberal humanisms call into question the "structures and processes of (e)valuation that subtend the sensus communis," offering alternate, disavowed, or subjugated sensibilities that might form the grounds of a currently uncommon common sense.[26]

"Foreclosure" resonates with the illiberal humanisms Chuh describes insofar as it contests the foundational bond between personhood and property, suggesting that only a radically reconstituted model of self and society will enable the production of "peace." In addition to the ways in which the poem contests liberalism's bounded, self-sufficient, and propertied subject, the speaker's repeated plea that the law not only "leave" her but leave her *something* can be read as the demand for a less-cruel set of terms, and for a different type of contract altogether. "Foreclosure" calls for not just a different mortgage contract but a different social contract: a different understanding of how society ought to be structured. At first pass, the repetition of the word "leave" seems to refer to what remains after the foreclosure. However, to "leave" something is also to bequeath it in one's will. When the speaker begs, "Leave me the land," she seems to ask that the law not take everything, that her relationship to the land remain unaffected by the foreclosure that will take her home. But then she revises her terms: we might think of the first couplet as a negotiation, because the speaker asks that her interlocutor "scratch out," or delete, "the land" from the contract. Rather than working within the system of property law and begging for scraps, Niedecker's speaker instead calls for the death of this system and demands a kind of bequest. If this suggestion of a bequest seems to limit the critical thrust of the poem, rejecting one part of property law, mortgage contracts, in favor of another, trusts and estates, or the generational transfer of wealth, what we need to bear in mind is that the speaker calls for "property" itself, not merely one its parts, to "die out." When property as a system dies, the poem suggests, the speaker will be able to remake her selfhood and to reconstitute her relationship to her home and to her land. The end of legalized possession and dispossession will provide the foundation for peace, a profoundly new kind of freedom.

Positioning aesthetic inquiry as a crucial response to crisis, Chuh suggests that the kinds of aesthetic inquiry performed in minoritized art and writings can teach us about "the conditions of possibility that subtend the dominant order, . . . the production and sustenance of the sensus communis—of common sense."[27] Such minor and minoritized writings, she suggests, stage a collision between "what is held to be reasonable and what is viscerally experienced"; they give texture and specificity to the contrasts between what we feel and experience through our senses and what we know is recognized socially as being sensible.[28] In its performance of this kind of collision, we could say that "Foreclosure" is a poem about what ends and what continues. Etymologically, the word "clause" comes from the Latin *clausula*, where it describes the close of a period, a formula, or a conclusion. The "clause of claws" enforcing the foreclosure redoubles and layers the connotations of dispossession and exclusion; it makes the violence of termination vivid. The repeated instruction to "leave me" does the opposite: it emphasizes what survives, what remains, and what lasts beyond. It banishes the law and its agents from the speaker's presence, pointing to the things that the law cannot prevent the speaker from enjoying, and to what escapes commodification as property. That this phrase is the only one repeated in the poem insists upon the existence of a future beyond foreclosure—*when* "prose and property both die out." It counterbalances the rapacious "clause of claws" and concludes the clanging, contractual off-rhymes with its inauguration of "peace," that is, of the silence that comes after the poem's end. What is "illiberal" about this poem, in Chuh's sense of the term, is that it insists on a different kind of order: that there is something possible that would make more sense than this, that there is another way of doing things that might make other relationships possible and might provide more freedom. If the final line seems to retreat, I don't think this is a resigned reassertion of the private: the poem does not say "leave me *in* peace." Instead, the poem suggests, in a small and quiet way, that without the violent ordering imposed by the common sense of "prose and property," some other, more restful possibility might emerge.

So how is the speaker left at the end of the poem? Her "bare walls" are "down," or at least it seems that they will be soon. This image identifies the speaker's bodily self with a physical structure in ways that connote pallor—walls, stripped of their decorations, may not be white, necessarily, but they are blank, neutral, usually pale. But the word "bare" subtly shifts this meaning. Rather than connoting the kind of blankness that we might associate with neutrality—and perhaps therefore with racial whiteness—Niedecker's "bare walls" offer a recoding of whiteness that dissociates whiteness from property and possession.[29] Niedecker's use of the word "bare" refers more specifically to being "without possessions," to a kind of lack.[30] This is not the neutral blankness that constitutes a presumptive center; it is instead the blankness of that which has been stripped, even ravaged. Her "cement abutments," too, will come apart. Can we read these structural supports as also referring to racial whiteness in some way? Perhaps it's a stretch to suggest a metaphorical reading in a poem so sparsely and insistently literal, but if we consider cement as that which makes other things "cohere firmly," then we might think of it in dialogue with the theories of property that I referenced at the beginning of this essay, wherein whiteness and possession are bound "firmly together" in a "stony consistency."[31] In calling for "prose and property [to] both die out," the speaker divests from these structures of racialized possession; left bare, she suggests that a relationship to "the land" must be based on something other than possession if "peace" is to be achieved.

"Foreclosure" describes one moment—a moment where its speaker loses everything. But the poem makes clear that such moments pervade the reign of "prose and property." These are the waves constantly lapping on our shores. At its most expansive, "Foreclosure" suggests that the history of the United States could be described as the taking down of "bare walls" and "cement abutments," the scratching out of connections to land. The poem's seemingly contemporary title reminds us that the foreclosures taking place in our own time echo and intensify long histories of dispossession, beginning with the US's colonial foundations—contemporary crises are not so unique, and there is nothing exceptional about foreclosure. It is integral to the governing system of property. There is something exceptional about "Foreclosure," though: this poem looks to a future beyond property and beyond predation, and to a selfhood whose structure inheres in something other than possession. It insists upon the existence—and the necessity—of something else and something more. In the silence that follows the closing demand for "peace," we readers are asked to imagine what that might be.

Notes

1. Jenny Penberthy, "Life and Writing," in *Lorine Niedecker: Collected Works* (Berkeley: University of California Press, 2002), 1.

2. Rachel Blau DuPlessis and Peter Quartermain, introduction to *The Objectivist Nexus: Essays in Cultural Poetics* (Tuscaloosa: University of Alabama Press, 1999), 2, 3.

3. Interestingly, one of the institutions that has yet to crumble in this crisis era is the state's role as guarantor of private property. Even as midcentury social programs, such as the GI Bill, that eased the white, male Fordist subject's access to housing have vanished or atrophied, the right to protect one's property through the use of lethal force (the "castle doctrine") has intensified in recent decades.

4. Kandice Chuh, *The Difference Aesthetics Makes: On the Humanities "After Man"* (Durham, NC: Duke University Press, 2019) 3.

5. Jeremy Waldron, "Property and Ownership," in *The Stanford Encyclopedia of Philosophy* (Summer 2020), ed. Edward N. Zalta, https://plato.stanford.edu/archives/sum2020/entries/property/.

6. C. B. MacPherson, *The Political Theory of Possessive Individualism: Hobbes to Locke* (Oxford: Oxford University Press, 1962).

7. MacPherson, *Political Theory of Possessive Individualism*, 3. For a version of the claim that MacPherson's theory can be used to explain the 2008 financial

crisis, see Hugh Breakey, "C. B. MacPherson, *The Political Theory of Possessive Individualism: Hobbes to Locke*," in *The Oxford Handbook of Classics in Contemporary Political Theory*, ed. Jacob T. Levy (Oxford: Oxford University Press, 2016), 10.1093/oxfordhb/9780198717133.013.42.

8. Cheryl I. Harris, "Whiteness as Property," *Harvard Law Review* 106, no. 8 (1993): 1707–1791. I am thinking of the murders of Trayvon Martin and Colten Boushie in particular, although the valuation of property over racialized lives is a critique often raised by the Black Lives Matter and Idle No More movements.

9. Brenna Bhandar, *Colonial Lives of Property: Law, Land, and Racial Regimes of Ownership* (Durham, NC: Duke University Press, 2018).

10. Amy Carillo Rowe and Eve Tuck, "Settler Colonialism and Cultural Studies: Ongoing Settlement, Cultural Production, and Resistance," *Cultural Studies ↔ Critical Methodologies* 17, no. 1 (2017): 3–13.

11. Rowe and Tuck, "Settler Colonialism and Cultural Studies," 4, 5.

12. Eileen Moreton-Robinson, *The White Possessive: Property, Power, and Indigenous Sovereignty* (Minneapolis: University of Minnesota Press, 2015), xii.

13. Moreton-Robinson, *White Possessive*, xii.

14. Moreton-Robinson, *White Possessive*, xii.

15. Moreton-Robinson, *White Possessive*, xix.

16. See Moreton-Robinson, *White Possessive*, xiii, xix, xx, 53, 54–55, 60, 191, 192, and elsewhere.

17. Bhandar, *Colonial Lives of Property*, 8.

18. Bhandar, *Colonial Lives of Property*, 25.

19. Bhandar, *Colonial Lives of Property*, 8–9.

20. For a helpful summary of the debates over settler-colonial racialization, see Iyko Day's *Alien Capital: Asian Racialization and the Logic of Settler Colonial Capitalism* (Durham, NC: Duke University Press, 2016).

21. "Abutment, n." *OED*, 2011.

22. "Party, n." *OED*, 2005.

23. Chuh, *Difference Aesthetics Makes*, 3.

24. Chuh, *Difference Aesthetics Makes*, xi.

25. Chuh, *Difference Aesthetics Makes*, xi.

26. Chuh, *Difference Aesthetics Makes*, 3.

27. Chuh, *Difference Aesthetics Makes*, 15.

28. Chuh, *Difference Aesthetics Makes*, 15.

29. For an extended discussion of whiteness in midcentury US lyric poetry, see Kamran Javadizadeh, "The Atlantic Ocean Breaking on Our Heads: Claudia Rankine, Robert Lowell, and the Whiteness of the Lyric Subject," *PMLA* 134, no. 3 (2019): 475–490.

30. "Bare, adj., adv., and n." *OED*, 1989.

31. "Cement, n." *OED*, 1989.

Chapter 2

The Poetics of Drift

Coloniality, Place, and Environmental Racialization

Samia Rahimtoola

> So we say, *vacancy* and *abject*, against the was, against a philosophy of once and then not.
>
> —Dawn Lundy Martin, *Discipline*

When an unnamed reviewer writing in *Publisher's Weekly* complained of Dawn Lundy Martin's 2009 book of poems *Discipline* that "one feels that Lundy Martin refuses to see compassion where it exists," they unwittingly linked the relentless negativity of Martin's text to a politics of refusal.[1] In a half-echo of what might seem a politically dubious stance, poet Ed Roberson called his 2006 volume of poems *City Eclogue* "a pessimistic statement, in that I'm going to have to live through this pessimistic time."[2] Taking up these ambivalent declarations about the prominence of negativity in recent experimental African American poetry, this essay examines the complex political significance of the refusal to move beyond or redeem the damages of racialized dispossession. Situated beyond a liberatory politics of resistance, this minoritarian politics and poetics of refusal enables these poets to approximate a liberatory mode that is distinct from the one offered by possessive individualism.

Both *Discipline* and *City Eclogue* are haunted by the racialized urban poor who are perennially out of work, sick without hope of cure, homeless and destitute, and physically and psychically shattered from serving in the endless wars of the post-9/11 era. Figures of negativity, these characters drift through landscapes of destitution where municipal services have been cut, public goods have been privatized, and houses topple into ruin. These are cities, as Martin puts it, "in the middles of nowheres."[3] Roberson describes the dismantling of cities "leveled," "mowed down / to vacant lots of garbage lawn," by intertwined processes of capitalist expropriation, racialized dispossession, and civic neglect.[4] In the face of this negativity, both authors refuse narratives of individual overcoming, urban reconstruction, and environmental repair that would heal or redeem Black suffering. Theirs are, in other words, relentlessly ugly books.

Together, they speak to the uneven distribution of precarity that is produced, as Judith Butler has warned, not by our basic existential exposure to injury in the world, but by uneven vulnerabilities that are organized by our "economic and social relationships [and] the presence or absence of sustaining infrastructures and social and political institutions."[5] Taking up the infrastructural dissolution manifest in the racialized urban landscapes of the early years of the twenty-first century, *Discipline* and *City Eclogue* guide their readers toward a politics and poetics of reinhabitation of landscapes of dispossession. The difficulty of imagining modes of liberation beyond coloniality has long preoccupied critical race theorists. Reaching beyond the blocked, impoverished political imagination that can conceive of liberation only via the very forms of freedom and self-possession that renew dispossession, these negative modes of reinhabitation offer an anticipatory glimpse of decolonial liberation. In the wake of the renewed reciprocal construction of race and place under neoliberal policies of urban development, such reinhabitations of place may be understood as salient strategies of resisting racialized dispossession and, more broadly, of resisting antiblackness itself. Far from pessimistic wallowing, then, the poets' shared impulse to dwell within landscapes of destitution is a politically urgent and historically necessary maneuver that opens up critical possibilities of decolonial resistance.[6]

Central to this shared political and poetic intervention is the complex and, at times, self-contradictory figure of *drift*. On the one hand, drift is thematically embodied by the chorus of drifters and vagrants whose muted, directionless wanderings reflect the nonteleological arcs of those absented from the rights and property relations central to self-making as it has been patterned by Enlightenment thought. This subjective state of drift bears with it a particular environmental orientation, also registered thematically, which embodies the racialized subject's unstable, tenuous relation to landscapes produced by the ongoing dispossessions of chattel slavery, settler colonialism, and racialized capitalism. On the other hand, the image of drift refracts the formal difficulty of articulating a mode of inhabiting place that resists coloniality's twin logics of possession and dispossession. This formal difficulty, as the epigraph of this essay suggests, is itself caught up in the attempt to escape a broader set of structural antagonisms—master and slave, white and Black, or "being" and "nothing," to use Martin's words—inaugurated by a modernity in which humanity is defined against the racialized subject. Seen from a Black perspective, these structural antagonisms, in which the Black subject is extinguished, entail "a philosophy of once and then not."[7] Tracing the wayward gestures of those who live "near not being," and who appear to be merely borne along by the currents of historical violence, this essay uncovers incipient forms of decolonial repossession.[8]

Blight: Race and Environment

Blight has a relatively recent history when applied to urban environments. Originally used by farmers to describe a disease or other "baleful influence" that damaged plants, the term was transplanted to urban contexts by social reformers in the early twentieth century.[9] Designations of blight were soon accompanied by remedies of urban renewal, which rebranded infrastructural dissolution as infrastructural improvement. As property law expert Wendell Pritchett has argued, designating an area as blighted—as in the case of Stuyvesant Town on the eastside of Manhattan—enabled cities to clear desirable neighborhoods of the poor.[10] By the mid-1940s, blight had become a racialized term applied to Black, Hispanic, and Jewish neighborhoods.[11] In its racialized deployment, blight enabled the reciprocal construction of poor urban landscapes and racialized subjects. Turning to Dawn Lundy Martin's *Discipline*, a book that dwells in landscapes of Black dispossession, I argue that Martin's poetry enables us to diagnose *and* resist a contemporary situation in which race is environmentally produced through discourses of blight.

Critical race theory has long taught us that race is a social invention that stabilizes phenotypical difference into cultural meaning. Just how race has been socially produced has varied historically. Writing in the early nineteenth century, Alexander von Humboldt contended that environment particulars determined the vast cultural and material differences encountered by a globalizing, colonizing West. Climate and geography, von Humboldt felt, were responsible for character differences between the dark-skinned inhabitants of the tropics and lighter-skinned Europeans. Competing theories of race, which held that race inhered in the "blood," also circulated in the nineteenth century, often servicing a slaveholding agenda. Just think, for example, of the "one drop rule," which meant that any American with "one drop" of African blood would be considered Black. Locating and stabilizing race—does it emerge from environmental conditions, or is it encoded in the organism itself?—persist as major preoccupations of a modernity spurred by global encounters. By reaffirming the links between poverty, criminality, place, and race, blight participates in processes of environmental racialization. Far from a repetition of the tenets of environmental determinism, however, Martin's poetry short-circuits the links that would bind race to place. For Martin, there is nothing natural about the racialized environments of our time.

The title of *Discipline* directs our attention to the ways in which the bodies, desires, and environments of its racialized, gendered, and queer subjects are brought under regulation by disciplinary power. The book's visual layout reinforces this thematic interest in the Black female body and the Black environment's repeated framing by power. Most poems comprise a short block of text suspended within the white page, and the boxlike layout of the poems evokes the numerous forms of captivity—from slave ships to incarceration to racial-gender stereotype—in which the Black female body has been historically confined. These formal enclosures also evoke a parallel history of Black geographic containment that has persisted from the plantation to Jim Crow segregation to the federal housing programs pursued in the post-1965 era by the US Department of Housing and Urban Development.

Interleafed among these claustrophobic lyric prose poems are a series of short poems composed entirely from binary code. With their sequences of "0"s and "1"s, these poems refract the lyric "I"—visually and thematically—through the automated instructions of machine technology. As "I" becomes "1," the poems ask us to see the racialized subject and the racialized environment as social and technological artifacts of a diffuse disciplinary network of power that includes housing law, police procedure, social discrimination, and stereotype. The code poems evidence both the difficulty and the urgency of decoding and interrupting the multiple scripts that reinforce prevailing social and racial inequalities. Take, for example, the following code poem:

> 0110010001100001011101001101011011
> 01110011001010111001101110011/01110
> 00001101100011000010110001101100101[12]

Translated into text, it reads: "darkness / place." For Martin, a central mechanism of the reproduction of racial inequality is the reciprocal construction of race and environment. As "darkness" tips into "place," racialization is sustained and underwritten by it. Read this way, Martin's poem participates in the suturing of race into place. But by interjecting the slash mark, a grammatical feature not found in the two-symbol system of binary code, the poem disrupts the seamless conceptual passage between race and place. In so doing, the poem halts what we could name the ideological reification of race as landscape.

In another poem that short-circuits the reciprocal construction of race and place, Martin begins:

> I am from an undone city, a killing here, a killing there city. Safe enough. You want to hear that story. Falling people and birds. All that hanging from wires. Being adrift in place. Unweeded gardens. . . .[13]

The poem locates the speaker in a non-site—an "undone city"—that has been unraveled through violence and unnamed dispossessions that likely include slashed municipal services, deindustrialization, and decades of underinvestment in urban infrastructure. Even murder, usually understood as an intersubjective act committed by an individual or social group, is projected onto the landscape—an environmental violence that occurs "here" and "there." Alert to the ways in which blight's racialized landscapes work to naturalize and individualize racial inequalities, the poem's "unweeded gardens" explain urban dispossession as an outcome of the racialized subject's character and ethos rather than infrastructural neglect.

But the poem soon interrupts its description of urban blight to "call out" the (white) reader's desire to aesthetically consume the spectacle of Black suffering as landscape: "You want to hear that story," taunts Martin. Amy De'Ath has argued that such strategies of readerly antagonism seek to turn away from the liberal politics of recognition that usually sustains the racialized artist's presence in a majority white literary scene.[14] Drawing on the writings of Jodi Melamed, De'Ath argues that because such recognition relies on categories of difference produced by the differential value-making processes of racialization, it "actually serve[s] to reproduce colonial structures of domination."[15] Martin's taunt certainly antagonizes the liberal scene of recognition, but it also antagonizes the desire to locate race in place. Read this way, the poem recalls geographer Katherine McKittrick's warning against the "the ideological assumption that blackness is equated with the ungeographic and a legacy of dispossession."[16] For McKittrick, the too-easy equation of blackness with poverty, ghettos, and blight is dangerous because it reifies race as a property of place *and* because it casts the Black subject as nongeographic. As Martin puts it in another poem, "abandonment figure waits atop grassy hill."[17] The floating signifier of dispossession, able to stand in at once for the subject and their place of inhabitation, reinforces their mutual negation. Whatever side of the political spectrum they emerge from—whether their hope is to repair or extend racialized dispossessions—such reifications cast the racialized subject as a victim to, rather than agent of, place. Learning from McKittrick, then, we can see Martin's "call out" as a mode of antagonism that resists the too-easy yoking of the racialized urban environment with dispossession.

The provocation here is clear. Even as she dismantles the reciprocal construction of race and blighted environments, Martin refuses to offer the reader optimistic images of the reclamation of urban Black life or avenues to its improvement. There are no colorful bursts of flowers trellising the rough edges of the city, no smells of cooking or sounds of children laughing; there's no relief at all. Against the unnamed reviewer's disappointment that Martin "refuses to see compassion where it exists," I argue that this refusal is a meaningful one for both decolonial resistance and Black repossessions of place. Understanding this significance, however, requires a detour into the ambivalent history of improvement in US urban centers. In this history, what appear to be acts of repair and betterment frequently mask episodes of dispossession and harm.

Take, for example, social reform movements for urban sanitation and social services, including those that culminated with the founding of Jane Addams and Ellen Gates Starr's Hull House in late nineteenth-century Chicago. Established in the 1890s in an area of the city densely populated with European immigrants, Hull House offered an employment bureau, English classes, and daycare services for working mothers. By the 1920s, the house incorporated African American residents newly arrived to the area. Because urban reformers sought to modify the built environment to create better health conditions for vulnerable populations, ecocritic Lawrence Buell has argued that they may be seen as early campaigners for environmental justice who sought to "green" the city through better sanitation and increased access to green space.[18] Like the wilderness conservation movement that Buell argues is environmental justice's companion piece, urban reformers believed that health and well-being could be improved through human management of the physical environment.[19]

Yet, schemes for the improvement of the racialized urban poor often were symptomatic of the racist and technocratic desire to manage allegedly unruly, primitive races. Jane Addams herself bemoaned the American city's internal "colony of colored people who have not been brought under social control."[20] However, improvement didn't simply imply a managerial attitude toward empirically stable racial pathologies. Far from improving preexisting racialized pathologies, pathologies that included licentiousness, laziness, and other morally dubious qualities assigned to the city's darker residents, urban reform movements often produced them. In her investigation of sociological surveys and photographs of Black urban life in early twentieth-century Philadelphia and New York, Saidiya Hartman has shown that social reformers documented only what was to be "targeted for destruction and elimination."[21] Improvement, in other words, was a means of producing and policing the urban Black poor. And, as improvers selected scenes from and provided captions to Black urban life, they actively created the very blight they sought. Stamping Black homes as "moral hazards" and reframing urban interracial intimacy into "Negro quarters," improvement naturalized both the supposed social inferiority of the Black subject and the racial geographies of Jim Crow.[22] Hartman's archival recoveries of Black life beyond these framings reveal the ways in which improvement campaigns were not simply efforts to manage physical environments to produce health; they were also efforts to manage physical environments to produce race. Little more than a euphemism for new environmental strategies of racial formation, improvement targeted the Black body, and especially the Black female body, as an unruly object in need of control.

The afterlives of these early campaigns for urban improvement continue to refract within strategies of twenty-first-century urban redevelopment. Consider, for example, recent efforts to "green" low-income, minority, and industrial areas of the urban landscape. Empirical studies have long shown that residents of poor and minority neighborhoods experience negative health impacts due to greater exposure to environmental risk and limited access to green space when compared with their wealthier and majoritarian counterparts.[23] Paradoxically, however, efforts to remediate brownfields into green space, to repurpose obsolescent infrastructure into urban parks, and to construct parklets in densely urban areas often spur gentrification and racialized displacement as low-income, minority, and industrial sections of the city are newly perceived to be more livable.[24] Perhaps best emblematized by the transformation of New York City's former West Side Elevated Line—a railroad transporting meat, dairy, and produce to and from the factories of West Chelsea—into first an abandoned infrastructural zone and then a revived urban greenway known as the High Line, such efforts recast capitalism's ongoing enclosures as public services. Flanked by multi-million-dollar condominiums whose property values have skyrocketed due to their proximity to the park, the High Line extends, rather than undoes, such enclosures.

To return to Martin, we may interpret the desire to stay with the damage as both an incipient critique of urban planning and a critical acknowledgment of the yoking of race and landscape within the broader discourses of improvement in which planning takes shape. In this sense, *Discipline* corrects environmental justice scholars who often treat race as a stable empirical category rather than a product of social and material practices.[25] But, the subject of *Discipline* is not only that of racial and environmental subjugation; it is also the struggle for resistance through repossession of both self *and* environment. Going back to the poem that began this extended meditation on race and the urban landscape, I'd like to suggest that we can find a figure for this ambiguous repossession—one which never quite seems to "belong" or to be capable of sustaining an uncomplicated relation to place—in drift. The poem offers only a fleeting glimpse of the subject condemned to live among blight: "Being adrift in place." Read across the book as a whole, the figure of drift flickers across the pages of *Discipline*, interweaving scenes of subjugation and resistance. One poem casts it as an interruption to the will that complicates the agency of the Black female subject: "The body drifts off to fuck like a ghost."[26] Another poem develops it as a psychic refuge from the unending nightmare of colonial dispossession: "We drift inside dreams to escape the dislogic of hunger."[27] A third pursues it as a state of being: "I'm drifting."[28] Complex and ambiguous, drift, for Martin, names the racialized subject's precarious relation to space in a social and material world fully structured by coloniality's dispossessions.

According to the *OED*, to drift is "to move as driven or borne along by the current; to float or move along with the stream or wind."[29] Like the Situationist *dérive* with which drift shares a name, Martin's term evokes "a technique of transient passage through varied ambiances," usually urban ones.[30] For the Situationist International, the European avant-garde collective active from 1957 to 1972, the *dérive* was a central strategy for the transformation of everyday life under late capitalism. As a mode of exploratory, open-ended passage, it enacted an alternative both to a city structured to ease the flows of commodities and to the passivity the group saw at the basis of spectacular capitalism.[31] With its quest to transform the alienated city into a Hegelian landscape of self-recognition and collective liberation, the *dérive* promised to unleash all the "possibilities and meanings" of the rehumanized city.[32] To achieve this, Guy Debord urged, the drifter must "drop their usual motives for movement and action . . . and let themselves be drawn by the attractions of the terrain and the encounters they find there."[33] Paradoxically, passivity leads the way toward active engagement with the urban environment.

Notwithstanding their shared interest in passivity, one would be hard-pressed to read the liberatory potential of Situationist practice into Martin's figure of drift. And, while this difficulty is no doubt compounded by the broader Situationist silence on the ways in which spatial mobility and identity reciprocally shape one another, it also and more broadly speaks to the ways in which the master-slave relation, as Frank Wilderson has argued, may not be easily analogized to the capitalist-worker relation.[34] The Situationist drifter is able to overcome alienation through acts of perception, recognition, and performance that restore the city to its human dimensions. But, Martin's speaker is not alienated. She is, as Martin repeatedly reminds us, abjected. Cast in the position of inhumanity, she is unable to find herself within the "human" architecture of the modern city.

If the avant-garde practice of the *dérive* offers one interpretative anchor for the passive, aleatory condition of drift, another might be found in a crucial archetype of the (de)colonial imaginary: the zombie. A racialized figure of the subject turned object, stripped of sovereignty and life, the zombie is a central figure of Haitian folklore. In seventeenth- and eighteenth-century Saint-Domingue, enslaved persons believed death could free them from the brutal conditions of plantation slavery through opening a passage back to Africa. Those unable to make this passage, however, were condemned to endure as zombies. Like these figures of the living dead, the one who drifts is held captive by the very racialized geography from which she longs to escape. In an essay on *Life in a Box Is a Pretty Life*, which Martin published three years after *Discipline*, Marius Henderson interprets Martin's figures of negativity—those subjects who meander aimlessly and hopelessly through the book's pages—as images for the ways in which Black life has been "positioned as socially dead."[35] Henderson draws on the work of Afro-Pessimist scholar Frank Wilderson to show that Black life is rendered as "anti-Human, a position against which Humanity establishes, maintains, and renews its coherence."[36] Approached this way, the psychic and corporeal condition of drift is part and parcel of the curse of inhabiting the position of death-in-life embodied by the zombie.[37]

But, to read "drift" in these terms is to mistake a relationship to damage and dispossession for an identity with it. To align oneself with drift, to return again to this essay's epigraph, is to position oneself slightly askew from the self-extinguishing "philosophy of once and then not." According to the *OED*'s definition, to drift is to admit the self's vulnerability to the social and material forces in which one is immersed, but it is also to adopt an oblique, even disinterested stance in these forces. If, as Martin puts it, "what the body resists the body is," drift salvages a mode of nonrelation—aloof but not outside, willed but not willful—to the damaging conditions of racism, capitalism, and patriarchy.[38] It also, as I will soon show, opens a quaver in the interstices between life and social death, possession and dispossession, that is crucial for addressing the unresolved struggle over race and landscape. In the next section of this essay, I turn to Ed Roberson's *City Eclogue* to address drift as a practice central to reinhabitations of the racialized urban environments. To attend to such repossessions of place, however, we must first come to grips with its ruination.

The Color Line and the Dialectic of Development

At least since Marshall Berman, modernity has been understood as "a maelstrom of perpetual disintegration and renewal" with paroxysms of creative destruction that rip urban space apart to remake it in the name of capitalist development.[39] Taking up the Faustian development projects of Robert Moses—the famous "power broker" whose imprint can still be felt in the racialized geographies of New York City—Berman confirmed Theodor Adorno and Max Horkheimer's warning that "the fully enlightened earth radiates disaster triumphant" for the urban landscape.[40] For Berman, the geography of the city is sculpted within a capitalist dialectic of enlightened development and disastrous dispossessions. Echoing Marx's dictum that under capitalism "all that is solid melts into air," Berman saw, in the instability of the modern city, the dispossessions and attenuations that accompany accumulation and development. Neighborhoods are razed; new towers rise.

In an essay adapted from the final lecture he gave before his death in 2013, Berman clarifies the extent to which firsthand experiences of displacement—his family moved from their home in the South Bronx when the area was cleared for the Cross-Bronx Expressway in the 1950s—shaped his own study of urbicide.[41] Despite appearances, Berman insists, "ruin was a process" rather than an event.[42] Indeed, if Moses's mythic attempt to remake the urban landscape was soon thwarted by Jane Jacobs and other community activists in the 1960s, urbicide would continue through more covert means. Throughout the 1970s, Berman writes, banks redlined areas to which they would not lend, buildings were set on fire so that landlords could collect insurance payouts, and cities redrew their limits to avoid providing municipal services to the racialized urban poor.

In his book-length exploration of the devastations of the urban Black environment, *City Eclogue*, Ed Roberson depicts this dialectic of development as it fractures along the color line. This color line, which W. E. B. Du Bois declared "the problem of the Twentieth Century," regulates the production of race through the division of place—from lunch counters to neighborhoods.[43] It also recasts the dialectic of development along racial lines, segregating costs from profits and dispossessions from expropriations. As Lynn Keller has argued in her analysis of Roberson as an environmental justice poet, the poem's depiction of the costs of urban redevelopment resonates with the analysis of urban sociologists like Michael Bennett.[44] Roberson describes the delirious remaking of the city in the name of development as a form of "vagrant progress," which continually displaces and unhouses Black life, "whose any settlement / is overturned for the better / of a highway through to someone else's possibility."[45] The poem references the historical razing of Black neighborhoods—from Chicago to Oakland to the Bronx—to make way for urban developments, including highways to the suburbs. Such progress is "vagrant" because of its restless and reckless pursuit of development no matter the cost. It uproots and annihilates, turning the racialized urban environment to rubble.

In what follows, I address two serial poems that explicitly address the ways in which Black urban life, whether it remains standing or falls before the bulldozer, is structured in relation to dispossession. Reminding us of McKittrick and Martin's warnings against the fixing of race in landscape, such a relation should not be taken to be exhaustive. Alert to this crucial difference—between a relation to dispossession and an identity with it, between an annihilated sense of place and a precarious, unstable one—I will ultimately guide us toward moments of resistance that open up alternatives within scenes of racialized, place-based dispossession. Reading two back-to-back poems published in *City Eclogue*, "Beauty's Standing" and "The Open," I argue that, however provisional and hesitating, these moments of resistance help move us beyond the conceptual impasses that block our current imagination of decolonial liberation and repossession.

Both poems narrate the destruction of an urban housing project to make way for an unnamed new development. The chronological structure of the two poems invites readers to create a linear narrative that moves from possession to dispossession through the unhousing of a poor Black community. Indeed, the parallel structure of the poems' opening lines appears to structure demolition as a singular and climactic event that ends one history and launches another: "The buildings stood," begins "Beauty's Standing," while "The Open" launches with "their buildings razed." Roberson, however, frustrates this desire for a clean temporal and conceptual break between possession and dispossession. Indeed, "Beauty's Standing," the poem sited prior to the destruction of urban housing, might better be described as the *with*standing of municipal cuts, environmental toxicity, and the privatization of basic public services, like waste management. If the buildings stand, Roberson suggests, they do so only as "a bunch of / garbage odd-sized barges / lashed together."

Together, the poems suggest that understanding dispossession as a singular event is untenable because dispossession has always already happened for the colonized, racialized subject. Such ordinary ruination may remind us of what Lauren Berlant has described as "slow death," or "the physical wearing out of a population in a way that points to its deterioration as a defining condition of its experience and historical existence."[46] While Berlant grants us the terms to differentiate the abeyance and even fraying of life under the conditions of late capitalism from discrete events of "memorable impact," Roberson's poems point to the ways in which divergent temporalities of racialized dispossession can amplify each other's resonances within the synchronizations of lived time. Ordinary ruination intersects with extraordinary demolition, and "slow death" travels alongside traumatic events, as the various tempos of racialized dispossession at times coincide and at times peel away from one another.

Far from reinstating a distinction between the event and the episode, Roberson's poems show us that the undeniably dramatic and spectacular event of slavery may, paradoxically, best be captured by the episodic scale and tempo of everyday attenuations. Throughout "Beauty's Standing" and "The Open," Roberson reveals the ways in which Black life continues to be structured by the long aftermath of slavery. So, in one passage of "Beauty's Standing" that meditates on the dispossession of racialized subjects in relation to waste and urban waste management, Roberson reflects on the complex temporality of living in the aftermath of destitution:

The other side of the idea
of having anything
to throw away to be collected is *après*
the collections—

is our territory
After empties us
out into the local dump
to turn what we can find over

to make up
into something we can use.[47]

To be without waste, here, is to build one's livelihood in relation to what others have cast off.[48] It is, in other words, to be rendered waste, as the community finds itself to be when it is "[emptied] / out into the local dump" along with discards and junk.[49] To be "*après* / the collections" is to live the condition of dispossession, which Roberson suggests needs to be seen as the "other side" of the excesses of consumption and accumulation that structure possessive individualism. "After" slips from temporal index to a noun in ways that reflect what Frank Wilderson and others have described as Black life's structuring by the ontological antagonisms inaugurated by slavery: white and Black, free and enslaved, possessor and dispossessed. If slavery generates a rupture that continues to shape the meanings of Black life, this reification of *after* points to the ways that contingent histories become dangerously ossified, appearing as uncontestable conditions.

In "The Open," Roberson again places the twenty-first-century urban Black environment in relation to the temporal horizon of slavery. In the opening cleared by the developers' bulldozers, he depicts residents who wander like "ghosts / their color that haze of plaster dust."[50] The image draws on literary traditions of African American haunting to cast displaced residents in relation to the social and corporeal deaths produced by enslavement. The newly razed city, too, resembles the landscape of the plantation, which, as Simone Brown has shown, facilitated surveillance and segregation.[51] To live in the "open" of the plantation was to live where one would be dehumanized and disciplined. Survival was tethered to the capacity to find shelter. As Roberson puts it, "People lived where it weren't open."[52] The demolition of housing unshelters, and so undoes, the subjects who reside there.

The figurative layers of Roberson's poem sediment the multiple clearings that have comprised African American history, from the fields of the plantation to the urban ruin. Such sedimentations gather the multiple, nonlinear unfolding of slavery's long aftermath. One can't, he suggests, effectively read the racialized landscape of dispossession outside of its relation to the afterlives of slavery. And, if one doesn't perform this reading, one not only certainly misinterprets the duration of dispossession for more dramatic, singular events of expropriation; one also misses the temporal drift by which seemingly closed historical processes like coloniality may be reopened and resisted. With slavery as his horizon, Roberson guides us toward Black resistance as it flickers within the figure of drift.

Life in the Ruins: Drifting on the Ghost Ship

How can resistance be reconceptualized within ruins generated within and through discourses of repair? To answer this question, I turn to a final image of "The Open": the ghost ship. The ghost ship has a long history in literary and visual representations of Black mutiny, including Herman Melville's famous depiction of the *San Dominick* in "Benito Cereno." For Roberson, as for Melville, the ghost ship serves as a central ground for the interrogation of liberation, (dis)possession, and place-based reclamation. Melville's depiction of the *San Dominick* is famously bleak. With its "hearse-like roll," ruined lettering, and skeleton masthead, the ship recalls the reciprocal construction of race and place through blight.[53] What better proof that enslaved persons' enslavement is justified than their inability to care for the ship once it falls into their own hands? Despite this apparent reinscription of race in place, the repossession and reclamation of the ship generate a momentary opening in the spatial capture of Black life from within the condition of damage.

It is this echo that Roberson carries into "The Open" when he reimagines Black repossession. After the neighborhood has been cleared, one house still stands within the ruins of urbicide. A "ghost ship" adrift in "a flattened sea of housing brick rubble," the house persists in the clearings of "what is not even a place anymore."[54] Only one man remains, "standing in the last building standing."[55] A squatter inhabiting the site of damage, he is:

> standing there, late foot on the sill as if
> balanced on the prow of his ghost ship he
> hasn't even had to take over.[56]

Captain of a ship "he / hasn't even had to take over," the man, at first glance, can hardly be taken as exemplary of liberatory struggle. Captain and crew have voluntarily fled their leaking vessel, leaving it to the only incidentally liberated, and likely doomed, subject of slavery who can be made exemplary neither of insubordination nor domination. Keller has named this tenuous figure of resistance "no champion."[57] Reading the squatter through Agamben's concept of "bare life," Keller finds him "a vulnerable figure stripped of political significance."[58] Roberson's gamble, as I see it, is that the squatter is, in fact, a meaningful political figure of decolonial resistance. In this mutinous figure, the poem grounds its imagination of liberation and the repossession of place.

At once capable of standing in for domination *and* liberation, dispossession *and* repossession, Roberson's squatter reveals an unfinished struggle over place in which meaning remains up for grabs precisely because it is still in the making. One can, in other words, understand the ambivalence of this image as a reflection of the hermeneutical and representational difficulties of "fixing" the meaning of provisional, as yet incomplete struggles for decolonial liberation. Such figurative ambivalence may also be found in the poem's depiction of Black housing. In the image of a vacant, blight-ridden building with "doors off the building, panes gone from / the frames," an unfinished struggle for meaning once again becomes visible.[59] Are these signs of dismantling indicative of damage, or do they embody explosive insurrection?

The ramifications of this question extend beyond the unfinished story of struggle to speak to our collective imagination of decolonial liberation. Inspired by Fred Moten's construction of "blackness" as "the place that has no place," Angela Hume has argued that Black radicalism's pursuit of a negative political ontology speaks to the belief that it is only by ending a world whose every social and material fiber has been built through colonial processes of racism that a liberated Black world may be founded in its place.[60] Following Hume, we might read Roberson's depiction of the devastated house-turned-slave ship as a shattering "repudiation" of a racist world.[61] Even Melville's "hearse-like" *San Dominick*, read this way, might signal an end to racism's discursive and material structures. Roberson's poem, however, strikes a more ambivalent note, one which makes all the difference between the liberatory politics of the 1960s and today. If Amiri Baraka, writing in "A Poem Some People Will Have to Understand," could make his famous appeal for Black liberation by asking for "the machinegunners [to] please step forward," Roberson's poems disclose an imaginative impasse in which there appears to be no conclusion to the process of living with the damage.[62] Neither apocalyptic devastation nor remediation of harm promises to end racialized dispossession. Only by maintaining an affinity with Roberson's squatter can we take up the urgent project of reimagining decolonial liberation.

Critical race theorists have long noted the ways in which race underwrites modern concepts of freedom, possession, and even humanity itself. Sylvia Wynter, for one, argues that race serves as the central—if elided—basis for definitions of Man in the secularizing West, separating him from his less than human Native and Black others.[63] Hartman has similarly shown that Western conceptions of freedom arise in relation to the historical and philosophical development of Black slavery.[64] More specifically to the terms of this chapter, McKittrick has shown that possessive individualism relies on racialized dispossession, posing a difficult quandary for imagining decolonial liberation. She warns that emancipatory projects that stake their claims on possession and ownership reinforce the existing "bifurcation-segregation system" on which coloniality depends. Recalling Roberson's representation of those dispossessed who live *after* the collections as the inverse image of possessive individualism, McKittrick argues that under coloniality, liberation can only be conceived as "being with," and "being with" is always defined by, and so dependent on, the condition of "being without."[65] To be clear, the problem is not Black possession in and of itself. Such a claim, which simply inverts the terms of the "bifurcation-segregation system" to praise dispossession erroneously *instead of* possession, speciously repackages all too common discriminatory practices—from federal housing policies to predatory lending by banks—as resistance. The problem, as McKittrick puts it, is the discursive and material coupling of liberation and possession. Put differently, can we nudge our imaginations of liberation beyond possession, ownership, and the condition of "being with"?

Such a project might usefully be cast as a minoritarian one because it points to the ways in which political resistance may require aesthetic experimentalism. Faced with the impasse—an impasse at once political and aesthetic—of reimagining Black relations to place beyond coloniality, both Martin and Roberson respond with a poetics of repossession that enables them to find a way through. The concluding lines of Roberson's poem guide us toward such a repossession of place, all the while withholding its more reparative forms:

> a lone survivor, a squatter keeping it
> open
> drifts out into the open[66]

No longer comprised only of the exposures generated by place-based dispossession, "the open" becomes a means of holding open the enclosures of Black place. Rather than reaffirming the squatter's rights to ownership, the poem articulates a nonpossessive relation to place. As the poem puts it, to "[keep] it / open" is not the same as keeping. Far from depicting an act of possession, the poem points toward a mode of inhabiting place that resists the flawed desire to erect a liberatory politics through the possessiveness that is merely one side of coloniality's coin. And, if openness speaks to a place held open for repossession, drift names the subject's precarious reoccupation of that place, a reoccupation which unfolds without the guarantees of possessive individualism. Far from an artifact or emblem of dispossession, then, drift enables a theory and practice of reinhabitation that dismantles the "bifurcation-segregation system" that McKittrick puts at the heart of coloniality. For Roberson's ghostly squatter, drift at once reopens the contingency of present conditions *and* teaches us to refrain from the too-easy translation that would understand liberation as simply that which passes for freedom in our modern world.

Coda: *The Last Black Man in San Francisco*

The question of who, exactly, owns the towering Victorian house that Jimmy Fails and his friend Mont painstakingly maintain—touching up its paint, watering the garden—haunts Joe Talbot's film *The Last Black Man in San Francisco*.[67] Located in the Fillmore District, the heart of San Francisco's African American community prior to its demolition and redevelopment during the contested urban renewal policies of the postwar decades, the house stands in a geography where racial struggle appears to be at once finished and failed. At the film's opening, a middle-aged white couple occupies the house. To the annoyance of the couple, Jimmy and Mont frequently return to the house, even bringing tools to carry out minor repairs. This iterative and self-undoing practice marks an ephemeral place-making that challenges both racialized discourses of blight and the property relations that undergird possessive individualism by staging care, rather than ownership, as the criterion for relations to place. A dispute over inheritance leads to the white couple's displacement from the property, and Jimmy and Mont promptly reclaim the vacated house, which, we are told, had once been owned by Jimmy's father. Soon after, Jimmy and Mont are thrown out by a real estate company.

One might be tempted to interpret the film as a lament for an interrupted chain of patrilineal transmission, one in which the property fails to be passed down from Jimmy's father to his children due to the neoliberal forms of racialized dispossession I have been tracing in this essay. However, the question of what constitutes possession in the first place is complicated by the protagonist's claim that his grandfather built the house with his own two hands in 1946, exactly one year prior to the publication of the San Francisco City Planning Commission's report, *New City: San Francisco Redeveloped*, which advocated for the urban renewal of the allegedly blighted African American neighborhoods of the Fillmore and Western Addition. This temporal coincidence—in which Jimmy's grandfather's claim is made on the eve of racialized displacement—is the first hint that the family mythology may have no basis in fact. More overtly, Jimmy's fantasy is exposed when the realtor selling the home informs Mont that the house was, in truth, built in 1857.

If the failed transmission of property from Jimmy's father to Jimmy can be blamed on racialized dispossession, the failed fantasy by which Jimmy justifies his reclamation of place has more ambiguous significance. Ultimately, Jimmy's reclamation of the Victorian rests on a dubious claim, but this, despite the realtor's revelation, does not invalidate his repossession. The first failed inheritance—from father to son—leaves open the possibility that proper forms of possession can be restored within the colonial framework of McKittrick's "bifurcation-segregation system." The second failure, however, speaks to the tenuousness of decolonial Black reclamations of place that venture outside the framings of coloniality. Jimmy's grandfather didn't build the house.[68] But, the historical speculation that *he did* not only reopens a seemingly settled racial history by exposing it as provisional and open to change; it also searches out an avenue of reinhabiting place that does not simply reproduce the structure of dispossession. Rather than reasserting proper patrilineal property relations, this reinhabiting interrogates them by asking us to consider what constitutes possession in the first place. In the terms of this essay, however fictional Jimmy's assertion may be, it inaugurates a temporal and spatial practice of drift that, despite its failure as fantasy, opens up imaginative possibilities of decolonial repossession.

In the film's final scene, dusk falls on San Francisco as Mont makes his way through a silent vigil of black-hoodied protesters—a nod to the numerous shootings of unarmed Black youth and to the protests against them—to a dock that reaches into the bay. The scene is dark, a palette of deep blue skies and seas. Suddenly, the film cuts to a brighter, fog-tattered sky on the same bay. There, Jimmy furiously rows against the swells that surge, one after the other, into the bay from the open sea. Still paddling as he exits the frame, Jimmy's exertions, at first glance, appear as the inverse of the passive, nonsovereign, and inconclusive practice this essay has named drift. The more crucial difference between this final disappearing act and the poetics of drift, however, might better be articulated through Jimmy's determination to unmoor himself entirely from place when all his claims, rights, and reclamations—fantastic and real—have, one by one, been stripped away.

Notes

I would like to thank Colby College's Center for the Arts and Humanities for inviting me to deliver an earlier version of this essay during their 2019–2020 Energy/Exhaustion lecture series. I would also like to acknowledge the debt this essay owes to conversation with Christopher Walker, Lisa Bartfai, Nina Hagel, and Angela Hume, as well as to the brilliant editorial pens of Drew Strombeck and Jean-Thomas Tremblay.

1. "Discipline," Review of *Discipline* by Dawn Lundy Martin, *Publisher's Weekly*, June 20, 2011, https://www.publishersweekly.com/978-0-9844598-4-1.

2. Ed Roberson, "'We Are Not the Language': An Interview with Ed Roberson (Part II)," interview by Kathleen Crown, *Callaloo* 33, no. 3 (Summer 2010): 754.

3. Dawn Lundy Martin, *Discipline* (Callicoon, NY: Nightboat, 2011), 14.

4. Ed Roberson, *City Eclogue* (Berkeley, CA: Atelos, 2006), 64.

5. Lauren Berlant, Judith Butler, Bojana Cvejić, Isabell Lorey, Jasbir Puar, and Ana Vujanović, "Precarity Talk: A Virtual Roundtable," *TDR: The Drama Review* 56, no. 4 (2012): 170.

6. In this, Roberson and Martin's project is shared by recent critical work in queer theory, disability studies, and the environmental humanities that has framed staying with social and material damage as both a pragmatic acknowledgment of a world riven by conflict, extraction, and exploitation *and* a crucial aspect of political resistance. See Heather Love, *Feeling Backward: Loss and the Politics of Queer History* (Cambridge, MA: Harvard University Press, 2007); Eli Clare, *Brilliant Imperfection: Grappling with Cure* (Durham, NC: Duke University Press, 2017); Anna Lowenhaupt Tsing, *The Mushroom at the End of the World: On the Possibility of Life in Capitalist Ruins* (Princeton, NJ: Princeton University Press, 2015).

7. Martin, *Discipline*, 7.

8. Martin, *Discipline*, 7..

9. "Blight, n.," *OED*, 2019.

10. Wendell E. Pritchett, "The 'Public Menace' of Blight: Urban Renewal and the Private Uses of Eminent Domain," *Yale Law and Policy Review* 21, no. 1 (2003): 33.

11. Pritchett, "'Public Menace' of Blight," 33–35.

12. Martin, *Discipline*, 31.

13. Martin, *Discipline*, 48.

14. Amy De'Ath, "Decolonize or Destroy: New Feminist Poetry in the United States and Canada," *Women: A Cultural Review* 26, no. 3 (2015): 285–305.

15. De'Ath, "Decolonize or Destroy," 296, 290.

16. Katherine McKittrick, *Demonic Ground: Black Women and the Cartographies of Struggle* (Minneapolis: University of Minnesota Press, 2006), 14.

17. Martin, *Discipline*, 52.

18. Lawrence Buell, *Writing for an Endangered World: Literature, Culture, and Environment in the U.S. and Beyond* (Cambridge, MA: Harvard University Press, 2001), 8.

19. Buell, *Writing for an Endangered World*, 13.

20. Addams blamed the unruliness and licentiousness of African Americans on segregation, which separated the "barbarous" races from their more civilized and restrained counterparts. See Jane Addams, "Social Control," *The Crisis* 1 (January 1911): 22.

21. Saidiya Hartman, *Wayward Lives, Beautiful Experiments: Intimate Histories of Social Upheaval* (New York: W.W. Norton, 2019), 20.

22. Hartman, *Wayward Lives, Beautiful Experiments*, 20.

23. For a history of the struggle for environmental justice, see Robert Bullard, ed., *Unequal Protection: Environmental Justice and Communities of Color* (San Francisco: Sierra Club Books, 1994); Luke W. Cole and Sheila R. Foster, *From the Ground Up: Environmental Racism and the Rise of the Environmental Justice Movement* (New York: New York University Press, 2001).

24. Jennifer R. Wolch, Jason Byrne, and Joshua P. Newell, "Urban Green Space, Public Health, and Environmental Justice: The Challenge of Making Cities 'Just Green Enough,'" *Landscape and Urban Planning* 125 (2014): 239.

25. For just one example of this trend, see Cole and Foster, *From the Ground Up*, 10–18. Cole and Foster put grassroots movements at the heart of their analysis of environmental justice, and perhaps because of this focus on political strategy, they treat race as a stable, empirical category. Thus, while the introduction reflects on the "environment" as a term, no such reflection accompanies the referent of race.

26. Martin, *Discipline*, 11.

27. Martin, *Discipline*, 23.

28. Martin, *Discipline*, 59.

29. "Drift, v.," *OED*, 2019.

30. Guy Debord, "Theory of the Dérive," in *Situationist International Anthology*, ed. and trans. Ken Knabb (Berkeley, CA: Bureau of Public Secrets, 1989), 50.

31. For a historical analysis of the broader political goals of the *dérive* and a theoretical analysis of its ongoing relevance for contemporary struggles against late capitalism, see Carl Lavery, "Rethinking the *Dérive*: Drifting and Theatricality in Theater and Performance Studies," *Performance Research* 23, no. 7 (2018): 1–15.

32. Tom McDonough, Introduction to *The Situationists and the City*, ed. Tom McDonough (London: Verso, 2009), 3. On the "possibilities and meanings" of the rehumanized city, see Debord, "Theory of the Dérive," 51.

33. Debord, "Theory of the Dérive," 50.

34. Lavery, "Rethinking the *Dérive*," 4. Tom McDonough also discusses the ways Situationist *dérives* were, "at some essential level, the search for an encounter with otherness, spurred on in equal parts by the exploration of pockets of class, ethnic and racial difference in the postwar city, and by frequent intoxication" (10–11). On the bad analogy of capitalism and slavery in Marx, see Frank Wilderson, "Blacks and the Master/Slave Relation," interview by C. S. Soong, "Against the Grain," KPFA, March 4, 2015, reprinted in *Afro-Pessimism: An Introduction* (Minneapolis: racked and dispatched, 2017), 16–17.

35. Marius Henderson, " 'Here is the trash heap, nothing there except a muted wailing': Dithering in Negativity and the Failure to Move On," in *The Failed Individual: Amid Exclusion, Resistance, and the Pleasure of Nonconformity*, ed. Katharina Motyl and Regina Schober (Frankfurt: Campus, 2017), 231.

36. Frank Wilderson, *Red, White, and Black: Cinema and the Structure of U.S. Antagonisms* (Durham, NC: Duke University Press, 2010) 11.

37. Like Hume, Henderson locates Black resistance in "the enactment of a destructive negation of an anti-black world." Reading this negation in Martin's images of "bombarded and voided" containments of Black life, Henderson recuperatively uncovers the emergence of Black collectivities from social negation. See Henderson, " 'Here is the trash heap, nothing there except a muted wailing,' " 240.

38. Martin, *Discipline*, 7.

39. Marshall Berman, *All That Is Solid Melts into Air* (New York: Penguin, 1988), 15.

40. Theodor Adorno and Max Horkheimer, *Dialectic of Enlightenment*, trans. John Cumming (New York: Continuum, 2000), 3.

41. For Marshall Berman's discussion of this term, which is meant to capture the deliberate murder of urban neighborhoods through practices of underinvestment and redevelopment, see "Emerging from the Ruins," *Dissent* (Winter 2014): https://www.dissentmagazine.org/article/emerging-from-the-ruins.

42. Berman, "Emerging from the Ruins."

43. W. E. B. Du Bois, *The Souls of Black Folk* (Oxford: Oxford University Press, 2007), 3.

44. Lynn Keller, *Recomposing Ecopoetics: North American Poetry of the Self-Conscious Anthropocene* (Charlottesville: University of Virginia Press, 2017), 215–216.

45. Roberson, *City Eclogue*, 64.

46. Lauren Berlant, *Cruel Optimism* (Durham, NC: Duke University Press, 2011), 95.

47. Roberson, *City Eclogue*, 54.

48. As Margaret Ronda has argued, Roberson "refuses to romanticize this state." Instead, "thrifty resourcefulness" exposes the limits of " 'bootstrap' ideologies

of social betterment through hard work." See Margaret Ronda, "'Not Much Left': Wageless Life in Millenial Poetry," *Post45*, October 9, 2011, http://post45.org/2011/10/not-much-left-wageless-life-in-millenial-poetry/.

49. In her essay on waste and wasting in Claudia Rankine's *Citizen*, Angela Hume argues that figures of waste speak to "how certain bodies are attenuated or made sick under capitalism and the state, while simultaneously being regarded as surplus by these same structures." Roberson's *City Eclogue* adds another dimension to waste's persistence as a crucial racial metaphor in contemporary American poetry. See Angela Hume, "Toward an Antiracist Ecopoetics: Waste and Wasting in the Poetry of Claudia Rankine," *Contemporary Literature* 57, no. 1 (2016): 79.

50. Roberson, *City Eclogue*, 63.

51. Simone Brown, *Dark Matters: On the Surveillance of Blackness* (Durham, NC: Duke University Press, 2015), 51–55.

52. Roberson, *City Eclogue*, 63.

53. Herman Melville, "Benito Cereno," in *Billy Budd, Bartleby, and Other Stories* (New York: Penguin, 2016), 58.

54. Roberson, *City Eclogue*; 70.

55. Roberson, *City Eclogue*, 70.

56. Roberson, *City Eclogue*, 70.

57. Keller, *Recomposing Ecopoetics*, 219.

58. Keller, *Recomposing Ecopoetics*, 219.

59. Roberson, *City Eclogue*, 70.

60. Hume, "Toward an Antiracist Ecopoetics," 101–102.

61. Hume, "Toward an Antiracist Ecopoetics," 102.

62. Amiri Baraka, *S.O.S.: Poems 1961–2013* (New York: Grove Press, 2014), 123.

63. Sylvia Wynter, "Unsettling Coloniality of Being/Power/Truth/Freedom: Towards the Human, After Man, Its Overrepresentation—An Argument," *CR: The New Centennial Review* 3, no. 3 (2003): 257–337.

64. Saidiya Hartman, *Scenes of Subjection: Terror, Slavery, and Self-Making in Nineteenth-Century America* (Oxford: Oxford University Press, 1997).

65. Katherine McKittrick, "On Plantations, Prisons, and a Black Sense of Place," *Social and Cultural Geography* 12, no. 8 (2011): 950.

66. Roberson, *City Eclogue*, 70.

67. *The Last Black Man in San Francisco*, dir. Joe Talbot (New York: A24, 2019).

68. In the mythology of Jimmy's grandfather, one might also hear the elided history of Black labor. Building, in other words, is unyoked from possession in ways that further racialized expropriations.

Chapter 3

Pansexual Public Porn

Trans Gender Docu-Porn in the Long 1970s

RL Goldberg

Porn is dirty. This is, at least, one way to summarize the attitude underpinning the ninety-two-recommendation conclusion of the *Final Report of the Attorney General's Commission on Pornography* (1986).[1] Porn is, the *Report* would have us believe, fundamentally degrading and antisocial. Despite disagreement in their policy recommendations, or on a coherent definition of *pornography*, the commissioners tended to agree on one thing, best summarized by commissioner Dr. Park Elliott Dietz: "a world in which pornography were neither desired nor produced would be a better world."[2] Desperately troubled by pornography's proliferation in public, Commissioner Diane Cusack makes the case more muscularly:

> For 2500 years of western civilization, human sexuality and its expressions have been cherished as a private act between a loving couple committed to each other. This has created the strongest unit of society—the family. If our families become less wholesome, weaker, and less committed to the fidelity that is their core, our entire society will weaken as well. . . . These materials, whose message is clearly that sexual pleasure and self-gratification is paramount, have the ability to seriously undermine our social fabric.[3]

Though the *Report* attended to many of the nuances of pornographic genre and medium—magazine, film, photograph, erotic fiction, softcore, hardcore—the distinction between mainstream pornography and avant-garde pornography was hardly relevant to the commission. For commissioners, harm was harm. Yet this distinction is crucial, I argue, in tracing the representation of trans sexualities in its passage from 1960s avant-garde porn into the mainstream in the late 1970s and its return to avant-garde film in the 1980s and 1990s. We might be tempted to think of the 1970s as the moment when trans sexuality leaves the avant-garde and is assimilated into the mainstream. A liberal reading might correlate increased visibility with political inclusion; but, as I will argue, this reading would be incorrect. While 1970s trans porn depicted trans sex acts, trans sexualities and identities remained taboo. Trans porn's return to the avant-garde in the late twentieth century enables us to see why this narrative of incremental inclusion is insufficient, and what minoritarian politics were constituted on its margins.

In this chapter I trace the historical enclosure of porn publics. By *enclosure* I mean the self-righteous, sanitizing zeal that led to the regulation and broad circumscription of public depictions of sexuality, whether this occurred in the rezoning laws that closed adult bookstores or in the Disneyfication of Times Square and the shuttering of porn theaters. As a guide for public policy, the *Report* decisively reshaped pornographic imaginaries, legitimizing what Whitney Strub describes as attempts—both internal to the pornography market and governmentally imposed—to "sanitize" the mainstream porn industry.[4] In his study of mainstream porn, Strub traces the industry-wide sanitization back to the 1970s, when the confluence of right-moralist, antiporn activism, and later, feminist antiporn activism—the latter coalescing into what came to be known as the feminist porn wars—resulted in a large-scale reshaping of pornography. Pornography's sterilization thus coincided with social and political closures and enclosures throughout the long 1970s: New Right bigotry, HIV/AIDS, and restrictive antisex zoning laws. What did enclosure mean, then, for trans minoritarian pornography contra mainstream pornography?

While important work has been done to historicize sexual enclosure in the United States in the latter half of the twentieth century—Samuel Delany first comes to mind—such accounts tend to center gay male sexualities and socialities. Turning to trans sexualities is an occasion to consider the ways in which another minoritarian community struggled to coalesce under conditions of spatial privation and nomenclatural instability.[5] As I will argue, though trans sex continues to be represented after the sanitizing impulses of the 1970s, what is effectively elided from mainstream trans porn isn't so much sex acts, as Strub claims in the case of cisgender pornography, but representations of trans gender as an autonomous political identification outside of pornography. Del LaGrace Volcano's *Pansexual Public Porn* (1998), which indicates an avant-garde engagement with pornography, intervenes in this history by refusing a neat bifurcation between trans sexuality and transsexuality. Volcano's film points to the violent history of enclosure in trans porn by turning toward trans identity and identification as a sexual fantasy that organizes subjects in forming political solidarities, friendships, and networks of care. Produced at the height of the HIV/AIDS epidemic, *Pansexual Public Porn* models a sexual-ethical practice of care, compellingly exemplifying avant-garde attempts to reopen planes and fields of enclosure and "make space" for minoritarian communities. The film flips the *Report*'s findings: if the film can be called *antisocial*, it is only to the degree that it rejects a civilizational definition of society like Cusack's and yearns for a less enclosed, more *public* public.

The social and political enclosures that precede the 1986 *Report*, from the Meese Commission, to restrictive zoning laws, confirm Commissioner Cusack's polemical, sanctimonious sense that what was under threat was the social fabric, the family, and public morality. Though the impact of this text is debated—as Michael McManus notes in the introduction, it was notoriously difficult to find anyone willing to publish it—the *Report* is indicative of, perhaps, the only generalization one can make about the porn industry: that like a coastline, its irregular shape is almost entirely dictated by tidal pressures. The ebb and flow of social and political mores yield an uneven landscape of sexual acceptability, sometimes more permissive, sometimes less so. The 1986 *Report* failed to define pornography adequately, and Volcano's film also allows us to recognize the ways in which the *Report* was similarly not up to the task of defining several other key terms it relied on: *antisocial*, *degrading*, and *family*.

Is Pornography Harmful to You?

Trans porn—or porn depicting trans people—has long been part of the mainstream media landscape, despite both industry and governmental attempts at sanitizing more hardcore depictions. Al Goldstein, the founder of the magazine *Screw*, put it this way in 1981: "There is a pattern to American life that what is avant-garde becomes commonplace. The mass market eventually assimilates that which is innovative or revolutionary."[6] Though trans porn was once niche, produced primarily as sleaze paperbacks and distributed by such outfits as the mob-run Star Distributors, from the late 1980s onward the mainstream market proved, as Goldstein suggested, adept at absorbing trans porn. Video production companies began capitalizing on the technological shift from print media to video. Production companies like Grooby, Pleasure Productions, Heads or Tails Productions, Boy Chick Productions, He Girl Video, and Blue Sands Productions rapaciously produced trans gender pornography for broader audiences.

As trans representation moved into the mainstream, concurrent advances in media practices—specifically the proliferation of VHS and video-editing technology—helped to engineer a self-censorship in hardcore porn film. In the brief gap between films' availability in porn theaters and on VHS, whole scenes were often omitted, rendering those porn films available for private consumption far more normative than the same films as audiences would have seen them in theaters. As film distributors repressed scenes of fisting, piss play, and simulated rape, they reconfigured porn's sexual landscape into what Strub describes as "a flattened one of penetration and orgasm rather than polymorphously perverse play."[7] Strub concludes that by 1987—the same year that VCR ownership reached 50 percent of the US public—"pornographic sex of the 1970s looked very different from its original version. It looked suspiciously like the ideal market conditions for the 1980s: frictionless, vanilla, safe."[8] When viewed against the decade more broadly—which was, on the whole, one of mounting precarity for trans people—the sanitizing idealization of pornography into something "safe" is ironic and perverse. As mainstream pornographic representations of trans people proliferated and became "safer," the material conditions of trans people dramatically deteriorated and became considerably *less* safe.

Though it was far more sexually graphic, mainstream trans porn of the 1980s was politically prudish. This is not to say that earlier producers of trans pornographic texts, like Andy Warhol and Paul Morrisey, had consistent or radical political agendas, or that other producers during the Golden Age of pornography were producing ideologically inflected porno-polemics. Rather, what was really scandalous in the 1970s was not simply depictions of fisting, or transsexuality, or of transsexuals fisting; it was depictions of trans gender as a publicly viable identity rather than merely a kink. It was depictions of trans gender as an identity capable of occupying the public outside of pornographic representation. *Transsexuality*, a fetishized practice often stylized as "Shemale" or "tranny" porn, comes to obscure *trans sexuality*, a gender and sexual identity that exists outside of porn.[9]

Pitched to a mostly cisgender, heterosexual-identified audience of men, trans porn of the 1980s hewed closely to the generic contours of mainstream heterosexual porn. These films merely add the sensationalization of transness—often figured through some filmic reveal—as a key element in pornographic trans representation. Indeed, the most obvious feature of analog trans porn in the 1980s is its sensationalizing depictions of trans gender, uprooting transness from any social or political critique. Such porn privileged the sudden *reveal* of transness, in which the expectations of cisgender sex were suddenly, thrillingly disabused. This is not to say that sensationalization in trans porn was new: one need look only so far as the lurid, vibrant, caricatures on the covers of Trisexual Books, a Star Distributors series, or the photographs on the covers of the Transvestia series, to detect the ubiquity of trans sensationalism.

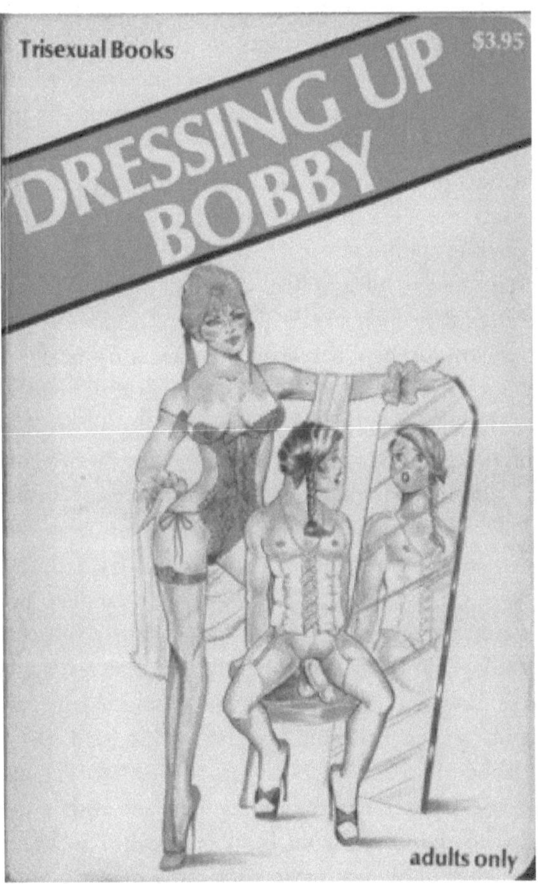

Figure 3.1. Cover of *Dressing Up Bobby* by Trisexual Books. From the author's personal collection.

But 1980s and 1990s directors of "shemale porn" took prurient interest in sensationalization itself, in the moment in which it became clear that someone could or couldn't be said to be "really" a woman. It is this moment of ontological uncertainty, or belated recognition, and the shock that at once sexualizes and desexualizes, that characterizes the kind of trans porn that managed to emerge into the mainstream, where it remains rather popular today. Compared to Warhol's work—films like *Flesh* (1968), *Trash* (1970), and *Women in Revolt* (1971), which featured trans superstars Candy Darling, Holly Woodlawn, and Jackie Curtis—1980s trans porn might appear far more scandalous, and thus a reaction against the industry-wide sanitization that Strub describes.[10] Though the sex acts included are indeed far more graphic in their staging—a Grooby film might depict anal sex in closeup, while Warhol might more suggestively show characters rooting around together, larvally, on a sofa—these films are powered almost exclusively on the salability of trans sensationalism to mainstream markets. What they don't accommodate—what is scrubbed clean from them—is any engagement with the material, lived, conditions of transness in the latter decades of the century.[11] Sanitized of sociopolitical content, these hardcore films mirror more convincingly the ideal market conditions of the 1980s: graphic but defanged, vulgar but apolitical.

At the start of the twenty-first century, political reticence was still the industry standard in mainstream pornographic representations of trans, exposing the enormous gap between transsexuality and trans sexuality. Nowhere is this clearer than in the Cambria List. Circulated in January 2001, shortly after the election of George W. Bush, the Cambria List is a baggy list of objects, sex acts, and kinks whose representation defense attorney Paul Cambria thought might trigger obscenity investigations into porn productions. The Cambria List—something of an unofficial, political extension of the sanitizing project that the mainstream porn industry first implicitly imposed on itself in the 1980s—is an attempt to preempt exactly the sort of government intervention that might put production companies out of business. A chain of negative imperatives that reads as something of a pornographer's Leviticus, the list's disavowal, selected in part, reads: "No bukkake; no spitting or saliva mouth to mouth; no food used as sex object; no coffins; no shot of stretching pussy; no fisting; no degrading dialogue, e.g., 'Suck this cock, bitch' while slapping her face with a penis; no menstruation topics; no transsexuals; no black men-white women themes."[12]

The list's inclusion of "no transsexuals" as a proscription is a standout: while the list refers almost exclusively to acts or to kinks—which, to be sure, transsexuality is often framed as, or conflated with, in much mainstream pornography, from "Shemale" to "Sissy porn"—it is unclear whether Cambria proscribed transsexuality as a fetish category for porn, or, more broadly, as an unacceptable identity for potential performers. The distinction between trans as *kink* and trans as *viable identity* is not merely one of qualitative representation: to proscribe transsexuality as a kink is to consider transsexuality as an obscene act or behavior, rather than as an identity for actors. By extension, to refuse transsexuality as a personal, embodied identity removes transsexual actors—that is to say, transsexuals—as possible subjects of erotic and pornographic imagining.

In what follows I trace Del LaGrace Volcano's reconfiguration of enclosure, rending the landscape of trans sexuality open and public. I argue that Volcano reimagines trans fetishization, staging the trans actor not as fetish object, as in trans porn aimed at heterosexually identified cisgender men, but as an eminently agential figure in gay porn. The filmmaker's interest in the public dimension of pornography seeks to redirect the future of trans gender representation in porn. With VHS technology came increased emphasis on private consumption. This meant, as Jon Davies notes, a new "viewing practice that dispatches with the myriad possibilities of social conflict and intimacy of the cinema theater."[13] Volcano's film, then, reverses the porn industry's privatization and privation, creating, in both production and content, public spaces of viewing, cruising, and collaboration. Further, in its nonprescriptive and direct addressing of safe sex practices, Volcano's film consciously situates itself within the context of the ongoing global HIV/AIDS epidemic. Especially attentive to the impact of HIV/AIDS on trans populations, the film consciously reflects on the pedagogical role docu-porn might play in advocating for informed and intentional sex practices.

Volcano's intervention reconsiders how the sanitization of porn in the long 1970s was not simply a project of excising obscene, or hardcore, sex acts; rather, this sanitizing project elided any understanding of the increasingly precarious material and political positions of trans people, and the ways in which national legal and economic policy founded this precarity. By showing how these spatial and psychic sites of enclosure are far more porous than we're led to believe, Volcano gestures toward a time and place in which we might claim and reclaim public space for trans sexualities.

Ourselves, in the Pursuit of Pleasure

Against a colorful shimmering background, the following artist statement introduces Volcano's *Pansexual Public Porn aka The Adventures of Hans and Del*:

> Hans and I have been talking and dreaming about making queer porn for queer people for as long as we've known each other. The idea has always been to include ourselves, in the pursuit of pleasure, as well as in the means of production. If we had made this five years ago it would have been called Dyke Porn, but as we've changed our sexual and gender identities that doesn't quite fit anymore. We are two Pansexual TrannyBoys trying to make a space for ourselves (and others like us) in that big bad world out there.
>
> Welcome to the world of Pansexual Public Porn![14]

The film begins, then, with two bold claims before offering viewers an invitation that is less contractually consensual than it is performative. (As if to say, *Welcome! You're already here!*) First, Volcano posits the political significance of porn in queer communities. In a subsequent claim, Volcano acknowledges queer sexual and gender fluidity as, itself, a project of discovering and creating publics. Porn and transness are defined here as two distinctive—though imbricated—means of pursuing pleasure, where pleasure is constituted simultaneously by productions of gender and gendered desire. Taken together, gender production and pornographic production, Volcano suggests, efficaciously produce politicized identities, or space for us (and others like us). But making space is also a project of intervening, or carving out room, within an already constituted site, such as kink/SM iconography and practice, so much of which has been borrowed from gay male culture.[15] Claiming space, then, is not only making public queer practices and identifications but also assuming a history and genealogy within the narratives of these established practices. Volcano denaturalizes conventionally gay cruising spaces as cisgender: in one scene, a trans masculine person is pumping (using a cylinder pump to draw blood flow into the genitals and increase their size), an activity hardly standard-practice within gay male cruising sites. Yet the pumping warrants neither explanation nor apology; it simply *is*. In one of the few spoken moments in the film, a tourist describes watching Hans cruise in an abandoned building. When this tourist realizes that Hans is trans, the tourist tells a convoluted story of encountering a trans man at a restaurant, once, and his surprise at how well this man passed. Within the scene, these moments both illustrate a kind of trans male infiltration of cisgender gay spaces and convey the sense in which these spaces are themselves enclosures: cordoned off from the mainstream—whether by a surrounding brush of trees, or the seclusion of a beach—and further including trans masculine people.

Insofar as pornography, or the potential to make pornography, maps onto identity's vicissitudes, it offers an occasion both for "making space" for nonnormative identities and for welcoming others into this shared space. This seems true both in terms of production, with Volcano as director, and for Volcano as character, as Del. For as long as they've known each other, Volcano writes, Del and Hans have been dreaming of and discussing making porn, for themselves and for other queer people. The duration of their conversation tracks their change in sexual and gender identity insofar as they no longer identify as dykes, but now as "TrannyBoys." By planning and making porn, Del and Hans are able to limn the boundaries of fantasy, where *fantasy* dually means the fantasy of pornography and the fantasy of identity construction.

There's something remarkably understated about the way Volcano positions the project—as an attempt to, simply, make space for themselves and for others like them. Though we may recognize that, for Volcano, pornography has expansive potentialities, the framing of the project hardly seems revolutionary. And yet Volcano's understanding of pornography as something identity-fulfilling could not be further from the definition of pornography offered by Franklin Mark Osanka and Sara Lee Johann in their 1989 *Sourcebook on Pornography*, an academic account, roughly contemporaneous with Volcano's film, of pornography's dangers:

> Pornography is an $8 billion a year business that legitimizes and encourages rape, torture, and degradation of women. It is created by filming real or simulated sexually explicit acts of sexual torture, abuse, degradation or terrorism against real people. Written or verbal descriptions and drawings of these same types of sex acts are also pornography. Pornographic scenarios are fantasy and fiction. Real women, children, and men do not enjoy being raped, tortured, bound, gang raped, mutilated, penetrated by dogs, horses or snakes, or being murdered. Yet these types of bizarre image are frequent pornographic fare.[16]

In the book's preface, Osanka and Johann describe the virulent danger of porn in terms of its capacity to refashion public sexualities, or to refashion sexualities in public: "what used to be considered weird is now considered chic—an area of sexual freedom among consenting adults." The threat for Osanka and Johann appears to be that pornography is "a directory of mayhem in a sense that it is saying that any possible activity can be done in the name of finding sexual satisfaction. The danger of this kind of thinking is that it can destroy sexual responsibility. The danger includes the breakup of marriages, sexual abuse, and violence and aggression against persons."[17] Their position reveals what artist and cultural theorist Barbara DeGenevieve might describe as the confluence of "irrational individual fears that mirror the cultural fears and obsessions surrounding the body, pleasure, and the difficulty of controlling bodily sensations that arise when looking at something that turns you on."[18] To be sure, Osanka and Johann would likely not concede their fear to be either irrational or a result of being turned on. Rather, their anxiety was grounded, I think, in a large-scale preoccupation with unstable norms: what used to be considered weird is now considered to be chic. How might one keep up? Or, perhaps more terrifyingly, what next will skid down the slippery slope? This fear plays into the logics of various phobic discourses—fear of queer contagion, fear of queerness as mere fad but one that presages something far more deranged to come, fear of being left behind—without necessary allegiance to the specificity of any one discourse. Even as they weave through discourses, they imagine marriage and responsibility as unsedimented, atemporal, undeviating certainties. The zealous pitch of their anxiety, however, belies any sense that they truly recognize these norms—marriage, heterosexuality, sexual responsibility—to be, in fact, permanent.

Pitched at two opposing ends of the pornography debates, Volcano and Osanka/Johann represent the intractability of the two positions, and the visions of public space each permits. Volcano presents porn as promising, as offering space for exploration, community building, and identity formation. Osanka and Johann define pornography as the moral problem par excellence, poised to destroy, first the family, then any semblance of interpersonal restraint. Indeed, it is unclear whether Osanka and Johann see this list of social and moral descent—the breakup of marriages, sexual abuse, and violence and aggression against persons—as some sort of necessary chronology. Intractably informed by the kinds of selfhood seen as valuable, necessary, and legible, these opposing positions—pro-porn and antiporn—dramatize representations of desire as both an individual problem and a sociopolitical one. That is, Osanka and Johann understand the nuclear family to be under threat; their position is reactionary, exclusive, and defensive. Their response is thus to batten down the hatches, to quarantine the heterosexual family from queer annihilation.

I don't think, however, that Volcano would disagree with Osanka and Johann's claim that "pornographic scenarios are fantasy and fiction." Instead, Volcano suggests that these scenarios are fantasies and fictions we need, and, in fact, need *more* of: they make life intelligible and livable for those as yet only able to "talk and dream" of making their identities publicly recognized. Moreover, these fantasies and fictions draw attention to the fragility of sexual orientation and identities—especially the ways in which identity is constructed in and through public spaces. In picking apart the various layers of received sexual practice—that is, how SM iconography or practice were associated with some communities to the exclusion of others—their work confirms the ways in which identity categories are not themselves fields of ahistorical foreclosure. In this way, I think Volcano might insist that Osanka and Johann consider how the marriage industry, too, is a fiction and is, among other things, *also* a multibillion-dollar-a-year business that, in far too many instances, legitimizes and encourages the rape, torture, and degradation of women. Which is to say: by what standards do we grant legitimacy to some fictions and fantasies and not others? How do public-facing identities not only assume but also accumulate a misguided sense of their own solidity?

Volcano also offers, by way of this introduction, a pair of existential conditions of involvement that circumscribe the film's interests: as filmmakers and actors, Hans and Del will be both *in the pursuit of pleasure* and *in the means of production*. I want to suggest that this has two implications for how we understand trans fetishization in porn. First, showing themselves in pursuit of pleasure stages the trans actors as agential in their own pleasure; these actors are thus not merely figures propping up the desire of mostly cisgender viewers, the conventional "objects" of fetishization. Compared to mainstream porn, where decisions are made based on producers' understanding of market desire, ceding agency back to performers is one way in which to show actors inhabiting their own pleasure in and through their relationships to trans embodiment. It is also a mode in which Hans and Del are able to act autonomously, and on their own terms, in a social context that largely has made trans lives unlivable—or lived with much difficulty.

We might also think about the fetishization inherent to the labor process even as—or *especially* as—Del and Hans control the means of production. Mireille Miller-Young argues about pornography, feminist or mainstream, that "its structure, networks, and modes of representation are regulated and sanctioned by the State, dependent on access to new media technologies and embedded in the flows of global capitalism. . . . theorizing a feminist pornography then means thinking about a dual process of transgression and restriction, for both representation and labor."[19] But what, exactly, does Volcano mean by showing themselves in the means of production? Taken at face value: Volcano directed and wrote *Pansexual Public Porn aka The*

Adventures of Hans and Del. Directorial control allows Volcano an opportunity rarely afforded in mainstream pornography: to "create a space for authentic sexual representations."[20] But Volcano also acts in the film; Volcano is "in the means of production" insofar as Volcano's physicality is the literal means of the film's production, its condition of possibility. As Talia Mae Bettcher reminds us, "one's own body is necessarily included in the erotic content," or, said differently, we cannot separate the penis from the fellatio, nor can we separate the mouth from it, either.[21] Their bodies thus become the site of both production and pleasure.

Del has explained that this film was neither put up for sale nor meant to garner any profit.[22] Still, it is important to consider, I think, the ways in which this film is embedded in the flows of global capital, especially as an avant-garde text. We might, here, begin by thinking how pornographic fetishization intersects with commodity fetishism. That is to say: even as Volcano seeks to reorient trans masculine fetishization, how might commodity fetishism, intrinsic in the pornographic genre, constrain Volcano's project? How does commodity fetishism look when what is being exchanged is sex work, albeit in no clear relation to financial exchange? Is fetishization—either of trans porn performers or of the commodity—inescapable? I'd argue that one aspect of the film that undercuts fetishization is its unscriptedness. The film is not tied to normative notions of the working day or of teleological production. Because the film was entirely unscripted, this meant not only the impossibility of a clear sense for a final project or product but also that each scene was undergirded by a general unpredictability. The cis men in the film were not hired as actors: they were simply men cruising for sex. Having to wait for men cruising, or men who would consent to be on film, or for the right conditions, colored the project with a fundamental indeterminacy: How might waiting and fetishization be rendered together? In one sense, waiting, delay, pause, and interval compellingly disrupt a linear narrative that happens on a productive timetable. The public Del and Hans create is one that takes time; but it is also one in which there is time to waste. Or, more properly, time cruising isn't exactly wasted: it's built into the activity of cruising itself.

What feels most public about *Pansexual Public Porn aka The Adventures of Hans and Del* is not just that the film tracks scenes of outdoor cruising and public sex. The film conjures a trans masculine public legible to a wide community of trans and cis men interested in sex with other masculine people; it thereby manages to imagine a material practice of public polymorphous sexuality that extends beyond the world of the film. From one angle, this looks like appropriation of gay male culture, a requisition of a history that is, in fact, kaleidoscopic and shared. On the other hand, this public porn is also considered an adventure: a going out into or toward. There's something of *adventure*'s etymology in their project: a sense of arrival, a future orientation, an encounter with wonder, with risk, with danger. To that end, it is unclear what, precisely, the adjective *pansexual* modifies. Are we meant to read it as pansexual *public porn*? Or *pansexual public* porn? Do the stakes change if it is the public, rather than the porn, that is pansexual and/or public? What would a pansexual *public* look like?

Certainly, a *pansexual public* was not the public Volcano was writing against. Porn's migration from public spaces and eventual self-imposed sanitization meant that public opportunities for viewing porn, cruising, and spontaneous sexual experimentation steeply declined. Attempting to reverse the privatization of porn by reopening a space for it in public, Hans and Del's project presents itself as antithetical to privacy. Their work tacitly, if ever, responds to the various changes in the sexual-social landscape—from social policy that rezoned and shuttered adult bookstores, to technological changes like the prevalence of VHS—that made porn, in effect, something to explore only at home. The *pansexual public* might look, then, rather simply, like most of the scenes in this film: roving indoors to outdoors, from empty buildings to public parks, disarticulating privacy from private life, turning "public" spaces into private ones, and making the most private ones public to minoritarian communities. This is not to say Volcano is imagining a public that is constituted exclusively by pansexuals; rather, perhaps we are meant to read Volcano's intention as a public that offers the conditions for pansexuality to visibly persist. Strikingly, such a public doesn't look remarkably different from the public we're accustomed to—one, that, though decidedly not pansexual, offers pockets of perverse and diverse sexualities. And, moreover, this relatively familiar public is not one that Osanka and Johann seem to predict in their disquietude. The social order, in a pansexual public, does not disintegrate; heteronormativity does not become less of a norm. If only to underscore this: while Hans and Del move through the public, engaging and disengaging in sex acts, their sexual adventures a kind of *Pilgrim's Progress*, Volcano's camera tracks the various passersby as they move through the world—cycling on a paved path, wandering through the park, packing up and leaving the beach. The film throws open the scrims that conventionally divide public from private. Happening in plain sight, operating on the same planes, public sex and private life—or private sex and public life—are nearly indistinguishable. This is the adventure, the new territory that Hans and Del plumb, that they bring into visibility. Public sex, though perhaps interesting to Hans and Del, is less compelling to Volcano, who is preoccupied, instead, with the ways in which public sex might become private life, and private life might become public sex. The adventure Volcano pursues is adjacent to, but different than, that of Hans and Del. Volcano's filmic adventure is concerned with citizenship, with public responsibility, and private desire. This is the adventure—the risk and desire—Volcano aspires to.

Crucial to Volcano's film, however, is the refusal to demand a moralistic public confessional about safe sex practices. If *The Adventures of Hans and Del* compasses various kinds of sex, various kinds of publics, and various ways of identifying, it also traverses the HIV/AIDS crisis. Though Volcano's project is one of far-reaching externalization, the artist also recognizes that any project of externalization has necessary and important limitations. If pansexual public porn externalizes a form of desire that Volcano wished to see in the world, Volcano's treatment of HIV/AIDS operates similarly by reorienting conventional understandings of public and private. HIV/AIDS was certainly a public health crisis at the time of the film's production, and it remains one today. Yet Volcano is unwilling to treat one's sex practices as a public health issue open to public debate, regulation, and surveillance. Safe sex, instead, becomes a matter of private consideration, to be determined individually with the support of a broader public. This is not to say that public discussions of safe sex oughtn't happen, or that public resources ought not be made easily accessible and freely available to those who might seek them out. By maintaining the integrity of individual choice, rather than prescribed social practices dictated by logics of public health, Volcano effaces the boundaries between public and private sex, arguing that there remains something ineffably private about safe sex practices—even within the frame of a global public health crisis—while simultaneously insisting that public attitudes about HIV/AIDS need not regulate private behavior.

Safe Sex

In *Speaking Sex to Power*, Pat Califia quotes a quip that the trans activist, historian, and writer Lou Sullivan made before his death. Having been, for many years, denied access to medical transition because he identified as a gay man, Sullivan commented on the devastatingly ironic notion of poetic justice of his AIDS diagnosis: "I took a certain pleasure in informing the gender clinic that even though their program told me I could not live as a gay man, it looks like I'm going to die like one."[23] Califia explains that "during most of the '60s, '70s, and '80s, gender reassignment programs affiliated with universities and medical schools would only accept transsexuals who said they were heterosexual."[24] As a self-identified gay trans man, Sullivan was excluded from trans health care. At a time when HIV/AIDS was still considered to be a gay man's disease, Sullivan is devastatingly correct in pointing to the poetic irony of his diagnosis, notwithstanding the fact that HIV/AIDS affected, and affects, those heterosexual and queer alike.

But in the late 1990s, the conversation around trans gender and HIV/AIDS was limited. A 1998 study published in *AIDS Care* sought to examine the lack of information about transness and HIV prevention. The study found that living with a stigmatized identity, in this case trans gender, often resulted in shame, low self-esteem, depression, and isolation. As the study reported, "these are all known correlates of HIV risk behavior . . . thus, stigmatization compounds transgender persons' overall risk for HIV."[25] The study also suggested that targeted preventative education would provide positive sexual role models and encourage candid conversations about sexual health among trans populations. The study was not the first to suggest, too, that trans sex workers—particularly male-to-female sex workers—were at higher risk for HIV than many cisgender sex workers were. A 2005 study, also published in *AIDS Care*, pressed further on this lack of knowledge: the study concluded that "there was a significant gender difference in HIV risk among the survey respondents. Compared to MTFs, FTMs were significantly less likely to have used protection the last time they had sex and significantly more likely to have engaged in recent high risk sexual activity."[26] This second study concluded, rather simply, that more knowledge was needed, both on the part of scientists and academics studying HIV/AIDS and for those trans people vulnerable because of a lack of knowledge of risk factors.

Within this context, Volcano's film makes a crucial intervention by acknowledging the importance of informed choice among the trans community. The film's final disclaimer is nothing if not pedagogical: Volcano pulls back and identifies, materially, how safe sex was performed in this film. The statement Volcano provides is direct, sheared of any moralizing.

The final lines do a good deal of work: Volcano offers an imperative, interpellating the viewers into a kind of sexual-ethical practice that can't be preordained by Volcano. The onus is on the viewer to inform themselves and make their own choices. These lines are less didactic than careful. That is to say, they're full of care. In these final lines, Volcano seems to simultaneously extend a kind of attention and loving care to those who might find

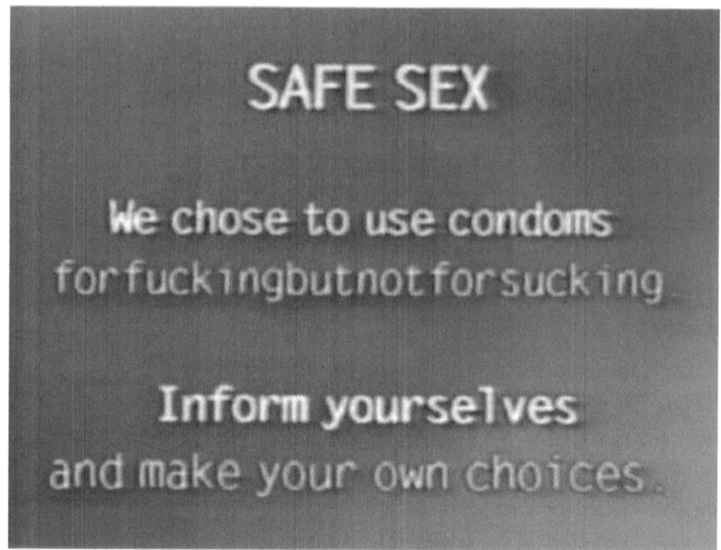

Figure 3.2. Still from *Pansexual Public Porn.* Courtesy of Del LaGrace Volcano.

themselves watching the film. In its direct address to viewers, these final lines presume that there is an audience that might be captured and might heed the call: "Inform yourselves and make your own choices." Whether or not viewers initially bought into the community—the public—when they were first welcomed in at the film's beginning, these final lines suggest, I think, that the pansexual public is one into which we're going to be welcomed regardless of our different choices and the ways in which we arrive at them. That's just the way that choice works, especially around sex: we're not atomistic. There is always a negotiation, a relationality, a context, a public we are accountable to, a public through which we must shape our very private and very public desires.

What seems crucial to me about Volcano's intervention here is the earnest call for—and opening up of—space to embrace pleasure in a time of danger. On the one hand, we might reflect on the fresh challenges to public sexualities we face in the twenty-first century. Or, we might take account of what hasn't changed: HIV/AIDS remains a global crisis. Hewing closely to Volcano's film, we might continue to hear the invitation to pleasure in the face of danger. But we might also recognize the ways in which the call has been answered and new space provided. Of course, the task then becomes to reckon with the ways this new space—promising, open, polyvalent, for some—is also an enclosure that we must continue to crack open. Perhaps, then, in this sense the commissioners of the 1986 *Report* were correct all along: porn—at least some porn—is vitally, stridently, antisocial.

Notes

1. Chartered in 1985, Reagan's Meese Committee was tasked with updating the decidedly obsolete 1970 Commission on Obscenity and Pornography. Fifteen years of technological advances in the production, distribution, and availability of pornography meant that the findings and recommendations of 1970 could hardly keep pace with the new landscape of pornography that threatened fresh moral, political, and social challenges.

2. *Final Report of the Attorney General's Commission on Pornography* (Nashville, TN: Rutledge Hill Press, 1986), 492.

3. *Final Report,* 486.

4. Whitney Strub, "Sanitizing the Seventies," *Feminist Media Histories* 5, no. 2 (2019): 33.

5. Though trans gender had been, by that point, part of the public discourse for at least two decades, there was little linguistic consolidation. After World War II, increased media representation of trans identities led to the rise in public-facing organizations that sought to establish trans communities and promulgate knowledge for those curious to know more about their own trans desires. The Virginia Prince–founded *Transvestia,* one of the earliest trans magazines, "excluded explicit sexual content and focused on social commentary, educational outreach, self-help advice, and autobiographical vignettes drawn from her own life and the lives of her readers. The magazine significantly shifted the political meaning of transvestism, moving it away from being the expression of a criminalized sexual activity and toward being the common denominator of a new (and potentially political) identity-based minority community." Susan Stryker, *Transgender History* (Berkeley, CA: Seal Press, 2008), 54. Though the magazine sought to consolidate gender-divergent experiences under a political, rather than primarily sexual, identity, it was this politicization, and its educative rather than salacious purpose, Stryker suggests, that made Prince a target of federal investigation, offering a key example of trans knowledge-production butting up against dissemination of texts deemed dangerous to the public. Prince's federal case reveals both the problem of linguistic consolidation from the 1960s onward, and the problem of government management into "obscenity"—especially when intervention sought to criminalize pedagogical, rather than sensationalizing, accounts of trans gender. Throughout the sixties and seventies the language around trans continued to shift unstably: transvestite, transsexual, hermaphrodite, intersex, cross-dresser, drag queen, and, to a lesser degree, transgender, were terms that were used interchangeably and often conflated. This is undoubtedly true of popular press

representations of Christine Jorgensen, for instance, who was differentially identified in the media as a "hermaphrodite," as a "transvestite," and as a "transsexual." Taxonomic slippage is also replicated in the 1970s boom in the production of trans print periodicals, as Nicholas Matte has illustrated in "The Economic and Racial Politics of Selling a Transfeminine Fantasy in 1970s Niche and Pornographic Print Publications," in *Porno Chic and the Sex Wars: American Sexual Representation in the 1970s*, ed. Whitney Strub and Carolyn Bronstein (Amherst: University of Massachusetts Press, 2016), 154–177.

6. Andy Newman, "Al Goldstein, a Publisher Who Took the Romance Out of Sex, Dies at 77," *New York Times*, December 19, 2013, https://www.nytimes.com/2013/12/20/nyregion/al-goldstein-pioneering-pornographer-dies-at-77.html.

7. Strub, "Sanitizing," 33.

8. Strub, "Sanitizing," 41.

9. That is to say: in terms of intention, aesthetics, audience, and sexual imaginary, this genus of trans porn—one that nearly exclusively depicts trans women to the exclusion of trans men and nonbinary people—has little in common with Andy Warhol's porno-chic auteur films of the 1960s and 1970s, trans print sleaze of the 1970s and 1980s, or the identity-affirming trans porn increasingly produced in the 1990s and 2000s by queer and trans directors. As Chauntelle Anne Tibbals notes, "Aside from featuring performers of various gender identities and sexual orientations, TS content does not overlap with queer porn in any way. TS scenes generally feature at least one performer who is in the midst of a male-to-female transition. TS performers are generally partnered with cis-gender men or other male-to-female TS performers, although I have noticed a slight increase in cis-gender women performers working in TS scenes. The majority of TS content parallels production patterns of relatively mainstream porn—mostly all-sex and occasional features, much of which can be accessed via VOD or digital download." Chauntelle Anne Tibbals, "Gonzo, Trannys, and Teens: Current Trends in U.S. Adult Content Production, Distribution, and Consumption," *Porn Studies* 1, nos. 1–2 (2014): 132.

10. Strub's claim that porn underwent an internal and reflexive sanitization in the 1980s is, perhaps, more accurate in the case of cisgender porn than it is in the case of trans gender porn. Indeed, the trans porn that appeared in the 1980s and 1990s was significantly more hardcore than it had been during the early 1970s. What seems to have been sanitized most effectively, however, was its overt political content.

11. Tobi Hill-Meyer also describes how mainstream trans-feminine porn offers no space for someone like her, a self-identified butch dyke "with short hair and unshaved legs wearing a dapper vest and fedora while packing a strap on and engaging in non-genitally focused sex." According to Hill-Meyer, "with rare exceptions, trans women are not cast in any genre of mainstream porn (gonzo, features, girl/girl, and so on) except 'tranny/shemale porn,' the derogatory phrase use to market trans women porn in the mainstream industry. Not only does that mean having your image publicized with derogatory terms, but 'tranny/shemale porn' producers

have a very specific list of conventions that they expect their 'shemale' performers to follow. These include: wearing makeup and high heels, shaving one's legs, appearing traditionally feminine, getting and keeping a strong erection, ejaculating, and either penetrating someone with your genitals or being penetrated . . . when mainstream producers are challenged to change their conventions, they fear losing their existing audience that has been trained to expect and respond to those conventions. However, they sacrifice authenticity for convention. Mainstream sex work often (if not inherently) requires that the workers conform to someone else's desires rather than express their own." Tobi Hill-Meyer, "Where the Trans Women Aren't," in *The Feminist Porn Book: The Politics of Producing Pleasure*, ed. Tristian Taormino, Celine Parreñas Shimizu, Constance Penley, and Mireille Miller-Young (New York: Feminist Press, 2013), 157.

12. "The Cambria List," American Porn, *Frontline*, PBS, 2002, https://www.pbs.org/wgbh/pages/frontline/shows/porn/prosecuting/cambria.html.

13. Jon Davies, "The Not-Quite-Forbidden Fruit: Sexploitation's Queer Temporalities," *GLQ* 25, no. 3 (2019): 499.

14. *Pansexual Public Porn aka The Adventures of Hans and Del*, dir. Del LaGrace Volcano (London: 1998).

15. Del LaGrace Volcano, interview by RL Goldberg, Skype, November 5, 2019.

16. Franklin Mark Osanka and Sara Lee Johann, *Sourcebook on Pornography* (Lexington, MA: Lexington Books, 1989), 3.

17. Osanka, *Sourcebook on Pornography*, vii–viii.

18. Barbara DeGenevieve, "The Emergence of Non-Standard Bodies and Sexualities," *Porn Studies* 1, nos. 1–2 (2014): 194.

19. Mireille Miller-Young, "Interventions: The Deviant and Defiant Art of Black Women Porn Directors," in *The Feminist Porn Book*, 107.

20. Hill-Meyer, "Where the Trans Women Aren't," 157.

21. Talia Mae Bettcher, "When Selves Have Sex: What the Phenomenology of Trans Sexuality Can Teach about Sexual Orientation," *Journal of Homosexuality* 61, no. 5 (2014): 609.

22. As Volcano explained during the interview, the film was entered into a few film festivals. But Del was embarrassed by the low production value. The Super 8 used to film belonged to Del; the digital camera operators hired were wedding photographers. Del borrowed a Casablanca editing machine from an ex-lover.

23. Pat Califia, *Speaking Sex to Power: The Politics of Queer Sex* (San Francisco: Cleis Press, 2002), 122.

24. Califia, *Speaking Sex to Power*, 122.

25. W. O. Bockting, B. E. Robinson, and B. R. S. Rosser, "Transgender HIV Prevention: A Qualitative Needs Assessment," *AIDS Care* 10, no. 4 (1998): 505–525.

26. G. P. Kenagy and C.-M. Hsieh, "The Risk Less Known: Female-to-Male Persons' Vulnerability to HIV Infection," *AIDS Care* 17, no. 2 (2005): 195.

Chapter 4

The Ethics of Provocation

Censoring the Past in German Cold War Punk

Priscilla Layne

When punk emerged in the late 1970s, movement participants and critics alike described it as the expression of a "blank generation" refusing their society's Cold War, unemployment, and austerity by piercing their ears with safety pins, dyeing their hair brash colors, and repurposing the mainstream's trash as clothing and art. No one could have imagined that over forty years later, punk would become a respectable part of Western culture, with a punk musical having succeeded on Broadway (*American Idiot*, 2010–2011) and conservative politicians like Boris Johnson proudly declaring their love of punk icons like The Clash. The Scottish punk band The Exploited may have desperately insisted that "Punk's Not Dead" on their 1981 release of the same name, but they were already fighting a losing battle. Despite the many subsequent revivals of the genre, from the US hardcore and British Oi! movements of the 1980s to the emo and pop punk variations that overtook the mainstream worldwide in the 1990s and 2000s, punk has never quite recovered its original ethics of refusal. As a "neo-avant-garde" form, to borrow a term from Peter Bürger's *Theory of the Avant-Garde*, punk was bound to become institutional because "the neo-avant-garde institutionalizes the *avant-garde as art* and thus negates avant-gardiste intentions."[1] Bürger insists, "If an artist today signs a stove pipe and exhibits it, that artist certainly does not denounce the art market but adapts to it. . . . Since now the protest of the historical avant-garde against art as an institution is accepted as *art*, the gesture of protest of the neo-avant-garde becomes inauthentic."[2] In lieu of dissonant music like Arnold Schoenberg's attacking the audience and the market, the audience and the market have now co-opted dissonant music, and this once "autonomous art" has adapted itself to the audience and the market in turn.

In contrast to Bürger's strict historical understanding of the avant-garde and dismissal of its revival, Hal Foster contends that the neo-avant-garde is not reactionary. Foster claims that neo-avant-garde movements attempt to "*re*connect with a lost practice in order to *dis*connect from a present way of working felt to be outmoded, misguided, or otherwise oppressive. The first move (*re*) is a temporal one, made in order, in a second, spatial move (*dis*), to open a new site for work."[3] In Foster's terms, punk qualifies as neo-avant-garde insofar as it connects to the earlier avant-garde of music by incorporating dissonance and atonal sounds and asking us to rethink our expectations of what music is, how it should sound, and what purpose it should serve. Moreover, punk opens up "a new site for work" by expanding on avant-garde music, which was, at the turn of the century, classical and infusing it with new technology: electric guitars and synthesizers. Foster redeems the neo-avant-garde by arguing that not only is it not reactionary, but it actually revitalizes the notion of autonomous art. While the historical avant-garde critiqued the institution, the neo-avant-garde critiques "the old charlatanry of the bohemian artist as well as the new institutionality of the avant-garde."[4]

In his response to Foster sixteen years later, Bürger concedes there are "artists who have endeavored to resume the program of the avant-garde. . . . Whether there are artists who elude my verdict is not a theoretical question, but of evaluating the artistic work."[5] Nevertheless, Bürger doubles down on his original argument to claim that most neo-avant-garde art cannot be considered as transgressive as the historical avant-garde:

> While the historical avant-gardes could rightly consider the social context of their actions to be one of crisis, if not revolution, and could draw from this realization the energy to design the Utopian project of sublating the institution of art, this no longer applied to the neo-avant-gardes of the 1950s and 1960s. The aesthetic context had also changed in the meantime. While the historical avant-gardes could still connect their practices with a claim to transgression, this is no longer the case for the neo-avant-gardes, given that avant-garde practices had in the meantime been incorporated by the institution.[6]

In this chapter, I take up Bürger's challenge of finding an example of neo-avant-garde that "resumes the program of the avant-garde" by examining the unique case of the German punk band OHL. OHL's example shows us the ongoing value of Foster's formulation for thinking through a minoritarian avant-garde. By rejecting all institutions, including those of the punk scene itself, OHL demonstrates, in the spirit of this collection, how a punk avant-garde can persist through and is energized by crisis.

Oberste Heeresleistung (OHL) formed in 1980 in the then–West German town of Leverkusen, a smaller city (ca. 168,000 inhabitants at the time) that borders the much larger cities of Cologne and Düsseldorf, which each had a population four to five times larger. This is what sets OHL apart from bands that stemmed from the big cities commonly known as the epicenters for German punk, such as Berlin, Hamburg, or Düsseldorf. Leverkusen is most commonly recognized as the home of the pharmaceutical company Bayer, known for both German innovation and its involvement in World War II and the Holocaust. The company not only used forced labor but also produced Zyklon B, the gas with which the Nazis murdered millions of Jews in the concentration camps. Despite the company's implications in the Holocaust, the British forces occupying the Rhineland were eager to keep the company active because of its important economic function for the region.[7] At any given time, so many residents of Leverkusen worked for Bayer that " 'the entire life in the city was influenced by Bayer' and 'no branch of its communal life was untouched by it.' "[8]

In their introduction, Andrew Strombeck and Jean-Thomas Tremblay note that, "paradoxically, crisis imperils artists but prompts new avant-gardes," and this is reflected in OHL's history on multiple fronts. OHL was formed during a time when Leverkusen was affected by the decline in industry in the Rhineland due in part to the oil crises of 1973 and 1979. As a more provincial town, Leverkusen grew much slower than bigger cities and for that reason its young inhabitants had less access to cultural offerings. Bayer was not only influential in the city's industry; since 1907, the company had also influenced the city's cultural life with the founding of its Erholungshaus (House of Leisure). It wasn't until 1969 that Leverkusen began to "emerge from the shadows of Bayer Inc." after the city finally had its own "house for theater and concerts at its disposal—the forum."[9] Even culture was affected by the oil crisis, with the city's culture budget cut by six hundred thousand marks until 1983.[10] What's more, Leverkusen didn't even have a youth club until 1985, even though the plan to create one had been passed in the 1970s (1978) like in other cities across West Germany.[11] Thus, OHL undoubtedly came about in both a time of financial and cultural crisis, as well as during the sociopolitical crisis of the Cold War.

Having grown up in the shadow of a company with such a complicated and somehow very *German* legacy as Bayer, the budding punk band unsurprisingly addressed issues pertaining to German nationalism and the Nazi past in their lyrics. From the very beginning, OHL did not comfortably fit in any category. Unlike their peers, OHL didn't espouse a leftist ideology. Yet they also rejected the glorification of the Nazi past. Nevertheless, the band was frequently misread as right-wing, as is indicated by this 1982 article from the West German fanzine *Sounds*: "The group's name and the soldier on the cover [of the debut album *Heimatfront*] were considered in many places to be proof of the politically right-wing orientation of the musicians and the entire label, even if the texts didn't offer any such indication."[12] As this review suggests, there may have been conflicting responses to the band's debut album, as German punks were unsure whether to read OHL's use of military imagery ironically or seriously. What confused both fans and critics about OHL's music was the fact that the band's punk vision rejected *both* communism and democracy. But unlike right-wing bands at the time, the band chose "no future" over reviving the Nazi past. In this respect, OHL's politics follows Cyrus Shahan's argument that West German punk "was acutely aware of the failures of previous interventions into the social but . . . never sought to rectify these to ensure its own duration."[13] For Shahan, to embrace the motto of "no future" meant to "[tap] strategies of European avant-gardes."[14] Echoing the Sex Pistols' flirtation with fascist symbols in the form of Sid Vicious's swastika shirt, OHL reappropriated imagery from Germany's fascist past, primarily images of the *Wehrmacht* (armed forces), such as on its debut album *Heimatfront*. In doing so, the band intended to shock, warn the public of persisting fascist tendencies, and embrace the dystopian belief that West German society had "no future" because fascism had not been defeated, and no viable alternatives had been provided.

If the intimate circle of the punk scene couldn't quite understand OHL's performance, it's no surprise that the band was misunderstood by the public as well. In 1987, the West German Federal Department for Media Harmful to Young Persons (or in German the Bundesprüfstelle für jugendgefährdende Medien, hereafter BPjM) indexed OHL's album *Heimatfront* due to the claim that it endangered young people with its right-wing ideology.[15] The BPjM was founded in the 1950s—a notoriously conservative era in the still-young country of West Germany, established in 1949. Texts like Uta Poiger's *Jazz,*

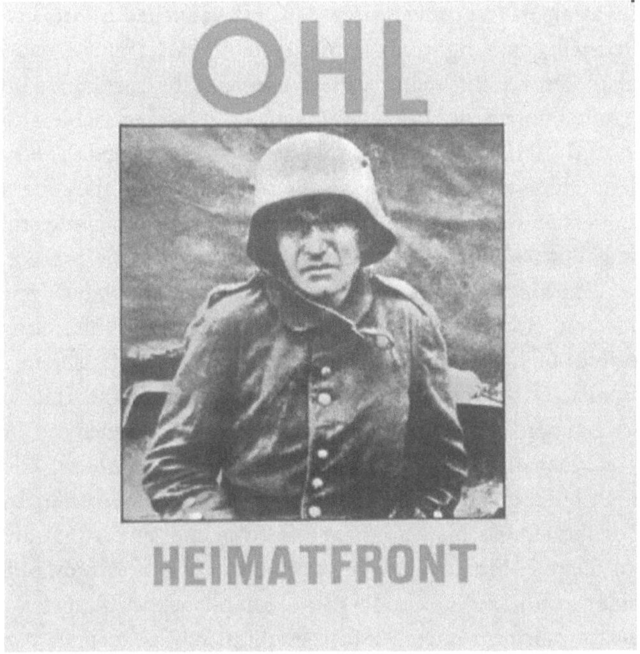

Figure 4.1. Cover of the album *Heimatfront* by OHL. Courtesy of the artists.

Rock, Rebels and Dagmar Herzog's *Sex After Fascism* have explored how the Christian Democratic Union (CDU), the ruling party in the 1950s, desired to return West German society to a prefascist Christian culture of modesty, hard work, and patriarchy. Part of this work consisted of staving off the influence of US popular culture in the form of jazz, rock 'n' roll, comic books, and movies, as well as condemning "deviant sexuality," including pornography and any nonheteronormative or extramarital sex.[16] Sharing the CDU's concerns for society, the BPjM's main task was to hinder the distribution of texts that endangered youth. Such hindrance meant that stores could keep indexed items on sale, hidden behind a counter, but they could not prominently display or sell them to people under the age of eighteen. Ultimately, two institutions are responsible for OHL's reputation as inciters of right-wing violence: the institution of the BPjM and the institution of the West German punk scene.

It is precisely because a range of voices of varying institutions unsuccessfully tried to constrain OHL to the binary of left- and right-wing politics, I argue, that their project makes sense as an avant-garde provocation. I read theirs as an *ethical* project because OHL launched a sarcastic critique of both left-wing *and* right-wing politics in its lyrics and artwork. OHL attempted to recover dissonant music's use-value by turning it into a critique of contemporary political systems and the lack of viable alternatives. To understand OHL's behavior in 1987, we have to situate the band as a Foucauldian ethical subject relative to the complexities of the time. Foucault helps us understand that the neo-avant-garde can function along ethical lines because it is not *only* acting in response to its avant-garde predecessors. In *The Use of Pleasure*, Foucault contends that we cannot reduce morality to one regime; rather, we must consider that an ethical subject can inhabit several regimes of morality simultaneously. Thus, when I refer to morality, I understand it, in Foucault's sense, as "a set of values and rules of action that are recommended to individuals through the intermediary of various prescriptive agencies such as the family (in one of its roles), educational institutions, churches, and so forth. . . . But 'morality' also refers to the real behavior of individuals in relation to the rules and values that are recommended to them."[17] Ethical work is work that "one performs on oneself, not only in order to bring one's conduct into compliance with a given rule, but to attempt to transform oneself into the ethical subject of one's behavior."[18]

Different moral codes may coexist in a society.[19] In order to understand the morality of OHL's behavior, we have to take at least two moral codes into consideration: the moral code of the Federal Republic of Germany and the moral code of the West German punk scene. I consider the most important moral code in West Germany to be the Grundgesetz (Basic Law), which was passed in 1949 in the united zones occupied by the US, French, and British armies following World War II. The Basic Law is meant to symbolize the redemocratization of West Germany and a decisive break from the country's National Socialist past. As such, Article 5 of the Basic Law grants freedoms of expression that would not have been guaranteed under National Socialist dictatorship. Nevertheless, Article 5, "Freedom of Expression, Arts and Sciences," should not be in conflict with those protected under Article 6, "Marriage–Family–Children." The second point in Article 5 makes clear that "these rights [to freedom of expression] shall find their limits in the provisions of general laws, in provisions for the *protection of young persons*, and in the right to personal honor."[20]

As a regime of censorship sanctioned by the Basic Law, the BPjM functions as an institution that determines who or what poses a potential threat to young people. Thus, I examine OHL as an ethical subject in relation to the West German punk scene, the moral codes of West Germany, and the BPjM and the historical moment—the Cold War and Germans' ongoing *Vergangenheitsbewaeltigung*, or their coming to terms with the Nazi past—in order to uncover the ethical potential of the band's performance as a neo-avant-garde entity. The best way to reject punk as institution was to refuse to promote an institutionalized political position and instead focus on critiquing all sides *and* expressing frustration that there were no other alternatives. To do so, the band appropriated Nazi imagery in a manner both unacceptable from the vantage point of the West German punk scene and inevitably in violation of the BPjM's moral codes.

Official Regimes of Morality

OHL's album was indexed despite the lack of any right-wing ideology in the album's lyrics—a point to which I return in the final section of this chapter. It was, I argue, the group's refusal to choose a side during the Cold War that went against the moral code of the Federal Republic of Germany, and this, in combination with their use of *Wehrmacht* imagery, is why their album was indexed. To grasp why such a stance might be so offensive to West Germans, we have to consider the sociohistorical context of the country's founding and the origins of the Grundgesetz (Basic Law). Since the founding of the Federal Republic of Germany (West Germany) in 1949, it was important for German politicians to set a course for the country that embraced democracy, tolerance, and civility.[21] But in fact, the culture of the 1950s, reflecting a CDU majority, was especially conservative on matters of gender, sexuality, and youth. As Dagmar Herzog investigates in *Sex After Fascism*, very conservative laws, such as the law against homosexuality and the ban on abortion as well as a conservative understanding of morality were passed on from previous regimes.[22]

On its website, the BPjM describes its task as protecting "children and adolescents in Germany from any media which might contain harmful or dangerous contents."[23] In its present-day incarnation, the BPjM examines videos, DVDs, computer games, audio records and CDs, print media, and internet sites. In order to behave morally according to the first and fifth articles of the Basic Law (and therefore promote free speech while protecting a vulnerable group of people: youth), media should be free of what the BPjM considers material harmful to minors. According to the BPjM, "Objects are considered harmful or dangerous to minors if they tend to endanger [minors'] process of developing a socially responsible and self-reliant personality. In general, this applies to objects that contain indecent, extremely violent, crime-inducing, anti-Semitic or otherwise racist material."[24] The BPjM acts as a regime of morality because it offers prescriptions for ethical subjects to follow in order to conform to the code of the Basic Law. Several changes were made to the law between its passing in 1954 and the indexing of OHL's album in 1987. On April 29, 1961, a new version of the law was passed to allow for decision making in smaller committees. A liberalization of the law happened on November 23, 1973, when § 6 Abs. 2 GjS (Gesetz über die Verbreitung jugendgefährdender Schriften [Law for the Spread of Texts Endangering Youth]) was removed, indicating that nude pictures were no longer harmful to youth. A change made on March 2, 1974, placed greater emphasis on texts that glorify war. In 1978, the number of institutions that could petition for a work to be indexed was increased considerably from eleven to around five hundred. The final significant change took place in 1985, when the GjS was combined with the Youth Protection Act (JöSchG), originally passed December 4, 1951. The motivation behind this merge was to tackle the sudden "video boom" of the 1980s and allow for laws written for theatrically released films to be applicable to video as well.[25]

OHL's album was indexed during the tenure of Rudolf Stefen, a member of the conservative Christian Democratic Union who led the BPjM from 1969 until 1991. Prior to 1969, the BPjM did not attract much attention. When Stefen entered office, however, he spearheaded the conservative backlash against the chaos of the 1968 student movement. He was intent on "making a point to crack down" on matters endangering youth.[26] In a 1986 interview with *Spiegel* magazine, Stefen describes the BPjM's indexing criteria as such: "products that lead adolescents on the wrong track 'of social and ethical disorientation' are not allowed to be advertised."[27] Based on these guidelines, OHL might be targeted by the BPjM because of the band's ample use of war imagery as well as the violence of its lyrics.

Achim Barsch recounts that one reason Stefen often cited for indexing media was the violation of human dignity. "According to Rudolf Stefen (1983, S. 101) . . . human dignity is violated if 'people are made into an object, purely to a means, degraded to a representative mass.' "[28] In a 1983 essay, Stefen explained that although some may mistakenly think that only sexual and erotic materials are dangerous to youth, the law explicitly includes materials that incite " 'violence, crime, and racial hatred, as well as media glorifying war.' "[29] Stefen adds that the BPjM considers something to be dangerous to youth if it " 'confuses [them] socioethically.' "[30] Out of a list

Stefen provides of eleven examples of what may be considered socioethically confusing, five have to do with National Socialism:

- Texts that attempt to recruit young people into National Socialism
- Texts that suggest that National Socialism is right for Germany and the rest of Europe
- Texts that glorify the SS as the military protectors of a united Europe
- Texts that question whether denouncing National Socialism is important for West Germany's identity
- Texts that affirm Hitler's rule[31]

In a discussion of the potential negative effects of the BPjM, Anja Ohmer is weary of the BPjM's status as a relatively independent institution, one that has its own budget, can function without the input from other organizations, and hides its deliberation from the public.[32] Ohmer's main issue with the BPjM is that its decisions ultimately come down to the way a small number of individuals happen to interpret a particular text. In line with this complaint, Barsch notes that one of the problems with the BPjM is that it makes no distinction between real, "fictional, [and] symbolic representations."[33] As an example of how this can lead to poor decision making on the part of the BPjM, Barsch offers the case of the science fiction novel *Der stählerne Turm* (The Steel Tower), written by the left-wing, German Jewish author and Hugo Award winner Norman Spinrad. The novel was indexed by the BPjM in 1982. *The Steel Tower* tells an alternative history of World War II, in which Adolf Hitler leaves Germany for the US in 1919. Although glorifying National Socialism was far from Spinrad's intent, Barsch reports that this is precisely what the BPjM accused the novel of doing.[34] In its justification for this decision, the BPjM completely ignores the details of the novel's organization, including the parallel worlds and the genre-specific typology of science fiction, resting its decision solely on the novel's fictionalization of Adolf Hitler.[35] As this case makes clear, an artist's critique of National Socialism could easily be misread as a glorification thereof by the BPjM, which ignores the aesthetic nuances of a text and simply focuses on its references to anything related to World War II and National Socialism. The BPjM's interpretive practice may pose a problem for punk acts, which, since the movement's inception, have frequently invoked Nazism in order to critique postwar society.

Punk and Fascism

West German punk emerged in the late 1970s, when youth were exposed to English and US punk thanks to "cassette recordings made of broadcasts and mailed to various cities—Düsseldorf, Berlin, Hamburg, Munich."[36] Part of what caused punk to take root in many locations was the sociohistorical situation—the "degree of garbage, concrete, boredom, and hate that the first generation of punks (around 1975–1979 in Great Britain, around 1977–1980 in Germany) had to deal with."[37] In West Germany, a constellation of social and political issues caused turmoil in everyday life. In the 1970s, West Germany was experiencing an economic downturn caused by the oil crises of 1973 and 1979, which triggered unemployment and wage stagnation. And while West Germans had never been particularly welcoming to the foreign guest workers who had been given contracts in German factories since the late 1950s, xenophobia increased as the economy slowed down. Moreover, there were new political frontlines: "The old war generation, against whom the student rebels and the hippies of the 1960s had fought, had stepped aside. And in the meantime the revolutionaries (*Revoluzzer*) had taken their place on the throne."[38]

Klaus Farin's use of the derogatory term *Revoluzzer* to describe the former rebels of the '68 generation indicates the bitter attitude of the younger punks toward their parents. The '68 students and hippies had wanted to reform German society, fight fascism and authoritarianism, and gravitate toward a more tolerant, open society. Rudi Dutschke, one of the prominent leaders of the movement, coined the slogan "long march through the institutions," riffing on the "Long March" of the Chinese Communist army across China (October 1934–October 1935) to describe what the German extra-parliamentary opposition was attempting to change in West German society and how it was going to do it. One may say that the opposition successfully enacted change with the founding of an additional political party, the Green Party, outside of the dominance of the two behemoths: the Christian Democratic Union (CDU) and the Social Democratic Party of Germany (SPD). However, the opposition's strategy of moving *through* institutions instead of working *against* them recalls what Bürger denounces about the neo-avant-garde of the time. With institutionalization comes complacency and settlement, as opposed to the constant change of revolution. As Farin writes, "The 'march through the institutions' had not seriously shaken the capitalist system, but many a '68er' now participated in the power—at least the power over the new young people."[39] The establishment of the Green Party had institutionalized protest and counterculture. Furthermore, the incorporation of a more radical wing of the '68ers into the Red Army Faction (RAF), an organization of domestic left-wing terrorists, had shaken the majority of nonviolent protesters, who preferred to voice their opposition with the ballot instead of the bullet.

By the late 1970s, as former revolutionaries had either joined the establishment or turned away from politics (as reflected by the writing of the New Subjectivity movement), young punks in their teens and twenties found themselves dissatisfied with meditations on inner turmoil. Like their predecessors, they wanted to reject what had come before them. However, they were no longer persuaded by the grand narratives of Communism or Socialism. For punk bands, there were three types of institutions in West Germany to contend with: mainstream music, the government (represented by the BPjM), and the institutionalized protest of the '68ers. And one way to offend all three of these institutions was through the use of Nazi symbolism and terminology.

Since its origins in the New York and London of the 1970s, punk has often flirted with provocative symbols. But while donning a swastika might have been an easy way for US and British youth to aggravate an older generation who had fought against the Nazis in the war, appropriating this symbol for such purposes proved much trickier in West Germany.[40] Nevertheless, German punk engaged with some of the same provocation strategies as their Anglophone counterparts, and as Cyrus Shahan argues, German punks' use of the swastika is part of what "binds this revolutionary, counter-discursive, and anti-institutional aesthetic to strategies of the avant-garde."[41] But because of West Germany's unique past and relationship to the former Third Reich, West German punks' adoption of Nazi or fascist symbols was not strictly a way for them to rebel against their parents and grandparents. Incidentally, the swastika and other references to Nazism were adopted by both leftist and right-wing bands, but for different reasons; the Left criticized the West German government by comparing it to the Third Reich and the Right glorified the National Socialist past to critique the present. Others deployed Nazi imagery in knottier ways.

The Moral Code of the West German Punk Scene

In the 1980s, the West German punk scene consisted of three currents. One current was the more commercial, pop-influenced, experimental, and electronic German New Wave. The second current was labeled *Deutschpunk* and was considered more underground and radically left-wing. The third current was an explicitly right-wing form of Oi—a successor of punk that emerged in the United Kingdom in the 1970s, when formerly apolitical punk bands like Skrewdriver adopted the racist agenda of the National Front.[42] While bands in all of those categories often made use of Nazi imagery, New Wave bands were read as doing so ironically, *Deutschpunk* as doing so more earnestly to critique the contemporary government, and right-wing bands as doing so to promote the National Socialist ideology of the past. Despite these assumptions, the lines between the categories were not always distinct. Consider, as an example of a German New Wave's more ambiguous treatment of Nazi symbolism, the band Deutsch Amerikanische Freundschaft (DAF), whose song "Der Mussolini" (The Mussolini, 1981) includes lyrics such as: "Turn to the right / Turn to the left / Clap your hands / And dance the Adolf Hitler / And dance the Mussolini." Similarly, the band Stahlnetz's song "Vor all den Jahren" (So Many Years Ago, 1982) is a satirical take on the Third Reich and postwar Germany. The song narrates the events of World War II—the bombing of German cities and the deaths it caused—and flippantly recaps the rebuilding period with the lyrics, "After the war comes peace / And after peace comes the victory victory victory victory / Can you remember, so many years ago?/ Can you remember, the beautiful nights? / Can you remember, so many years ago? / Can you remember how it was back then?" The repetition of the word *Sieg* (victory) and the ironic statement that the war years were "beautiful nights" reflect the band's attempt to critique an older generation nostalgic about the stability of the Third Reich and argue that the specter of fascism still haunts the Federal Republic.

The ambiguity in these West German bands' treatment of Germany's fascist past was investigated at the time. One particularly interesting study was done by Hermann Langer, an East German professor of history and German studies. In 1985, Langer published the study *"Wollt ihr den totalen Tanz?": Streiflichter zur imperialistichen Manipulierung der Jugend*, which documented what he perceived, in German New Wave, as growing fascist tendencies among West German youth. One must note that as an *East* German professor, Langer's analysis would inevitably reflect East Germans' bias against West Germany and Western capitalist culture more generally. East Germany viewed itself as a direct descendant of the Weimar Republic and therefore as not having inherited the fascist legacy of the Third Reich. The East German government's justification was that the founders of the German Democratic Republic had been the antifascist, Communist fighters who had resisted the Nazis and had either escaped to the Soviet Union or been imprisoned in camps. A self-declared antiracist nation, East Germany viewed neo-Nazism as related only to capitalist societies and therefore not a threat to their own. Furthermore, while they refused to acknowledge the presence of neo-Nazi skinheads in the East, East Germans did target punks as participants in a decadent subculture antithetical to Socialist ideals and thus necessarily exported by the West in an attempt to destabilize society. In line with East Germany's rhetoric about its neighbor, Langer believed conditions similar to those of 1933, such as high employment and heavy armament, suggested that fascism was alive and well in West Germany. Langer's evidence includes everything from a lyrical analysis of West German bands to observations about innocuous practices, such as the way DJs reportedly got the crowd going with lines like "Do you want total dance?," a reference to Goebbels's Nazi-era speech about total war.

As these brief examples suggest, if OHL had been considered a German New Wave band, its lyrics and use of Nazi-era terminology would not have stood out. And it is interesting to consider that while many German New Wave bands were guilty of such behavior, their albums were not indexed. Arguably, OHL faced more scrutiny because the authorities considered it a *Deutschpunk* rather than a New Wave band. Despite its experimentation, peculiarities, and tendency to push the limits, German New Wave was quite popular and had a mainstream following—possibly because musically New Wave relied more on melodic synthesizers than on dissonant electric guitars. In contrast, *Deutschpunk* was part of much more marginal scenes, and in the 1980s, your average German citizen would not have thought very highly of German punks. *Clockwork Orange*, a punk fanzine of the time, sarcastically claimed that "95 percent of punks consist of left-wing nutcases, people afraid of hard work, drunk bums, and scum."[43] Although OHL shared some lyrical similarities with New Wave bands, when it came to music, *Deutschpunk* was a more fitting label. Overall, within the *Deutschpunk* scene, the band did stand out. The following description of OHL also stems from *Clockwork Orange*: "They are in no way comparable to the average pig punks, because they believe in neither anarchy nor the proletarian world revolution. They're against left-wing nutcases and dreamy do-gooders."[44] Prominent music journalist Martin Büsser claims that OHL is "representative of historical revisionism that tries to relativize the crimes of the Nazis."[45] Büsser argues that instead of rejecting extreme political ideologies, OHL wishes to portray the German soldier as a victim. While their choice of album cover might suggest a desire to portray the suffering of German soldiers, the band also addresses the suffering of Holocaust victims in the song "Kraft durch Freude" (Strength through Joy), which I discuss further later in this chapter. Rather than simply painting Germans as victims, OHL sought to depict the misery of war for everyone involved.

What distinguishes OHL from the leftist *Deutschpunk* bands is its suspected glorification of Germany's role in the world wars. The band's name, OHL, is an acronym for Oberste Heeresleistung, the highest command in the German Army during World War I. The band has also used a lot of images from World War I on its albums, and the title *Heimatfront* (Homefront) evokes war. Fueling the band's controversy was the fact that some of its music was released on the German record label Rock-O-Rama, the same label responsible for all of the German releases of the neo-Nazi British Oi band Skrewdriver. In a 1982 interview, Rock-O-Rama's owner Herbert Egoldt claimed that the so-called "witch hunt" against OHL was unjustified. In Egoldt's words, the band had been misunderstood; it was unfair to consider them right-wing because their name stemmed from the German empire and they used a soldier on their album cover to express the misery of war in general. What makes Egoldt's defense of the band questionable at best is that he is now publicly known as a neo-Nazi. Since 1984, his label has concentrated on openly right-wing German and US bands and has been associated with the right-wing scene. In addition to OHL, numerous other LPs produced by Rock-O-Rama were indexed.

OHL as Ethical Subject and the Indexing of *Heimatfront*

OHL can be considered an ethical subject in Foucauldian terms because, with its album *Heimatfront*, the band attempted to articulate a political position vis-à-vis the multiple moral codes to which it was subjected. First and foremost, the band sought to critique West German society. Drawing comparisons between Nazi Germany and West Germany made this critique possible. OHL was also resisting the moral code of the German punk scene that insisted that a band fit into a particular category—either mainstream New Wave, *Deutschpunk*, or Oi—and adopt the corresponding political stance—either apolitical, leftist, or ring-wing. Ultimately, part of what made

OHL ethical from an avant-garde standpoint was its rejection of punk's ties to institutions and its rejection of art *as* institution. In the West Germany of the 1980s, apolitical New Wave was promoted by mainstream radio stations and record labels. Left-wing *Deutschpunk* represented the leftist institutions of the punk scene. And right-wing Oi conspired with likeminded movements and political parties.

Music sociologist Tia DeNora considers music a technology of the self in the Foucauldian sense. The subjects she interviewed in her monograph *Music in Everyday Life* describe using music to get what they need, which is "a common discourse of the self, part of the literary technology through which subjectivity is constituted as an object of self-knowledge."[46] I argue that OHL likewise uses music and style to form its social existence, which entails expressing to what extent it is willing, or not, to subject itself to certain West German moral codes. What is more, the band's violent lyrics may function as a way for listeners to manage destructive emotions. Listeners can instead choose to perpetrate "a kind of aesthetic violence, to 'scream,' 'punch' or 'kick' musically, and thus have power over [their] (aesthetic) environment."[47] While the BPjM accused OHL of spreading violence, their songs may actually be reducing violence and channeling it into a more private, less harmful outlet.

Five songs are named in the official letter from the BPjM regarding OHL's album. The song "Botschaftslied" (Embassy Song) encourages listeners to "Stürmt die amerikanische Botschaft" (storm the American embassy). This sort of sentiment, common among German punks, was directed not against Americans more generally but against their government. As OHL's lead singer Deutscher W (DW) sings, "[Ich] habe nichts gegen das Volk, aber gegen den Staat" (I'm not against the people, but the government). The roots of this sentiment lie in a sense of betrayal that had been felt since the 1960s. German youth had once looked up to Americans as decidedly different from authoritarian father figures because of their pop culture: their comic books, chewing gum, and rock music. The onset of the Vietnam War changed that image; now Americans were seen as the oppressors rather than the liberators. Thus, DW sings, "Ich halte nichts von deutsch-amerikanischer Freundschaft" (I don't think anything of German-American friendship). This last line could have also been a snide remark about the German New Wave band by the same name, DAF. Nevertheless, it was clearly not in the West German government's best interest to allow lyrics inciting violence against their closest ally since the war.

The second song listed, "Kraft durch Freude" (Strength through Joy), deals with the Holocaust. It is indexed because it contains the following phrases stemming from the National Socialist period: "Arbeit macht frei" (work liberates) and "Kraft durch Freude" (strength through joy). It is also indexed because of the lines "yellow star on my jacket" and "tomorrow I will be gassed." Yet, when considered in its entirety, the text of the song appears to be written from the perspective of the Jewish victim of the Nazis:

Kraft durch Freude
Saft und Treue
Kraftlos, saftlos den Todesstoß
Arbeit macht frei
Tod und Geschrei
Kraft durch Freude
Saft und Treue

Wenn wir viele Steine schleppen
Kann es uns das Leben retten
Ein gelber Stern auf meiner Jacke
Angebracht von Naziratte
Ein roter J in meinem Pass
Morgen sterbe ich durch das Gas

Translation:

Strength through joy
Sap and loyalty
Strengthless, sapless to the deadly shot
Work liberates
Death and clamor
Strength through joy
Sap and loyalty

If we carry stones
It can save our life
A yellow star on my jacket
Put there by a Nazi rat
A red J in my passport
Tomorrow I will be gassed

Rather than interpreting the song as an incitement to anti-Semitism due to its use of Nazi jargon, we may just as easily interpret it as sympathizing with Holocaust victims. DW sings in the first person, which can be understood as an effort to identify with the Jewish victims. The text in the second strophe may simply be a statement of fact—a reminder to West Germans of the atrocities of war. Furthermore, DW's declaration in the first strophe that he is marching "strengthless, sapless to the deadly shot" could be an expression of resignation. Skeptical of the Cold War, neoliberal promise that he could find freedom and purpose in the free market society of West Germany, DW succumbs to a lack of future.

Pr. 110/87

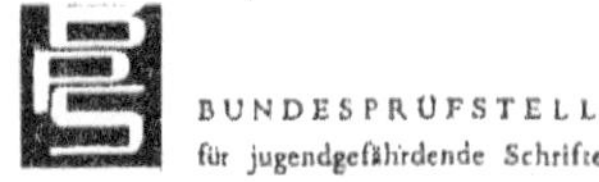

Entscheidung Nr. 3002 (V) vom 14.08.1987
bekanntgemacht im Bundesanzeiger Nr.152 vom 19.08.1987

Antragsteller:

Verfahrensbeteiligte:
1. Rock-O-Rama-Records

Bevollmächtigter Rechtsanwalt:

2. Rockgruppe Oberste Heeresleitung

Die Bundesprüfstelle für jugendgefährdende Schriften hat auf den am 03.03.1987 eingegangenen Antrag am 14.08.1987 gemäß § 15a GjS im vereinfachten Verfahren in der Besetzung mit:

Vorsitzender:

Literatur:

Jugendwohlfahrt:

einstimmig entschieden:

"Heimatfront"
Oberste Heeresleitung
Schallplatte (LP)
Rock-O-Rama-Records, Brühl

wird in die Liste der
jugendgefährdenden Schriften
aufgenommen.

Sachverhalt

1. Der Inhaber der Verfahrensbeteiligten zu 1., "produzierte die Langspielplatte "Heimatfront" der Rockgruppe OHL (Oberste Heeresleitung). Sämtliche auf der Schallplatte enthaltenen Lieder stammen von der Rockgruppe OHL.

Am Michaelshof 8 · Postfach 20 03 55 · 5300 BONN 2 · Telefon (0 2 2 8) 35 60 21

Figure 4.2. Excerpts from the BPjM decision. Courtesy of Bundesprüfstelle für jugendgefährdende Medien.

2. Folgende Lieder sind auf der Schallplatte enthalten:

Seite A:	Seite B:
Leverkusen,	Kernkraftritter,
Kraft durch Freude,	Widerstand,
Botschaftslied,	Hindustan,
Patte,	Sid,
Türkenlied (langsame Version),	Wir sind die unreparierten,
Deutschland,	A-Bombe,
Sterben ist menschlich,	Ist es erlaubt Fragen zu stellen?

3. Das hat beantragt,

   die Schallplatte "Heimatfront" der Gruppe Oberste Heeresleitung (OHL) in die Liste der jugendgefährdenden Schriften aufzunehmen.

   Das hält die Schallplatte für jugendgefährdend. Das Lied 1 auf Seite A "Kraft durch Freude" setze sich ironisch mit dem Schicksal der Jugen im Dritten Reich auseindander. In dem Lied "Deutschland" würden Textzitate der nicht zulässigen ersten Stophe der Deutschen Nationalhymne gebraucht. Im Lied "Kernkraftritter" rufe die Gruppe zu Intoleranz gegenüber Andersdenkenden auf und biete Gewalt als einziges Mittel zur Konfliktlösung an. Das Lied "Wir sind die Unreparierten" sei jugendgefährdend. Das Zitat "Wir spritzen unsere Kinder an die Wand" wird in diesem Zusammenhang angeführt. Der Antragsteller bittet darum, die Tatbestandsmäßigkeit im Sinne der §§ 131 und 184 StGB zu überprüfen.

4. Der Bevollmächtigte der Verfahrensbeteiligten dzu 1. wendet sich gegen eine Listenaufnahme der Schallplatte "Heimatfront". Die Antragschrift des gebe lediglich aus dem Textzusammenhang herausgerissene Textzitate wieder, so daß ein jugendgefährdender Inhalt der beanstandeten Lieder nicht substantiiert dargetan sei. Eine nähere Stellungnahme zu den in Frage stehenden Texten werde vorgenommen, sobald der Verfahrensbevollmächtigte die Texte von der Musikgruppe erhalten habe.

   Der Verfahrensbevollmächtigte hat beantragt

   von einer Entscheidung im vereinfachten Verfahren gemäß § 15a GjS abzusehen.

   Der Rockgruppe "Oberste Heeresleitung" wurde ein Doppel des Indizierungsantrages zugeleitet. Ihr wurde Gelegenheit gegeben, sich zu diesem sowie zu der Absicht der Bundesprüfstelle, im vereinfachten Verfahren nach § 15a GjS zu entscheiden, zu äußern. Von dieser Möglichkeit hat sie keinen Gebrauch gemacht.

5. Wegen der weiteren Einzelheiten des Sach- und Streitstandes wird auf den Inhalt der Prüfakte sowie auf den der Schallplatte Bezug genommen. Die Mitglieder des Prüfgremiums haben die Langspielplatte bei normaler Laufgeschwindigkeit in voller Länge abgehört. Mit ihrer Unterschrift erklären die Beisitzer ihr Einverständnis mit dem Wortlaut der vorliegenden Entscheidung. Ein Transskript der Schallplatte ist zur Akte und als Anlage zu dieser Entscheidung genommen worden.

Figure 4.3. Excerpts from the BPjM decision. Courtesy of Bundesprüfstelle für jugendgefährdende Medien.

G r ü n d e

6. Der Indizierungsantrag ist begründet. Die Schallplatte "Heimatfront" der Rockgruppe OHL (Oberste Heeresleitung) war in die Liste der jugendgefährdenden Schriften aufzunehmen. Die Schallplatte ist geeignet, Kinder und Jugendliche "sozialethisch zu desorientieren" wie der Begriff "sittlich zu gefährden" in § 1 Abs. 1 Satz 1 GjS auszulegen ist.

Das "Botschaftslied" hat folgenden Inhalt:

Stürmt die amerikanische Botschaft,
Stürmt die amerikanische Botschaft,
Stürmt die amerikanische Botschaft,
Ich halte nichts von amerikanischer Freundschaft,
hab nichts gegen das Volk, aber gegen den Staat,
darum mußt Du verstehen,   das Volk erst ab.

Stürmt die amerikanische Botschaft,
Stürmt die amerikanische Botschaft,
Stürmt die amerikanische Botschaft,
Ich halte nichts von deutsch-amerikanischer Freundschaft,
ich hab nichts gegen das Volk, aber gegen den Staat,
darum mußt Du verstehen,   das Volk erst ab.

I like to go to America,
everything is good in America
I like to be in America,
I like to stay in America.

My name is John F. Kennedy.
Ich bin ein Berliner.

Das "Botschaftslied" fordert dazu auf, die amerikanische Botschaft zu stürmen. Es wendet sich gegen amerikanische Freundschaft. Dieser erste Teil des Liedes steht im Widerspruch zu dem englischsprachigen zweiten Teil. Nach dem Inhalt des englischsprachigen Teils geht der Interpret gerne nach Amerika, meint, alles in diesem Land sei in Ordnung. Bezug wird genommen auf John F. Kennedy, der für die Stadt Berlin im Namen des amerikanischen Regierung umfangreiche Garantien in der Zeit des kalten Krieges abgegeben hat.

Dominant in dem Liedtext ist die jeweils dreimal wiederholte Aufforderung: "Stürmt die amerikanische Botschaft!" in Verbindung mit der Bemerkung "Ich halte nichts von amerikanischer Freundschaft". Durch diese Passage werden die Hörer aufgefordert, Gewalt gegen das Gebäude und die Mitarbeiter der amerikanischen Botschaft auszuüben. Zur bracchialer Gewalt wird aufgefordert. Wer das Lied hört, soll sich aus Protest gegen die Politik der amerikanischen Regierung deren Vertreter in der Bundesrepublik vertreiben.

Mit diesen Aufforderungen werden die Hörer aufgefordert, Straftaten zu begehen. Gewaltanwendungen gegenüber Personen, Sachbeschädigungen sowie das nicht erlaubte Betreten privaten Grundbesitzes ist unter Strafe gestellt.

Figure 4.4. Excerpts from the BPjM decision. Courtesy of Bundesprüfstelle für jugendgefährdende Medien.

Organe und Vertreter ausländischer Staaten sind im besonderen Maße strafrechtlich durch die §§ 102-104 StGB geschützt. Danach macht sich strafbar, wer Organe und Vertreter ausländischer Staaten angreift oder beleidigt, oder Flaggen und Hoheitszeichen ausländischer Staaten verletzt. Die Formulierung "Stürmt die amerikanische Botschaft" hält aber dazu an, die Botschaft samt Personal und Hoheitszeichen zu attakieren. Das Lied fordert damit in mehrfacher Hinsicht zu strafbewehrtem Tun auf. Es steht damit positiv formulierten, verbindlich postulierten Werten diamentral entgegen. Die Formulierung ist daher geeignet, eine sozialethische Desorientierung zu bewirken.

Dieser Tendenz des "Botschaftsliedes" steht nicht entgegen, daß sich das Lied nur gegen den "Staat", gemeint ist die Regierung, wendet; auch der englischsprachige Textteil und der Bezug auf das Zitat von John F. Kennedy "Ich bin ein Berliner" soll wohl nur Sympathie zum amerikanischen Volk bekunden, nicht aber die Aufforderung "Stürmt die amerikanische Botschaft" in Frage stellen. Die Formulierung soll sicherstellen, daß nicht das amerikanische Volk sondern die heutigen Machthaber mit der Gewaltaufforderung bedacht sein sollen.

Die Lieder "Kraft durch Freude", "Deutschland", Kernkraftritter" und "Wir sind die Unreparierten", enthalten nach Ansicht des Prüfgremiums ebenfalls jugendgefährdende Tendenzen; die Gefahr für Kinder und Jugendliche tritt in diesen jedoch nicht so stark hervor wie in dem "Botschaftslied". Der jugendgefährdende Inhalt eines der Lieder genügt indes, um die gesamte Schallplatte zu indizieren. Das GjS kennt nämlich keine Teilindizierungen, vgl. Urteil des BVerwG vom 16.12.1971, Az.: I C 41/70.

7. Die von der Schallplatte "Heimatfront" ausgehende Jugendgefährdung ist auch offenbar im Sinne von § 15a GjS. Anhand der Aufforderung zu Gewalt gegenüber einer anerkannten diplomatischen Vertretung wird dies für den unbefangenen Betrachter klar und zweifelsfrei einsichtig.

8. Ausnahmetatbestände im Sinne von § 1 Abs. 2 GjS kamen nicht in Betracht. Die Lieder auf der Schallplatte stellen weder Kunst dar noch dienen sie ihr, § 1 Abs. 2 Nr. 2 GjS. Weder der Text noch die Musik der Lieder erreichen ein Level, daß man ihnen das Prädikat "Kunst" zubilligen könnte. Gesang und Texte weisen in keinerlei Hinsicht Qualität auf; die niveaulose Gestaltung erscheint anderseits auch nicht als künstlerisches Stilelement. Der Ausnahmetatbestand des § 1 Abs. 2 Nr. 1 schied aus, weil die Schallplatte nicht allein wegen eines politischen oder weltanschaulichen Inhalts sondern wegen Aufruf zu nach dem StGB strafbewehrten Taten, unabhängig von dem jeweiligen politischen Gegner als jugendgefährdend eingestuft wurde.

9. Ein Fall geringer Bedeutung im Sinne von § 2 GjS schied wegen dem hohen Maß an Jugendgefährdung, bedingt durch die Aufforderung zu Straftaten, aus.

Rechtsbehelfsbelehrung

Gegen die Entscheidung kann innerhalb eines Monats ab Zustellung schriftlich oder zu Protokoll der Geschäftsstelle beim Verwaltungsgericht in 5000 Köln, Appellhofplatz, Anfechtungsklage erhoben werden. Die vorherige Einlegung eines Widerspruchs entfällt. Die Klage hat keine aufschiebende Wirkung. Sie ist gegen den Bund, vertreten durch die Bundesprüfstelle zu richten (§§ 20 GjS, 42 VwGO).

Figure 4.5. Excerpts from the BPjM decision. Courtesy of Bundesprüfstelle für jugendgefährdende Medien.

The third song named in the letter is "Deutschland" (Germany). This song was indexed because, in the words of the BPjM, it "quotes the impermissible first strophe of the German national anthem," the banned line being "Germany, Germany above all."[48]

Deutschland, Deutschland über alles
Das Leben in Deutschland
Die Scheisse an der Wand
Deutschland, wie hasse ich dich
An mich kommst du nicht
Deutschland du bist zu alt
Deutschland du bist zu kalt
Deutschland, wie hasse ich dich
An mich kommst du nicht
Deutschland, du hast kein Herz
Und sehnen Menschenschmerz
Deutschland, so lächerlich
Deutschland, wir hassen dich
Deutschland, ein Hinderniss
Für Menschen wie dich und mich
Deutschland, du hast die Macht
. . .
Deutschland, wie hasse ich dich
An mich kommst du nicht
Ich kotze dir ins Gesicht
Deutschland, ich hasse dich . . .
Deutschland, es geht Berg ab
Deutschland, wie hasse ich dich
An mich kommst du nicht
Deutschland, du bist verrückt
Deutschland, ein Murmelstück
Näher an den Abgrund ran
Und dann bis du dran
Deutschland, bald ist es vorbei
Und dann sind wir wieder frei
Deutschland . . . vorbei
Scheiss-Deutschland . . . Scheissland

Translation:

Germany, Germany above all
Life in Germany
The shit on the wall
Germany, how I hate you
You won't get me
Germany you're too old
Germany you're too cold
Germany, how I hate you
You won't get me
Germany, you have no heart
And long for the pain of others
Germany, so ridiculous
Germany, we hate you
Germany, a hindrance
For people like you and me
Germany, you have the power
. . .
Germany, how I hate you
You won't get me
I throw up in your face
Germany, I hate you . . .
Germany, it's all downhill
Germany, how I hate you
Germany, you won't get me
Germany, you're crazy
Germany, a piece of marble
Closer to the edge
And then it's your turn
Germany, soon it'll be over
And then we'll be free again
Germany . . . over
Shitty Germany . . . shitty country

After quoting the German national anthem in the first line, the entire song mocks and criticizes Germany, periodically returning to the chorus, "Germany, I hate you." The line "Germany, Germany above all" was originally penned by August Heinrich Hoffmann von Fallersleben in his poem "The

Song of the Germans," a prodemocracy song anticipating the attempted democratic revolution of 1848. In fact, von Fallersleben spent several years in exile to escape political persecution at the hands of the Prussians. The song would later be adopted by the Nazis and reappropriated as a nationalist anthem, in part because several of the German territories it names had been lost to other countries since the end of World War I. Instead of citing the song as an act of nationalism, OHL could very well be extending von Fallersleben's tradition of critiquing the state. In the second half of the song, DW implies that in order for the speaker to be liberated, Germany has to end: "Germany, soon it'll be over / And then we'll be free again." These lines are reminiscent of another punk anthem by the left-wing band Slime, "Deutschland muss sterben" (Germany must die, 1981). OHL's ode to Germany concludes with the singer repeating "Shitty Germany" to the tune of the national anthem, which could perhaps also be compared to The Velvet Underground's German singer Nico's subversive 1974 performance of "Song of the Germans" to discordant, atonal music.

The fourth song mentioned in the letter from the BPjM is "Kernkraftritter" (Nuclear Power Knights), which the BPjM deemed problematic because it "encourages intolerance against people who think differently and offers violence as the only solution." But the lyrics to this song clearly convey the punk performative gesture of rejecting what came before, in this case antinuclear energy activists, whom the band associates with the '68ers, those "alternative langhaarige Sau[e]" (alternative long-haired pigs):

Alternative langhaarige Sau
Du siehst aus wie deine Frau
Alles was du willst ist Frieden
Doch es gibt nur hass
Du bist jedem Menschen liebe
Aber du bist aus Glas
Ich sehe deinen gelb/roten Sticker
Du bist der Kernkraftritter
Ich sehe deinen gelb/roten Sticker
Du bist der Kernkraftritter

Alles tust du diskutieren
Doch das Leben ist hart
Du willst uns nur irritieren
Aber du bist zu schwach

Ich sehe deinen gelb/roten Sticker
Du bist der Kernkraftritter
Ich sehe deinen gelb/roten Sticker
Du bist der Kernkraftritter

Alles was du machst ist lachen
Doch man braucht Gewalt
Du willst uns nur überwachen
Aber du bist zu alt
Ich sehe deinen gelb/roten Sticker
Du bist der Kernkraftritter
Ich sehe deinen gelb/roten Sticker
Du bist der Kernkraftritter

Translation:

Alternative long-haired pig
You look like your wife
All you want is peace
But there's only hate
You're nice to everyone
But you're made of glass
I see your yellow and red sticker
You're a nuclear power knight
I see your yellow and red sticker
You're a nuclear power knight

All you do is talk
But life is hard
You just want to confuse us
But you're too weak
I see your yellow and red sticker
You're a nuclear power knight
I see your yellow and red sticker
You're a nuclear power knight

All you do is laugh
But one needs to have violence
You just want to supervise us

But you're too old
I see your yellow and red sticker
You're a nuclear power knight
I see your yellow and red sticker
You're a nuclear power knight

Against the claims made in the BPjM's letter, I argue that OHL does not promote violence against antinuclear energy activists. The band's tone is mocking. The nuclear power knights are "too old." They are the "alternative long-haired" hippies of the '68 generation. They want to "supervise" the youth. The nuclear power knights think that discussion is the answer and want to get along with everyone, but according to OHL, this is futile because "life is hard" and "there's only hate." The lyrics reflect resignation and nihilism. They insist that there is no way to win in the current system; one can only succumb to the chaos.

The final song mentioned in the letter is "Wir sind die Unreparierten" (We Are the Unrepaired), which was indexed solely because of the lyric "we splatter our children on the wall." This line is actually misquoted by the BPjM. The text is really "we splatter our children of tomorrow on the wall." This is a notable error, because the song is really about masturbation and the band's commitment to wasting their semen, rather than using it to reproduce:

Wir sind die Unreparierten
Und wir wichsen mit Verstand
Wir spritzen unsere Kinder von morgen an die Wand

Translation:

We are the unrepaired
And we wank with purpose
We spray our children of tomorrow on the wall

There exist several satires about killing children by US punk bands, from Dead Kennedys' "I Kill Children" (1978) to the Misfits' "Last Caress" (1978). But "Wir sind die Unreparierten" does not belong on this list, as it is actually rejecting heteronormative reproduction and the obligation to become a productive member of society. In this way, the lyrics are similar to those of the US punk band The Circle Jerks' "Operation" (1980), in which lead singer Keith Morris narrates his experience of getting a vasectomy in order to ensure that he doesn't bring any children into such a horrible world. It is also important to note that the song "We Are the Unrepaired" is a loose adaptation of an English song, "The Troops of Tomorrow" (1978), by British punk band the Vibrators, with which it shares a melody. The two songs convey the same sense of nihilism and hopelessness, but the British song is more violent:

> We ain't got a bright future
> We bought it on the never-never
> Don't wanna be city prisoners
> We ain't gonna live forever
>
> We gotta stop that dreamin'
> We gotta pick up that gun
> I said we're troops of tomorrow
> We got a new vision

The document from the BPjM concludes that "in the sense of article one, paragraph one, this record is perfectly capable of socially and ethically disorienting children and adolescents."

Conclusion

Instead of justifying OHL's behavior or denying that their language and the images they use could possibly fuel right-wing politics, this chapter has questioned why, even though several German and even British and US bands at the time behaved similarly, OHL in particular alerted the BPjM. In an informed discussion about right-wing tendencies in German music, I do not believe it is productive to categorize OHL or bands like it in binary terms without proper contextualization. Upon further analysis, we can just as easily read the band's behavior as a process of forming its social existence during turbulent political times. As one New Wave band stated to Hermann Langer, "What we distribute is not an ideology. We are the mirror image of our world."[49] Using provocative music and style, OHL attempted to situate itself in relation to the moral codes of Cold War Germany. In a style reminiscent of the *Zweckentfremdung* (purposeful estrangement) practiced by the avant-garde Situationists, OHL used war imagery and Nazi-era terminology to confront West Germany with both Germany's Nazi past and the alleged persistence of fascist and authoritarian tendencies. What sets the band apart from the German protest rock of the 1960s and 1970s is OHL's rejection of both right- and left-wing politics. Unlike the '68ers, for whom Communism seemed a viable alternative, punk bands like OHL saw both sides, East and West, as equally destructive; yet, the band also rejected the anarchist alternative that other *Deutschpunk* bands at the time embraced. OHL has always claimed to oppose all ideologies. For them, there is no difference between fascism and communism, as evidenced by the logos on their website: a fist smashing a swastika and a fist smashing a hammer and sickle.

OHL's position was not uncommon among young people during the Cold War, especially in the punk scene. The San Francisco–based punk band the Avengers once sang, "We are not Jesus Christ / We are not fascist pigs / We are not capitalist executives / We are not Communists / We are the ones." The argument in these lyrics is certainly simplistic. What the ambivalent "we are the ones" refers to is open to debate. But psychoanalyst Erik Erikson's work might provide some clarification as to the meaning of these lyrics. In a 1970 article entitled "Reflections on the Dissent of Contemporary Youth," Erikson offers that the large-scale destruction of World War II meant that young people afterward were destined to challenge their fathers and had to find new ways to do so that were not simply borrowed from the modernist revolutionary forms that had failed.[50] Perhaps OHL understood this "new way" as a rejection of the communist East, the capitalist West, Germany's fascist past, *and Deutschpunk*'s accepted leftist positions. Their "new way" was an argument against existing systems and institutions and a refusal to argue in favor of a specific alternative—a tension that led to extreme, abrasive, and nihilistic lyrics. And even though the Cold War is a thing of the past, this sentiment has not necessarily disappeared among young people. Despite Francis Fukuyama's 1989 declaration regarding the "end of history," we are not celebrating a world of democracies but witnessing an increase in skepticism toward democracy both in the US and Germany.

And while OHL continues to perform and record new music and still takes satirical jabs at contemporary politics—hence pseudonyms like Kalashnikov and Stalin—the group no longer stands out in the German punk scene or for the BPjM. In fact, on July 20, 2011, the BPjM removed *Heimatfront* from the list of indexed albums, confirming that it does not, and never did, pose an ethical threat to young people. While OHL's music may no longer be as controversial as it was in the 1980s, we could argue that a band like Rammstein has taken its place. Like OHL, Rammstein's tendency to flirt with shocking imagery and icons of Germany's past has led people to question their political allegiances.[51] The band's single "Deutschland" (Germany, 2019) recalls a few of the tactics from OHL's banned album. In the video for "Deutschland," Rammstein covers various scenes from German history, specifically the history of a mythical German national identity, including everything from Hermann's battle against the Romans in the Teutoburg Forest (AD 9) to the dissolution of East Germany (1989). A Black woman is featured throughout the video and at times appears to be standing in for the nation itself. Like OHL, Rammstein sometimes identifies with Jewish victims of the Holocaust—in one scene the band members don striped prison uniforms and yellow stars—as well as East German party bureaucrats.[52] Rammstein's lyrics, like OHL's, hold the key to the band's message:

> Deutschland, deine Liebe
> Ist Fluch und Segen
> Deutschland, meine Liebe
> Kann ich dir nicht geben
>
> Translation:
>
> Germany, your love
> is a curse and a blessing
> Germany, I cannot
> give you my love

While it shares OHL's critical view of Germany, Rammstein's music is much more mainstream and reaches a wider audience. The single "Germany" reached number one on the German charts when it was released in 2019. The appropriation of icons of the past and engagement with issues of national identity certainly didn't end with the Cold War and don't seem to be going away. Instead of condemning such performances outright, we should take the time to understand their appeal in order to gain insight into how fans view themselves within political landscapes and what listening to such music does to shape them as ethical and moral subjects.

OHL invalidates Bürger's 2010 claim that neo-avant-garde cannot be as transgressive as the historical avant-garde. Bürger argues that the avant-garde emerged amid crisis, and OHL certainly perceived the 1980s as a moment of crisis in West Germany. Moreover, while certain aspects of punk fashion, music, and politics were institutionalized by 1983, when the album *Heimatfront* was released, what had *not* been sanctioned by any institution was an unironic use of Nazi symbolism that claimed neither a left- nor a right-wing position. This is precisely what makes OHL an ethical, neo-avant-garde act in the context of the West German punk scene. According to Bürger, "The unification of art and life . . . can only be achieved if it succeeds in liberating aesthetic potential from the institutional constraints which block its social effectiveness," and OHL achieves such a unification by refusing to play by the rules established by moral codes to which it was subjected.[53]

Notes

1. Peter Bürger, *Theory of the Avant-Garde*, trans. Michael Shaw (Minneapolis: University of Minnesota Press, 1984), 58.

2. Bürger, *Theory of the Avant-Garde*, 52–53.

3. Hal Foster, "What's Neo about the Neo-Avant-Garde?," *October* 70 (1994): 7.

4. Foster, "What's Neo about the Neo-Avant-Garde?," 14.

5. Peter Bürger, "Avant-Garde and Neo-Avant-Garde: An Attempt to Answer Certain Critics of 'Theory of the Avant-Garde,'" *New Literary History* 41, no. 4 (2010): 713.

6. Bürger, "Avant-Garde and Neo-Avant-Garde," 712.

7. Gert Nicolini, "Leverkusen 1945 bis 1974," in *Leverkusen: Geschichte einer Stadt am Rhein*, ed. Gabriele John (Bielefeld: Verl. für Regionalgeschichte, 2005), 446.

8. Nicolini, "Leverkusen 1945 bis 1974," 468.

9. Matthias Bauschen, "Die neue Stadt Leverkusen 1975 bis 2004," in *Leverkusen*, 549.

10. Bauschen, "Die neue Stadt Leverkusen 1975 bis 2004," 549.

11. Bauschen, "Die neue Stadt Leverkusen 1975 bis 2004," 556.

12. Quoted in Martin Büsser, "Rebel in Society: Der Aufstand des Punks aus dem Geist der Pubertät," in *testcard: beiträge zur Popgeschichte* 9 (2000): 99. All translations from German to English are mine, unless otherwise specified.

13. Cyrus Shahan, *Punk Rock and German Crisis* (New York: Palgrave, 2013), 2.

14. Shahan, *Punk Rock and German Crisis*, 3.

15. Having your album indexed by the BPjM is the American equivalent of receiving a Parental Advisory label. It makes it more difficult for young people to buy the album without being accompanied by an adult.

16. See Dagmar Herzog, *Sex after Fascism: Memory and Morality in Twentieth-Century Germany* (Princeton, NJ: Princeton University Press, 2007); Uta Poiger,

Jazz, Rock, Rebels: Cold War Politics in American Culture and a Divided Germany (Berkeley, CA: University of California Press, 2000).

17. Michel Foucault, *The Use of Pleasure*, trans. Robert Hurley (New York: Vintage Books, 1990), 25.

18. Foucault, *Use of Pleasure*, 27.

19. Foucault, *Use of Pleasure*, 26.

20. "Article 5: Freedom of Expression," *Deutschland.de*, May 15, 2019, https://www.deutschland.de/en/topic/politics/the-german-basic-law-article-5-freedom-of-expression, emphasis added.

21. See Noah Benezra Strote, *Lions and Lambs: Conflict in Weimar and the Creation of Post-Nazi Germany* (New Haven, CT: Yale University Press), 2017.

22. Herzog, *Sex after Fascism*.

23. "General Information," BPjM, October 8, 2018, https://www.bundespruefstelle.de/bpjm/meta/en.

24. "Socialweb—Socialwork," *Socialweb—Socialwork*, n.d., https://www.socialweb-socialwork.eu/content/regulation/index.cfm/action.showfull/key.16/secid.25/secid2.51, emphasis added.

25. Digital copies of these laws can be found on the Bundesanzeiger Vergal website: https://www.bgbl.de.

26. Peter Stolle, "Die Harke im Garten der Lüste," *Der Spiegel*, February 10, 1986, 196.

27. Stolle, "Die Harke im Garten der Lüste," 196.

28. Achim Barsch, "Das Problem von Authentizität und Fiktionalität im Rahmen der Indizierungspraxis der Bundesprüfstelle für jugendgefährdende Schriften," in *Verbrechen—Justiz—Medien: Konstellationen in Deutschland von 1900 bis zur Gegenwart*, ed. Joachim Linder and Claus-Michael Ort (Tübingen: Max Niemeyer Verlag, 1999), 122.

29. Rudolf Stefen, "Jugendmedienschutz in der Bundesrepublik Deutschland," in *Jugendschutz und Massenmedien*, ed. George Wodraschke (Munich: Verlag Ölschläger, 1983), 99.

30. Stefen, "Jugendmedienschutz in der Bundesrepublik Deutschland," 100.

31. Stefen, "Jugendmedienschutz in der Bundesrepublik Deutschland," 100–101.

32. Barsch, "Das Problem von Authentizität," 135.

33. Barsch, "Das Problem von Authentizität," 122.

34. Barsch, "Das Problem von Authentizität," 124.

35. Barsch, "Das Problem von Authentizität," 124–125.

36. Shahan, *Punk Rock and German Crisis*, 11.

37. Klaus Farin, *Jugendkulturen in Deutschland 1950–1989* (Berlin: Bundeszentrale für politische Bildung, 2006), 102.

38. Farin, *Jugendkulturen in Deutschland 1950–1989*, 102.

39. Farin, *Jugendkulturen in Deutschland 1950–1989*, 102.

40. Dick Hebdige, *The Meaning of Style* (Hoboken, NJ: Taylor and Francis, 2012). See also Jon Stratton, "Jews, Punk and the Holocaust: From the Velvet Underground to the Ramones—the Jewish-American Story," *Popular Music* 24, no. 1 (2005): 79–105.

41. Shahan, *Punk Rock and German Crisis*, 5.

42. Fronted by Ian Stuart, Skrewdriver started out as an unremarkable British punk band but began adopting right-wing ideology with its second studio album, *Hail the New Dawn* (1984). Indicative of that album's title, the band embraced neo-Nazi ideology and frequently borrowed German terms like *Blood and Honor* (*Blut und Boden*). They advocated for British nationalism and white supremacy and their music helped recruit young people for the British far-right political party the National Front.

43. Klaus Farin, *Die Skins: Mythos Und Realität* (Berlin: Ch. Links Verlag, 1998), 48.

44. Farin, *Die Skins*, 48–49.

45. Büsser, "Rebel in Society," 99.

46. Tia DeNora, *Music in Everyday Life* (Cambridge, UK: Cambridge University Press, 2007), 50.

47. DeNora, *Music in Everyday Life*, 56.

48. All quotes are from the BPjM's index letter, retrieved in 2008 from the band's now-defunct website.

49. Hermann Langer, *"Wollt ihr den totalen Tanz": Streiflichter zur imperialistischen Manipulierung der Jugend* (Berlin: Verlag Neues Leben, 1985), 10.

50. Erik H. Erikson, "The Problem of Ego Identity," *Journal of the American Psychoanalytic Association* 4 (1956): 56–121.

51. For a discussion of Rammstein's aesthetics and politics see Corinna Kahnke's "Transnationale Teutonen: Rammstein Representing the Berlin Republic," *Journal of Popular Music Studies* 25, no. 2 (2013): 185–197; John T. Littlejohn and Michael T. Putnam, eds., *Rammstein on Fire: New Perspectives on the Music and Performances* (Jefferson, NC: McFarland, 2013).

52. Laina Dawes does an in-depth analysis of the video, including a discussion of its use of racialized and gendered tropes. " 'Die Schwarze Germania': Race, Gender and Monstrosity within Rammstein's Deutschland," *Ethnomusicology Review* 22 (2020): https://ethnomusicologyreview.ucla.edu/content/%E2%80%9Cdie-schwarze-germania%E2%80%9D-race-gender-and-monstrosity-within-rammstein%E2%80%99s-deutschland?fbclid=IwAR0a-j1qBlfmHyC1sR1VB2B8frlSWmddkS6ju9PDt9gLWesC-OKz1Q22Rmc.

53. Bürger, "Avant-Garde and Neo-Avant-Garde," 696.

PART II

INFRASTRUCTURES

Chapter 5

Indexing Post-Fordism at P.S. 1

Andrew Strombeck

In 1975, the curator Alanna Heiss leased the former First Ward School from the city of New York for $1,000 a month to use as an alternative art space. Built in 1892 to house the first public school in Long Island City, the building was closed by the city in 1963, after the surrounding neighborhood had transitioned from a residential area into a manufacturing district. By the mid-1970s, the building was in bad repair, with peeling paint, a damaged roof, old wiring, and a leaky plumbing system. With funding from the New York State Council on the Arts and a construction loan from Chemical Bank, Heiss repaired the roof, rewired the building, and completed whatever plumbing repairs were necessary. She left the rest of the building largely intact, because, well, all that decay looked fascinating and might provide a perfect space for artists to do the kind of site-specific work that had been popular since the late 1960s.[1]

For the space's first exhibit, entitled *Rooms*, Heiss invited the bright lights of 1970s site-specific art, including Richard Serra, Carl Andre, Gordon Matta-Clark, Vito Acconci, Lynn Hershman, Nam June Paik, and Michelle Stuart. These artists cut into the building, built concrete mounds in classrooms, suspended ropes from ceilings, created panels that intersected with peeling walls, and found other ways of engaging the building's space. In an important essay published in the newly founded *October*, Rosalind Krauss took up the exhibit to outline what she described as an "indexical" turn in the art of the 1970s. The work at *Rooms*, Krauss argued, represented nothing but the building itself. In the terms of the era's rising discourse of semiotics, such works collapsed signifier into signified. Krauss stopped there, refusing to consider how, in turn, the First Ward Building, as a closed school, itself indexed the withdrawal of the state's support for particular forms of life under conditions of austerity. In reading the works of *Rooms* as indexing the First Ward Building, Krauss develops the index as an influential framework for collating the aesthetic productions of the 1970s. Yet by foregrounding some of the exhibit's works—those that reference the building—over others—those that reference the school's lifeworld—she forecloses other important indexes of the era, in particular the Consumer Price Index, a crucial player in mediating the effects of the long crisis on impoverished populations. This chapter picks up where Krauss left off, asking how indexicality helps us think through the possibilities of the avant-garde under conditions of crisis.

The Dual Crises of the Art Institution and the Keynesian State

The particular characteristics of the First Ward Building brought *Rooms* into collision with forces in the city that sought to dismantle public institutions. Facing constrained budgets in the early 1970s, the city wanted the building off its books: after all, there were plenty of *functional* school buildings that needed maintenance and support. These budgetary constraints had ideological causes: the loss of tax revenue from white flight and demanufacturing were real, but these became an occasion for financial elites to argue that the welfare state had run its course. Schools, along with hospitals, libraries, and firehouses, became potent sites of conflict over how the city should distribute resources. These local debates relayed critiques of Keynesian governance occurring at the national level during the Ford and Carter administrations; Ford's famous decision to refuse federal aid for the city had roots in these discussions.[2] In parallel, but with common causes, the artworld was experiencing its own crisis of faith in institutions. Collating site-specific works in a former public school, Heiss's work operates at a crucial nexus between these economic and artistic critiques.

The name Heiss gave the new art space was Project Studios One, quickly shortened to P.S. 1. P.S. 1 is now part of the Museum of Modern Art and has, over the past forty years, been a major factor in the gentrification of Long Island City. Through the alchemy of art, a space of neglect became a space that the city could safely ignore. Even better, this space fostered the city's broad conversion from a local economy based on manufacturing to an outward-looking economy based on finance and real estate. This story should sound familiar. It continues to be told up to the present day: the old rails around Atlanta become greenspace that attracts galleries, condominiums, and upscale restaurants; a steel mill in Pittsburgh is converted into a shopping mall; a Nabisco factory in Beacon, New York, becomes a Dia museum. Heiss transformed P.S. 1 from a ruined leftover of the industrial age to a flourishing node in the international museum system that, by the 1990s, would become a model for economic development and, by extension, urban governance. While the postwar Keynesian consensus had treated the arts as a secondary beneficiary of economic expansion, after the 1970s the arts would come to be seen as a paradigm for economic development, through the interlinked processes of gentrification, the "creative economy," and the adoption of what Luc Boltanski and Eve Chiapello call the "artistic critique" into management models.[3] For Boltanski and Chiapello, the "new spirit of capitalism" that emerges in the 1970s—entailing flexible work schedules, contract-based employment, and the networked project—needed the artistic critique as a means of both justifying worker identity and insisting that every worker continually evaluate their work processes. These categories have yielded crucial insights into the embeddedness of even the most avant-garde artistic practices in networks of neoliberal governance after the 1970s end of the postwar economic expansion.

Each case—gentrification, the creative economy, and the artistic critique—augmented a wider tendency in the crisis-era economy: a shift away from centralized planning and toward local control. A corresponding tendency was at work in the artworld itself, as the postwar gallery and museum system came to be seen as unnecessarily narrow arbiters of value. Critics and artists alike questioned the terms with which art governed itself—in particular, the ways that the museum had come to dominate the reception, circulation, and production of art. These debates had simmered for decades, particularly under the sign of the avant-garde. With exceptions, the avant-garde had come to be seen as submerged beneath cultures of (often corporate-sponsored) modernism that were dominant in the 1950s and 1960s (think abstract expressionism). Minimalism, pop art, and institutional critique all posed versions of the same question: how could aesthetic autonomy persist when the fortunes of aesthetic creation were closely tied to the museums and galleries that authorized the circulation and production of aesthetic objects? Artists and critics alike would come to see the museum, as Douglas Crimp puts it in a 1980 essay, as a ruin whose authoritative claims were fragile.[4] In Crimp's view, the museum maintained a false "ordered discourse" that created the very categories it claimed to study, much like the way the asylum produces madness in Michel Foucault's analysis.[5] This discourse, which had "[determined] the order of aesthetic objects in the museum throughout the era of modernism," had been "broken" by the artworld disruptions of the 1970s, resulting, for Crimp, in "the fragility of the museum's claims to represent anything coherent at all."[6] For aesthetic autonomy to persist under these conditions, these institutions would need to be radically challenged. As chapters elsewhere in this collection demonstrate, in a good many sectors, like feminist art, conceptual art, and minoritarian art more widely, such challenges to art institutions drew attention to the ways that the artworld had fostered dispossession, patriarchal power, heteronormativity, and white supremacy. Often, though—as was the case with much site-specific art—these challenges served merely to renew aesthetic autonomy as a vital force, ensuring that art remained of interest to collectors and museums and providing an important set of signifiers for the artistic critique.

At this same moment, similar claims were being made about the Keynesian management of the economy. As Judith Stein documents in *Pivotal Decade: How the United States Traded Factory for Finance in the Seventies*, one by one, the pillars of the Keynesian economy—stimulus, progressive taxation, and regulation—fell in favor of market-based governance, tax cuts, and deregulation.[7] These reforms translated into a wide withdrawal of support for the institutions of the welfare state. The critique of the museum and the critique of Keynesian policies emerged in tandem: both responded to what seemed to be the hegemonic status of postwar institutions. Both critiques, too, emerged under the term *crisis*. While the realms of politics and art are not reducible to each other, the two realms are repeatedly bound—and here, gentrification, the creative economy, and the artistic critique form merely three nodes in a wider system of interconnection. As the central planning of the Keynesian era broke down, the arts not only followed but provided models for governance that emphasized entrepreneurialism and autonomy over support for institutions.

Embracing the Ruins at P.S. 1

In the hands of artists such as Richard Serra and Robert Smithson, site-specific art emerged as a particularly visible means to decenter the museum. Located in one place and impossible to move from gallery to gallery, site-specific work ostensibly formed a bulwark against the commodification of art. In interviews, Serra, for example, explained that site-specific work "[bypasses] commerce and cultural institutions by not being available for secondary sales or confinement in the ahistorical space of the museum."[8] Again in Serra's words, the postwar system was perceived to have made museums into "capitalist safe deposit boxes" that were "basically akin to bank structures or corporate structures."[9] But theoretically, at least, you could not bank a spiral in the desert or a bronze ring embedded in a Bronx street, to reference two works by, respectively, Smithson and Serra. Both alternative spaces and site-specific art served, as the critic John Roberts summarizes, to help art recover "its extra-institutional, interdisciplinary, performative and technological dimensions" after postwar modernism had run its course: "the street, the landscape and desert, the disused building, the abandoned factory become the sites of art's formal re-articulation and dispersal."[10] But inasmuch as site-specific work rebuked the closed world of the museum, the critical interpretation of these practices tended to insulate them from the historical and economic forces that made derelict sites and other noninstitutional spaces available. Often, artists and critics alike acted as though these works transformed sites that were only accidentally the products of 1970s decline.[11]

And yet by the mere fact of calling attention to sites of industrial decline—Matta-Clark cutting into an abandoned warehouse on the New York piers, Serra embedding a bronze ring into a decaying Bronx street—site-specific artists opened the possibility of returning viewers to the social engagement of the prewar avant-gardes. As Miwon Kwon has observed, these possibilities would burst forth in the coming decades. Under the influence of socially oriented art, site-specific art would become a potent vehicle for socially engaged art, as artists began to seek out sites with the goal of changing life. "The distinguishing characteristic of today's site-oriented art," Kwon wrote in the early 2000s, "is the way in which both the art work's relationship to the actuality of a location (as site) and the social conditions of the institutional frame (as site) are *subordinate* to a *discursively* determined site that is delineated as a field of knowledge, intellectual exchange, or cultural debate."[12] That is, as site-specific art evolves, it begins to look more like the prewar avant-gardes, seeking to change life, society, and the world.

By dispersing form into disused buildings and abandoned factories, site-specific artists stretched aesthetic categories such that, as Krauss pointed out in her landmark essay "Sculpture in the Expanded Field," the category of sculpture threatened to become "almost infinitely malleable."[13] By turning to the emerging field of semiotics, Krauss would rein in these dispersed forms.

In "Sculpture," she deployed semiotics to set up a series of oppositions for sculpture: site-construction versus sculpture, "marked sites" versus "axiomatic sculptures." Redefining aesthetic autonomy in terms of semiotics, Krauss replaced the narrow categories of the postwar museum with a flexible code that would reinfuse urgency and autonomy into the artworld, just as the artistic critique did for the new spirit of capitalism.

In an essay written contemporaneously with "Sculpture," Krauss drew on *Rooms* to announce an indexical turn in art. In "Notes on the Index: Seventies Art in America," she used the index to collate seemingly diverse strands of artistic innovation in the 1970s: photography, performance art, and site-specific installation. For Krauss, indexical works express "that type of sign which arises as the physical manifestation of a cause, of which traces, imprints, and clues are examples."[14] In taking up the index, Krauss was drawing on Roland Barthes's account of the photograph in "The Rhetoric of the Image" (1964; translated 1977). In that essay, Barthes describes the photograph as a special kind of image, one that evades the closed sign-system of drawing and painting.[15] The index is a sign, but one collapsed into its referent, as smoke is a sign of fire and a footprint is a sign of human presence. In this way, indexical works moved away from the closed system of postwar painting celebrated by critics such as Michael Fried—in which elements of the painting refer only to each other—but replaced one closed system with another, in which artwork and site refer only to each other.[16]

In Krauss's interpretation, a wide swath of work at *Rooms* was indeed not intended to function as a sign at all. Alan Daniel Saret cut an oval-shaped hole in the wall for *The Hole at P.S.1, Fifth Solar Chthonic Wall Temple* (1976), exposing crumbling brick and letting in light. (Saret's hole exists in the present-day P.S. 1.) Dale Henry carved into water-damaged walls, melding these cuts with canvas to create what he called a "site-specific painting." Lucio Pozzi hung two-color, painted panels in places where the school itself had shifted paint colors, such that panel matched the wall behind it.[17] For her *East/West Wall Memory Located*, Michelle Stuart used floor-to-ceiling sheets of paper to imprint the wall beneath: wainscoting, blackboard frames, and cracked plaster. She then transposed the sheets of paper to the opposite wall. The paper is smoke, and the wall is fire—the paper communicates nothing beyond "Here is a wall."

By asserting that, essentially, these works collapse the signifier into the signified, Krauss performed a move consistent with, though also orthogonal to, her account of sculpture in the "expanded field" essay. That essay presents

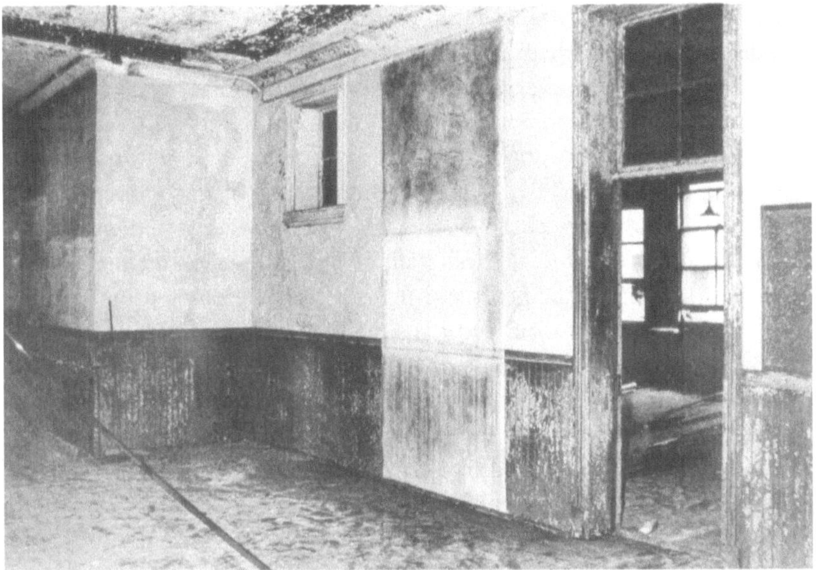

Figure 5.1. Installation view of Michelle Stuart's *East/West Wall Memory Located* in the exhibition *Rooms*, June 9 to 26, 1976, P.S. 1, Long Island City, New York. Courtesy of the Museum of Modern Art, licensed by SCALA / Art Resource.

sculpture as a series of floating signs, while the index describes a series of signs that are fixed in place. The works in *Rooms* could not mean anything beyond the building they referenced. For Krauss, this meant that the works at once intervened into notions of art as a closed sign system and presented themselves as autonomous, free from what Andreas Huyssen would later call "that overload of responsibilities—to change life, change society, change the world—on which the historical avantgarde had shipwrecked."[18] One of the purposes of this collection is to suggest that accounts of this shipwreck have been overstated. And yet it's true that Krauss, in defining the index along narrow lines, obscured work at *Rooms* that acknowledged the changes in life, society, and the world that roiled city and nation in the 1970s.

The terms in which Krauss defined this art would, over time, become as dominant as those of Fried. As a founder of *October* and the mentor of Hal Foster, Craig Owens, and Benjamin Buchloh, Krauss has exerted a powerful influence on the art theory of the past four decades, shaping received notions as to how site-specific art should be interpreted.[19] More widely, because *Rooms* was taken up by Krauss at the very birth of *October*, it undergirds the ways that the journal's critics would shape aesthetic debates in the 1980s, 1990s, and beyond. Notions of the expanded field, notions of the museum in ruins, and notions of the semiotic as the essential interpretive frame for art are all at work in Krauss's essay. Describing a set of signs that collapse into their referents, Krauss's theory became a touchstone moment for postmodern theories of art. By the mid-1990s, Foster would cite Krauss as foundational, explaining, "The shift to indexical marks of presence in this art was prompted by a crisis in representation, prompted by both the 'serial objects of minimalism and the simulacra images of pop' after which 'the move to reground art was urgent, almost necessary.' "[20] By the time Foster was writing, a decade of art criticism, much of it in *October*, had declared that the best art of the era—simulacral art, institutional critique, or conceptual art—intervened into semiotic systems.

But while Foster and others often framed their accounts of semiotics in terms of media saturation—what Guy Debord called the society of the spectacle—a longer view of the 1970s allows us to see how *Rooms*, by invoking the First Ward Building as a ruin, entered another system of signs that was vibrant in the 1970s: those asserting a failure of governance. Despite the fact that the site-specific works of *Rooms* were intended to be antirepresentational, their situatedness in a former public institution makes them representational by default: inasmuch as the school is, or was, what the political theorist Bonnie Honig describes as a "public thing," work done to alter the building cannot help but engage discussions of public institutions that were then under attack. Moreover, at least some of the artists of *Rooms*, including the Krauss favorite Matta-Clark, were well aware of how the dynamics of the 1970s crisis interacted with their work. When Krauss asserts that in these artists' works "the building itself is taken to be a message," it's hard to imagine that she didn't have Matta-Clark primarily in mind, even as she also highlights works by Kelly and Pozzi. Among the artists of *Rooms*, no one had better theorized the relationship between art and the built environment than Matta-Clark. Beginning in 1971, when he cut into Santiago, Chile's Museo Nacional de Bellas Artes to make a hole from gallery to roof, Matta-Clark sliced into many a building: an abandoned tenement in the Bronx (*Bronx Floors*, 1972), a suburban home (*Splitting*, 1974), a warehouse on New York's waterfront (*Day's End*, 1975). In explaining his project, he often used language similar to Krauss: "I'm interested in . . . somehow getting the building to talk," Matta-Clark told Lisa Bear in 1974.[21] Similarly, he described his project to Donald Wall as "a recognition of the building's total (semiotic) system, not in any idealized form, but using the actual ingredients of a place."[22] For Matta-Clark, the questions raised by a building were often architectural: what makes up the building, what is behind the walls, what is underneath the building. These notions are at the core of Krauss's analysis: indexical works are shifters pointing to the building itself as a structure.

Yet Matta-Clark was just as often interested in the social and historical forces that shaped buildings. In *Window Blow-Out*, Matta-Clark used an exhibit held at the Institute of Architecture and Urban Studies to call attention to deteriorating conditions in a Bronx housing project. For that work, Matta-Clark placed photographs of the housing project, in which windows had been broken, into the window casements at the institute. But recognizing, as Thomas Crow observes, that this might entail reproducing urban ruin as picturesque, Matta-Clark proceeded to break every window in the building with an air rifle. The windows were replaced almost immediately, and as Crow summarizes, the replacement became part of the project. Even amid the crisis of the 1970s, the institute's building, unlike the Bronx projects, could summon resources to repair it: it retained the care and interest of a certain public.[23] *Window Blow-Out* was not intended to call attention to the institute's well-maintained building; it was, instead, intended to call attention to the misallocation of resources in the city.

The Social Practice Art of *Rooms*

Taking place in an abandoned school at a moment of intense debate about city resources, *Rooms* raised questions similar to *Window Blow-Out*. While most of the artists developed work that engaged the building as they would any other readymade space, some also engaged the building's past use as a school. Marjorie Strider built a sculpture out of polyurethane foam and ladders, intended, she wrote, to "suggest the interminable fire drills of my younger days in school."[24] Bill Beirne's *Progress Through Education 1976* played a forty-minute recording of sounds that the artist had recorded in a New York public high school. Jeffery Lew's *Library 1976* featured sculptures of books. Joseph Koseth's *Ideology/Artifact* incorporated commendations that had actually been awarded to former pupils in the school. All of this work demanded that the viewer take stock of what the building had meant in the lifeworld it previously inhabited. Fire ladders, the sounds of children, sculptures of books, and commendations summon the children, teachers, and administrators who had once occupied the building. These artists' work pointed toward those future versions of site specificity analyzed by Kwon that would be socially oriented.

In this sense, the work of Strider, Beirne, Lew, and Koseth anticipates social practice art, which, as Claire Bishop and others have argued, would become the dominant form of art after the 1990s. Social practice art encompasses such projects as community-based practices and site-specific work in hotels and hospitals. At their best, as Shannon Jackson puts it, these projects are "art forms that help us to imagine sustainable social institutions . . . exploring forms of interdependent support—social systems of labor, sanitation, welfare, and urban planning that coordinate humans in groups and over time."[25] By foregrounding the school as an institution, Strider, Beirne, Lew, and Koseth anticipated, for example, the work of Theaster Gates, whose *A Game of My Own* (2017) used wood reclaimed from the gyms of closed high schools in African American neighborhoods in order to call attention to the constrained funding in such neighborhoods.[26] While the socially oriented works of *Rooms* lack the rich conceptual frameworks developed by Gates and other social practice artists, they nevertheless point toward the social problems of the 1970s crisis in ways that Krauss's account obscures.

To see ruins as beautiful is not necessarily to align oneself with the forces that made a thing a ruin, though as critics of "ruin porn" have observed in the context of Detroit, the depiction of urban ruins as aesthetically interesting can indeed obviate political and historical forces that produce ongoing suffering for impoverished, minority communities.[27] To convert a ruin into something that produces value in a different register at the least demands that one ask questions about the shift from one institution to another. The artists whom Heiss gathered looked at the peeling walls, empty floors, old ductwork, erased blackboards, bare courtyards, and saw spirals, cuts, color blocks, out-of-place writing, foam spilling out of windows, tiny cities, networks of string. They wanted to resist the weight of what, in an essay that circulated widely in the 1970s artworld, Walter Benjamin called the artwork's "aura"—that is, to bring something new out of what was already there, to embrace the readymade and the index—in order to reground art with an urgent autonomy.

No more making needed to be done. What artists needed to do was to salvage what had come before, to use and respect the collective labor of others, and to join an assemblage of unmediated signs in order to resist what *October*'s writers would later call "the value of authenticity, originality, and singularity."[28] Such salvaging would allow, as Serra put it, "the definition of the place to control the priority of relationships," or, in Krauss's words, allow "the building itself" to be "taken to be a message."[29] But this logic—that spaces contain their own definitions and are not the product of specific decisions—is also the logic of austerity. Planned shrinkage—a phrase that circulated widely in New York's 1975 fiscal crisis—means withdraw and let what happens happen. If a school, hospital, or firehouse was viable, market forces would reveal them to be such, unburdening governments from making difficult decisions about which forms of life the state supports. Indeed, as Honig suggests, under austerity, such institutions can become vital sites of activism through the mere reassertion that they are "public things"—sites that are part of a collective commons irreducible to the logic of privatization.[30]

As I noted earlier, this dispersal of authority was hardly limited to the artworld. In New York and elsewhere, workers, neighborhood organizers, activists, and others came to see the central planning of the Keynesian era as repressive. Under the influence of Jane Jacobs's *The Life and Death of American Cities*, for example, a vibrant neighborhood movement arose in cities. This movement agitated against the centralized planning represented by Robert Moses, which members associated with destructive forms of redevelopment. Movement activists contended that neighborhoods should be preserved as they are. Museums dictating particular kinds of art and city planners dictating particular kinds of neighborhoods: both came to seem flawed by the 1970s. Indeed, the same term—modernist—is often associated with both kinds of planning.[31]

As Jasper Bernes notes in *The Work of Art in the Age of Deindustrialization*, Krauss never identifies a structural cause beyond the artworld for the rise of indexical art. Bernes finds his answer in shifting work cultures: just as the clerical worker now moves information around, artists of the index move signs around. Bernes's account has a compelling symmetry, particularly because we can imagine the white-collar professionals of his study as actually being exposed to the work of professional artists: workers and artists occupy the same class strata. And yet, shifts in work cultures are only part of the story of the 1960s and 1970s. A much wider set of changes—the rising attack on the welfare state—would affect subjects of all classes but especially the working class and impoverished. For all the innovation of his intervention, Bernes is, in the end, working with the same terms as Foster, Crimp, Owens, and the rest of the *October* school, whereby the moment of modernism's relatively fixed meanings shifts into the expansive register of shifting signs.

The setting of *Rooms*—a school building—points to an analogous, yet distinct, mode of selection. This is the selection of who gets to live and who gets to die, not in the fullness of what Foucault describes as biopower but in the withdrawal of such fullness. By this I mean that we can read *Rooms*, as did some of its artists, not in terms of a crisis in art, or even a crisis in spaces that enable the production of art, but as a crisis in an institution that reproduces life. Institutions like schools, hospitals, firehouses, and libraries were all under fire in the austerity politics of New York's 1970s—politics that would spread throughout the nation and world in succeeding decades. The city's impending bankruptcy had resulted in its temporarily being taken over by, first, the Municipal Assistance Corporation, and then the Emergency Financial Control Board. Each group represented a group of bankers who immediately demanded broad austerity, resulting in cuts to city schools, police departments, fire departments, CUNY, direct assistance, and other areas. Support for the First Ward School itself had faded away long ago, but support for similar institutions—schools, firehouses, hospitals—was writhing under the austerity politics of 1975.

In this sense, the school building itself is a kind of index: of area population, of state funding for education, of a set of ideas about how educational institutions should be run, of childrearing, of shifting work habits. Public schools were intense sites of conflict even before the crisis; African American and Latinx parents had fought for the schools' desegregation in the 1960s, resulting in, among other things, a 1964 boycott involving 460,000 schoolchildren. In 1975, the city laid off seven thousand teachers, raising class sizes to forty-five students per class. Teachers went on strike, and when the union and city were unable to make a deal, the contract was resolved by the Emergency Financial Control Board.[32] School funding distribution was the object of intense debate. In the wake of the crisis, the New York City Board of Education dropped employment by 20 percent between 1975 and 1978.[33] Where and when schools would be closed, too, became the focus of intense community activism.

The uncanny resonance between some artists' insistence on foregrounding the school's lifeworld and the decline of this lifeworld elsewhere in the city prompts us to interrogate crucial questions of how art did, and did not, resist the moves toward dismantling happening elsewhere in the economy. The social-interventionist elements of Beirne, Strider, Lew, and Koseth remained, in Krauss's account, buried beneath the ruin of the First Ward School. These artists made claims on the school as a specific kind of place with a specific kind of life-giving history, resisting the life-denying circumstances that had led to the First Ward School becoming a ruin in the first place. From the perspective of the present, it is difficult to celebrate the museum or the school as a ruin, because so many other institutions are also in ruins.

In this sense, Heiss's value-extraction would not have been possible without the drive to destroy the commons that had simmered among the business class since the New Deal. In its pre–P.S. 1 state, the First Ward School exemplified a principle that undergirded the crisis: this neighborhood no longer supports a school, and therefore market logic dictates its closure. The architects of the crisis stressed that the city could not provide for everyone and would do best to withdraw capital from spaces deemed unproductive. This is the part of the crisis that was forced and ideological. Read in terms of such withdrawal, the works of *Rooms* emerge as compensatory and reactive instead of additive and innovative. From here on, if you wanted a school building to mean something, you had better find the resources to make it mean something yourself, because the state no longer cared about such things.

The First Ward School appeared to be simply sitting there, as do all of capitalism's ruins. But to understand capitalism's ruins this way is to validate capitalism's own logic: to imagine that things just die instead of being allowed, or made, to die. Things may be allowed to die because they promise future profits: this is what the geographer Neil Smith calls uneven development. At other times, things are allowed to die because someone does not want to provide them with the resources to live. The First Ward School, a ruin that was allowed to die, becomes the justification for allowing more things to die.

During the Keynesian era, an educated workforce came to be seen as an essential component of economic expansion. And yet, the promise of the democratic distribution of education and other goods and services proved to be not a national ideal but instead a momentary solution to the labor unrest of the early twentieth century. Once nonwhite and nonmale populations demanded that such distribution be extended to them, this promise was revealed to be fragile. The official logic goes thus: if these populations wanted education so badly, they should pay for it themselves. The underlying logic goes thus: the city is for us, and we will keep it that way. Still, the process of cutting the welfare state happens gradually, and it is here that other indexical measurements come into play: those used by government agencies to determine whether a social program, neighborhood, or school continues to be viable. The technocratic commitments of the Keynesian state would not disappear overnight, and the processes for measuring viability could, in some cases, offset the relentless logic of austerity. In this context, art that attends to technocratic measurement, particularly the Consumer Price Index, has a vital role to play.

In his contribution to *Rooms*, *Lament for the Children*, Carl Andre set one hundred concrete blocks into the former schoolyard, intended to represent the children who had once played there. Since the First Ward Building could hold one thousand students at a time, we can imagine that each block would, at the time the school was fully functioning, represent ten students. But as the neighborhood shifted, that number declined to nine, eight, seven, and finally zero. *Lament for the Children*, then, represents a quite different kind of index, that which the *OED* defines as "a number showing the variation (increase or decrease) in the prices or value of some specified set of goods, shares." As this index shifted, the school's resources declined, until it was closed.

Andre's work points, albeit obliquely, to another important sense of "index" under discussion in the inflation-worried 1970s: the Consumer Price Index. Since 1913, the CPI has served as the essential yardstick for the reproduction of life in the United States: it is a weighted average of the cost of fuel, housing, food, and other consumer goods. Aggregated together, these represent the cost of living (cost of living adjustments—COLA—are often based on the CPI). The CPI is a core mechanism through which wealth is redistributed in the United States. As inflation rose, benefits and wages that were tied to the CPI necessarily rose as well. This is what results in a strange paradox of 1970s governance, recently made clear by Melinda Cooper in *Family Values*. Late seventies inflation had been, as Cooper notes, "decried as a universal catastrophe for all social classes," and cutting inflation became, after the 1970s, the central driver of fiscal policy in the United States and elsewhere.[34] But the disaster was unevenly distributed: middle-class people might have paid more for essentials, yet an inflation-driven rise in the CPI meant that, for those at the lower ends of the economic spectrum, benefits momentarily increased. Inflation also lowered the value of wealth by reducing the purchasing power of the dollar. Because wealth declined and benefits increased in the late 1970s, that period actually saw a reduction in income inequality, fueled by a rise in the CPI.[35] As the primary measure of inflation, the CPI serves as a floor for austerity, often to the frustration of those who seek to slash benefits and wages. While recent attempts to reduce Social Security benefits have, by and large, failed, one of the subtle ways proposed to reduce such benefits has been to link them to a modified

CPI, because the CPI otherwise solidly grounds such benefits. The CPI itself, then, provides a technocratic limitation, at least in some cases, to austerity's ravages.

As a kind of index, Andre's work anticipates the work of the artist Loren Madsen, who in 1994 made an indexical sculpture that incorporates the CPI. To make *CPI*, Madsen gathered data on food, fuel, and housing. He used this data to form ovals that he then cut out of plywood and glued together. The taper begins in 1960; the dramatic bulge outward and upward shows how food, fuel, and housing costs increased from 1960 to 1994.

Madsen describes his project in terms of another set of students, noting that the inspiration for *CPI* began with the realization that "my students' experience as young artists differed so radically from my own. They pay

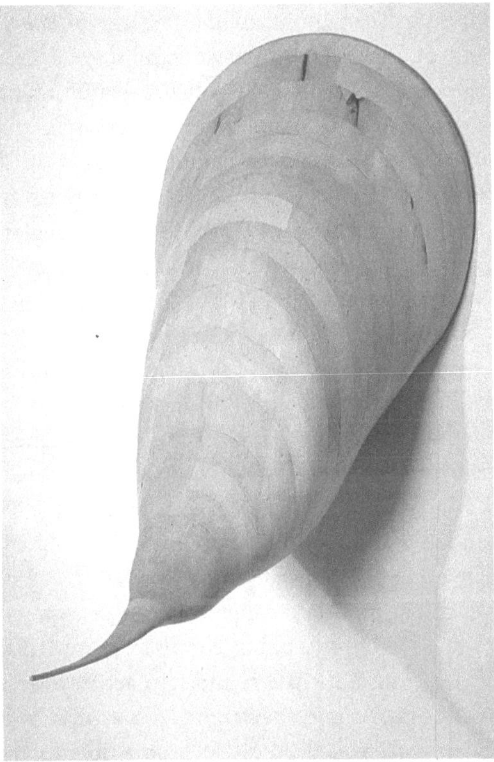

Figure 5.2. Loren Madsen's *Historical Abstract: CPI 1995*. 1 layer = 1 year (1960–1994). Horizontal dimension: fuel costs. Vertical dimension: food costs. Center line: housing costs. Courtesy of Loren Madsen.

unthinkable rents and leave school heavily in debt. They cannot, as I did, work part-time to finance time in the studio."[36] By transforming the abstract CPI into a physical sculpture, Madsen translates an economic index into the kind of aesthetic index that Krauss would recognize: *CPI* uses form to point to its own meanings. That is, *CPI*'s curves index changes in the CPI itself, just as the works of *Rooms* pointed to the building. But because *CPI* is, in effect, an index pointing to an index, the sculpture demands that viewers think through a doubled sense of index that Krauss's reading excluded. Viewing Madsen's sculpture, one can grasp the experience of Madsen's students, just as one could grasp the sadness of a school closing in 1975 by looking at a set of commendations in an abandoned school room.

Rooms, taking place in a specifically delineated space of public life, navigated between two poles: on the one hand, the attacks on public life happening in the city, and on the other, the revival of avant-garde work through site-specific art. The particular characteristics of *Rooms* highlight how prominent features of the avant-garde work of the 1970s, especially site-specific art, emerged out of the long crisis that began in that decade. Krauss, and later Foster, saw *Rooms* as responding to a crisis in the sign, situated within the society of the spectacle—a paradigm that, as Bishop notes, was all-consuming from the 1970s to the 2000s.[37] For Krauss and like-minded critics, the only recourse is to develop avant-garde strategies to recover the grounding that, within cultures of the spectacle, was gnawing away.

From the vantage point of the 2020s, this crisis in the sign looks like a crisis in the welfare state. Though some of its art dissented, *Rooms* was, by and large, a turn away from the life-sustaining networks of the welfare state and toward the logic of privatization. Emerging at a moment of austerity, which benefited it as an institution, *Rooms* straitened a vital public space into the segmented spaces of do-it-yourself. The possibility was there to produce work like Madsen's *CPI*: the events around the 1975 fiscal crisis might have demanded that the exhibit think through problems of withdrawn education funding occurring elsewhere in the city.

Rooms serves as an important hinge between discourses on the decline of the welfare state as a life-sustaining social force and discourses on the expanded field. *Rooms* thus anticipates, and retroactively interrogates, a host of discussions of the avant-garde. By staging *Rooms* in a public institution, Heiss, knowingly or not, yoked aesthetic production to the crises in the reproduction of life occurring elsewhere in the 1970s. By theorizing *Rooms* in terms of the index, Krauss, also perhaps unintentionally, suggested ways that the First Ward building indexes the social fallout from the crisis. If indexical works were the site of the avant-garde's renewal, these works point to the ways in which avant-garde art might take shape under new conditions of crisis. The index, then, offers a useful node between the avant-garde and the crisis of the 1970s: the core concerns of this collection. At the very moment that Krauss was developing her theories, institutions came to be seen as not oppressive conveyors of narrow ideas but as small protectors of life that were worth preserving, with the CPI serving as an important measure of how much life would be preserved. *Rooms* as well as Krauss's essay suggest another possible world that might have unfolded from 1976, wherein artists, as have Madsen, Gates, and others, index not just the ruins of artworld institutions but the ruins of the long crisis of the 1970s itself.

Notes

1. Grace Glueck, "Abandoned School in Queens Lives Again as Arts Complex," *New York Times*, June 10, 1976, 38. Martin Beck observes, "The building housing P.S. 1 was only slightly renovated for the exhibition; repairs were confined to such basic safety issues as the heating, wiring, and plumbing systems, but the building's decrepitude and material traces of long-term neglect remained visible. Paint was peeling, plaster was falling off the walls, and ceilings were in disrepair." Martin Beck, "Alternative: Space," in *Alternative Art, New York, 1965–1985*, ed. Julie Ault, Social Text Collective, and Drawing Center (Minneapolis: University of Minnesota Press, 2002), 258. For other accounts of artists' use of the disused city landscape, see Lynne Cook and Douglas Crimp, eds., *Mixed Use, Manhattan* (Cambridge, MA: MIT Press, 2010); John Alan Farmer and Bronx Museum of the Arts, eds., *Urban Mythologies: The Bronx Represented since the 1960s* (Bronx, NY: Bronx Museum of the Arts, 1999).

2. For important overviews of the 1975 crisis, see Kim Phillips-Fein, *Fear City: New York's Fiscal Crisis and the Rise of Austerity Politics* (New York: Metropolitan Books, 2017); William K. Tabb, *The Long Default: New York City and the Urban Fiscal Crisis* (New York: Monthly Review Press, 1982); Joshua Benjamin Freeman, *Working-Class New York: Life and Labor since World War II* (New York: New Press, 2000); Kim Moody, *From Welfare State to Real Estate: Regime Change in New York City, 1974 to the Present* (New York: New Press, 2007); William Sites, *Remaking New York: Primitive Globalization and the Politics of Urban Community* (Minneapolis: University of Minnesota Press, 2003).

3. On art-enabled gentrification, see Jason Hackworth and Neil Smith, "The Changing State of Gentrification," *Tijdschrift Voor Economische En Sociale Geografie* 92, no. 4 (n.d.): 464–477; Maria Gravari-Barbas and Sandra Guinand, *Tourism and Gentrification in Contemporary Metropolises: International Perspectives* (New York:

Routledge 2017). On the creative economy, see Richard L. Florida, *The Rise of the Creative Class, Revisited* (New York: Basic Books, 2012); Sarah Brouillette, *Literature and the Creative Economy* (Stanford: Stanford University Press, 2014); Justin O'Connor, "The Cultural and Creative Industries: A Critical History," *Ekonomiaz: Revista Vasca de Economía* 78, no. 3 (2011): 24–47. On the artistic critique, see Luc Boltanski and Eve Chiapello, *The New Spirit of Capitalism* (New York: Verso, 2007).

4. Douglas Crimp, "On the Museum's Ruins," *October* 13 (1980): 50.

5. Crimp, "On the Museum's Ruins," 56, 45.

6. Crimp, "On the Museum's Ruins," 53.

7. Judith Stein, *Pivotal Decade: How the United States Traded Factories for Finance in the Seventies* (New Haven, CT: Yale University Press, 2010).

8. Richard Serra, *Writings/Interviews* (Chicago: University of Chicago Press, 1994), 117.

9. Serra, *Writings/Interviews*, 108.

10. John Roberts, *Revolutionary Time and the Avant-Garde* (New York: Verso, 2015), 198.

11. Roberts, *Revolutionary Time and the Avant-Garde*, 194–195.

12. Miwon Kwon, "One Place after Another: Notes on Site Specificity," *October* 80 (1997): 92.

13. Rosalind Krauss, "Sculpture in the Expanded Field," *October* 8 (1979): 30.

14. Rosalind Krauss, "Notes on the Index: Seventies Art in America. Part 2," *October* 4 (1977): 59.

15. Roland Barthes, "Rhetoric of the Image," in *Image, Music, Text*, trans. Stephen Heath (New York: Noonday Press, 1977), 32–51. Krauss was working with her own translation.

16. This is only a rough summary of Fried's celebrated essay "Art and Objecthood," in which Fried negatively contrasted minimalism—a body of work that Fried dismisses as "theater" with what he described as the "presentness" of modernist painting and sculpture. Michael Fried, "Art and Objecthood," in *Minimal Art: A Critical Anthology*, ed. Gregory Battcock (New York: E. P. Dutton, 1968), 147.

17. Of Pozzi, Krauss observes, "The painting's colors, the internal division between those colors, are occasioned by a situation in the world which they merely register," in "Notes on the Index," 60.

18. Andreas Huyssen, "Mapping the Postmodern," *New German Critique*, no. 33 (1984): 40.

19. In *Revolutionary Time and the Avant-Garde*, Roberts asserts that "Sculpture in the Expanded Field," along with Foster's "What's Neo about the Neo Avant-Garde" and Fredric Jameson's "Postmodernism, or the Cultural Logic of Late Capitalism," are the three most important art-critical essays of the era (198).

20. Hal Foster, *The Return of the Real: The Avant-Garde at the End of the Century* (Cambridge, MA: MIT Press, 1996), 83.

21. Matta-Clark interviewed by Lisa Bear, "Gordon Matta-Clark: Splitting the Humphrey Street Building," *Avalanche*, December 1974, 37.

22. Gordon Matta-Clark, "Gordon Matta-Clark's Building Dissections," interview by Donald Wall, in *Gordon Matta-Clark*, ed. Corinne Diserens (New York: Phaidon Press, 2006), 181–186.

23. Thomas E. Crow, *Modern Art in the Common Culture* (New Haven, CT: Yale University Press, 1996), 134–135.

24. Institute for Art and Urban Resources et al., eds., *Rooms, P.S. 1: [Exhibition] June 9–26, 1976* (New York: The Institute, 1977), 125.

25. Shannon Jackson, *Social Works: Performing Art, Supporting Publics* (New York: Routledge, 2011), 14.

26. Sadie Dingfelder, "Why Theaster Gates Took an Ax to His Own Painting at the NGA," *Washington Post*, March 9, 2017, https://www.washingtonpost.com/express/wp/2017/03/09/why-theaster-gates-took-an-ax-to-his-own-painting-at-the-nga/.

27. See, for example, John Patrick Leary, "Detroitism," *Guernica*, January 2011, https://www.guernicamag.com/leary_1_15_11/.

28. Hal Foster, "What's Neo about the Neo-Avant-Garde?," *October* 70 (1994): 14.

29. Serra, *Writings/Interviews*, 7; Krauss, "Notes on the Index," 65.

30. Bonnie Honig, *Public Things: Democracy in Disrepair* (New York: Fordham University Press, 2017). Public things, Honig argues, "constitute us, complement us, thwart us, and interpellate us into democratic citizenship" (5). Honig offers as examples Occupy Wall Street's 2011 use of Zuccotti Park and the blocking of a Quebec bridge by Mohawk activists in 1993. For examples of activists making such moves in New York institutions, see Phillips-Fein, *Fear City*, 227–255.

31. In *The Invention of Brownstone Brooklyn*, Suleiman Osman describes New York mayor John Lindsay as a "local modernist hybrid" who hired McKinsey consultants to "centralize and rationalize city bureaucracy." Suleiman Osman, *The Invention of Brownstone Brooklyn: Gentrification and the Search for Authenticity in Postwar New York* (New York: Oxford University Press, 2011), 221.

32. Phillips-Fein, *Fear City*, 160.

33. Phillips-Fein, *Fear City*, 221.

34. Melinda Cooper, *Family Values: Between Neoliberalism and the New Social Conservatism* (Cambridge, MA: MIT Press, 2017), 125.

35. Cooper, *Family Values*, 125.

36. Loren Madsen, "Interview with Loren Madsen: The Birth of Data Sculpture," interview by Pierre Dragicevic, http://dataphys.org/list/loren-madsen-interview/.

37. Claire Bishop, *Artificial Hells: Participatory Art and the Politics of Spectatorship* (New York: Verso, 2012), 11.

Chapter 6

Under the Figure of the Palm Tree

Jennifer Wild

> Art is a prisoner of its phantasms and its function as magic; . . . it flickers along the peripeties of our history like a shadow-play—but is it artistic?
>
> —Marcel Broodthaers, "Notes on the Subject"

Scholars continue to show how, across a *longue durée* of the avant-garde, artists have been preoccupied with history, historical time, and the theory of history.[1] Even as this scholarly interest has developed into the exploration of concepts such as "deep history," which includes the "prehistoric" and the Paleolithic, it extends many of the critical, theoretical, conceptual, and also material legacies of 1970s art practice, especially surrounding the rise of installation art in general, and those practices associated with institutional critique in particular. While artists engaged in installation practice and institutional critique both responded to and amplified a crisis in the modernist concept of medium specificity, some also worked to foreground how the invisibility of colonialism and its history presented an equally urgent crisis concerning the museum's institutional role in legitimizing (or not) historical narratives. Forging an exploration of (post-)colonial reality and history as they broadly rejected medium-specific purity in favor of nontraditional media, artists working in the expanded field of the 1970s avant-garde increasingly turned to film and cinema as both concept and practice.

Key in this avant-garde genealogy are the 1970s works of Marcel Broodthaers. Having published his first poems in the late 1940s, within the context of late Belgian surrealism, he made his first film, *La Clef de l'Horloge*, which he called a "cinematographic poem in honor of Kurt Schwitters," in 1957. Film and cinema continued to be a conceptual and material support for Broodthaers both before and after he took a decided detour into the realm of conceptual art with *Pense-Bête* (1964), a sculptural object he made by anchoring his books of poetry in plaster. Although his short but prolific career as a conceptual artist is marked by a continued engagement with language, poetry, and filmmaking, he is perhaps best known for site-specific, mixed-media installations broadly organized as the "Décors" and the large-scale "Museum Fictions."

From the latter ensemble, *Musée d'Art Moderne, Département des Aigles*, divided into twelve separate "sections" over the course of four years, was the focus of Rosalind Krauss's 1992 meditation on the "post-medium condition."[2] For Krauss, the early cinema's *promesse de bonheur* was one crucial predecessor to Broodthaers's development of a conceptual practice that, through installation's relationship to history, technological media, and medium specificity, revealed the interplay "between a technical or material support and the conventions with which a particular genre operates."[3] With its guiding "principle" of the eagle, Broodthaers's museum "implodes the idea of an aesthetic medium and turns everything equally into a readymade that collapses the difference between the aesthetic and the commodified."[4] Douglas Crimp, who throughout the 1980s and 1990s contributed extensively to debates in the journal *October* (and elsewhere) concerning the art-institutional crisis, connected the critically historical drives of Broodthaers's use of institutional vocabularies and methods of display with Walter Benjamin's thought on both collecting and the critique of the idealist conception and function of art as structured by museums and markets.[5] "And this institutional 'overvaluation' of art," Crimp writes, "produced a secondary effect, which Benjamin called 'the disintegration of culture into commodities' and Broodthaers referred to as 'the transformation of art into merchandise.' "[6] At the core of these and other critical evaluations of Broodthaers's oeuvre is the sense that, in generating a conceptual, material, and also plastic language for institutional critique, the artist confronts the ahistorical myths generated by institutions. Insofar as history has been vigorously obscured by institutions of all kinds, a primary drive in Broodthaers's conceptual approach is to make history perceptible as one artistic medium—or "support," as Krauss would say—among others.

Across many stages of his oeuvre, Broodthaers's engagement with history can be located in his prolific application of the label "Fig. [ure]." When he applies it to the various objects corralled within the different sections of *Musée d'Art Moderne, Département des Aigles*, he does not merely appropriate the vocabulary of nineteenth-century museums and their classification systems. "Fig." is, rather, a critical term and an approach to dissecting the museum into the components that, as an aggregate, formerly maintained a stable, idealist conception of its institutionalized contents—whether those contents were artworks, ethnographic artifacts, or natural history specimens. Alongside other objects labeled or not as such, Broodthaers's "Figs." capably draw together disparate epochs, objects, and institutional, artistic, and economic discourses to advance thinking and perception about the present's relationship to history—including the historical "fictions" that arise in institutional frameworks concerning, for example, the violence of Belgian imperialism and the colonization of the Congo. His various figures constitute a figural but materialist tactic that queries how structural systems, including those related to colonialism and to a history of "art," have ordered history's in/visibility.[7]

There are recurring figures that stand out in Broodthaers's oeuvre, such as the mussels—an icon of Belgian cuisine—that are either piled within metal casseroles or affixed en masse to a vertical support, as we find in *Cercle des moules* (1966). There are the eggs and heaps of eggshells. And there is the repeated image of the pipe borrowed from René Magritte, himself an icon of the Belgian avant-garde. Another figure stands out: the palm tree. Appearing in his botanical gardens, or, more precisely, the winter gardens belonging to his late installations grouped under the heading of "Décors," the palms have an especially significant purchase over his works' visual, spatial, and historical dynamics.

In his last exhibit before his death, *L'Angelus de Daumier*, first mounted in Paris in 1975 at La Fondation Salomon de Rothschild (now the site of the Centre national d'art contemporain), domesticated, potted palms lined the walls of the show's *Salle verte*, or green room. In a photograph documenting the green room, visitors can be seen standing in pairs and conversing while a woman in the foreground of the image casts her gaze away from the palms positioned behind a row of outdoor folding chairs. *L'Angelus de Daumier* was planned as a self-curated retrospective, wherein Broodthaers successively reworked past installations, and the palms (and garden chairs) appearing in the green room are in fact an iteration of *Un Jardin d'Hiver II* (1974).[8] The palms are a key and repeated figure in Broodthaers's artistic enterprise, and the woman's errant gaze proves useful in glossing their figural charge: as banal, interior décor, potted palms are as unremarked upon as the violence that defines Belgium's colonial past. The palms figure the ordinariness

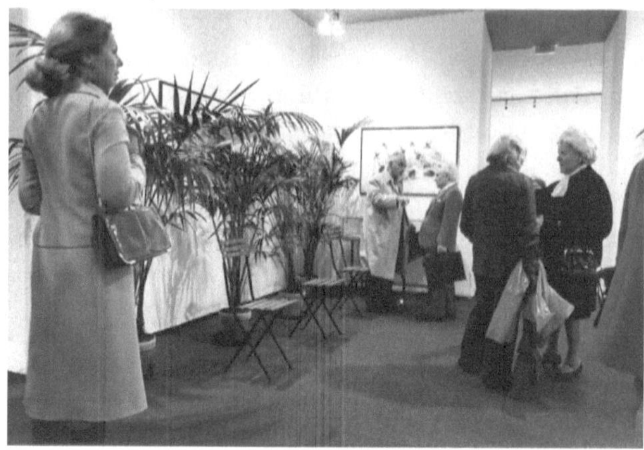

Figure 6.1. Marcel Broodthaers's *Salle verte* in the exhibition *L'Angelus de Daumier*, 1975, La Fondation Salomon de Rothschild, Paris, France. Anonymous photograph courtesy of Foundation Marcel Broodthaers.

with which historical violence is simultaneously effaced and emblematized, commodified and neutralized in the space of the museum-as-institution.

While Broodthaers' "Fig." might recall the "figures of history" in Jacques Rancière's approach to political aesthetics, they function more robustly in the Kristevian sense of *figura* or figure, especially insofar as they invite the viewer "to establish the *relationship between two historical realities*, to restore the historic depths of each event—its before and its after."[9] And while Broodthaers's figures demonstrate a strong connection to Walter Benjamin's "dialectal image," itself an approach to no-historicist thinking (Broodthaers praised Benjamin as a "model art critic" in 1976), Kristeva is particularly significant for the long 1970s.[10] Her conceptualization of the figure as it appears in 1998 demonstrates the consistent, if evolving, manner in which she has theorized historical time. From her earliest publications in 1969, through the 1980s, to her more recent work, Kristeva has pursued an "interrogation of various systems of historical thinking and their mutual dependence on certain fundamental conceptions of language—the speaking subject and religion," as Alice Jardine observes.[11] With *figura*, Kristeva's thought more directly addresses the domain of the visual, which Jean-François Lyotard, in *Discours, Figure* (1971), opposed to the dominance of language in structural and poststructural thought.

I pursue a figural mode of inquiry in this chapter by focusing on the specific figure of the palm tree and by drawing together its appearance in "two historical realities" of avant-garde and modernist art practice. Broodthaers's figural deployment of the palm tree during the mid-1970s is indeed "one historical reality" in this chapter. The other is Jean-Luc Godard's use of the palm tree in his massive 2006 installation at the Centre Pompidou, titled *Travel(s) in Utopia, Jean-Luc Godard, 1946–2006: In Search of a Lost Theorem.*[12] Like Broodthaers's *L'Angelus de Daumier*, *Travel(s) in Utopia* was commissioned as a self-curated retrospective of the filmmaker's career, and in it we find an array of potted palm trees and a variety of other plant specimens. For decades, Godard has openly engaged with film and art history in his work, not least in *Histoire(s) du Cinéma*, a "great metahistorical undertaking," as Erika Balsom has called the epic, multipart work of video collage.[13] His project for the Pompidou was equally ambitious in its approach to site-specific institutional space, having been originally titled *Collage(s) de France, archéologie du cinéma d'après JLG*. But whereas Broodthaers's palms operate figurally to make visible the persistence of large-scale historical denial, Godard's use of the palms in what became *Travel(s) in Utopia* rather affirms his commitment to a mythic sense of history wherein what we see of such history, by way of art or cinema, remains stubbornly mediated by the author. Godard's approach in 2006 appears unaffected by the long 1970s that saw the "death of the author" and championed textual autonomy.[14] Rather, cinema history "according to JLG" is tethered to the 1940s, when cinematic authorship arose as a dominant formal, theoretical, and also idealist approach to film form, industry, and politics.

By treating the palm tree as a figure rather than as a sign conceived from a structural linguistics model, we gain a more precise understanding of the different "historical realities" from which each artist emerged and conceived of his approach to history, institutionality, and site specificity. Broodthaers's and Godard's two "realities" might be summarized respectively as "the artworld" and the cinema milieu, with its industrial, narrative, and collective demands. But these "realities" are more complex than they appear, and I suggest they may be best perceived in relation to the concept of "peripety," or sudden reversals in (historical) narratives, to recall this chapter's epigraph by Broodthaers. Peripety encapsulates the disruption that cinema introduced into the history of art—its *promesse de bonheur*, as Krauss put it—and that installation inaugurated into the fabric of art more generally by further challenging the notion of unified aesthetics and medium-specific "supports," also emphasized by Krauss. The historical avant-garde of Dada was perhaps the first to seize upon the power of historical reversals when it challenged the museum's legitimizing function. In an abbreviated gloss, the most classic example of avant-garde peripety is found in Marcel Duchamp's *Fountain*, from 1917. With his signed, readymade urinal, submitted to and rejected from the Salon des Indépendants, Duchamp reversed the course of classical art history by making visible the structural pressures operating behind the designation of a "work of art." In so doing, he helped foster a conceptual revolution that was not beholden to idealist, transcendental models of the work of art and its effects.

The literary convention of peripety, whereby a character's fate is dramatically affected by a plot reversal, was also central to some of the most important literary criticism of the 1970s. For Peter Brooks, author of the field-changing book from 1976, *The Melodramatic Imagination: Balzac, Henry James, Melodrama, and the Mode of Excess*, understanding the genre of melodrama meant attending to the narrative, historical, and moral pressures of peripety.[15] Brooks's observations about theatrical and literary form and history demonstrate the importance of an expanded analysis of the crisis of the long 1970s and its repercussions across media. Perhaps surprisingly, Brooks's observations about literary genre convene in important ways with poststructuralist undertakings that consider the effects of history on art, literature, and language.

Possibly more surprising is how Brooks's intervention into literary history assists me in contrasting Broodthaers and Godard's use of the palm tree as a material convention—object or figure—that in turn illuminates what the editors of this volume perceptively describe as the "crisis" of the avant-garde in the long 1970s. My aim is not to frame these installations in terms of historical influence, wherein Godard's use of the potted palm emerges as a reference or symbol for Broodthaers's place in a history of site-specific installation art (which is nevertheless plausible). Rather, juxtaposing the artists' deployment of this specific type of flora, a living "figure," highlights the crisis that installation art in the 1970s created by unsettling the concepts of medium and medium specificity, and by problematizing the museum's institutional role as a gatekeeper of both colonial histories' in/visibility and "nontraditional" media's (such as film) legitimacy in the history of art.

Benjamin also helps me in assessing the historical pressures of the palm tree's specific charge as a figure or as an object of "décor." In his writing, palm trees and their fronds are dialectical figures for history and its indiscriminate flow across public and private spheres. Benjamin's thinking proves useful for clarifying Broodthaers's and Godard's site-specific and institutionally driven approaches to history, historical time, and the concept of art in ways that speak to another crisis of the avant-garde in the long

1970s: the struggle against idealist and also historicist approaches to art in the avant-garde's efforts to do away with "museum fictions" and everything they have historically suppressed.

For example, writing about the dream house in *The Arcades Project*, Benjamin oriented his thinking on the historical past toward the practice of excavation and the discovery of Pompeii and Herculaneum:

> It must be remembered . . . that the memory of the lava-death of these two cities was covertly but all the more intimately conjoined with the memory of the great Revolution. For when the sudden upheaval had put an end to the style of the ancien régime, what was here being exhumed was hastily adopted as the style of a glorious republic; and *palm fronds*, acanthus leaves, and meanders came to replace the rococo paintings and *chinoiseries* of the previous century.[16]

In this passage, we should recognize Benjamin's manner of thinking historically by traversing disparate epochs, spaces, and objects. Benjamin uses his acute dialectical and figural sensitivity in order to perceive, in this case, a transformation in the popular vernacular of interior décor as it relates to the emergence of bourgeois domesticity. Here, palm fronds, associated with experience's increasing mediation by technology and other temporal modalities of industrial late capitalism, are object-forms expressing how historical time either registers or appears in the private and public worlds of things. Although he begins by evoking how Pompeii survives despite being overcome by ancient "lava-death," Benjamin ends up excavating the French Revolution of 1789 as a perceptible figure therein. But rather than noting the Revolution as simply a historical event, Benjamin denotes its effect as a great, historical peripety whose volcanic magnitude forever changed the meaning of nature and the natural—a change that will be tracked in especially Broodthaers's art historical undertaking within the museum, and in the figure of the palm.

In her singular and important monograph on Broodthaers, Rachel Haidu reveals the Benjaminian drive that makes Broodthaers's palms multifaceted figures for conveying haunting historical transformations. Observing that the palms operate in a primary sense in Broodthaers's artistic language as signs for Belgian "ethno-botanical collecting and its impact on Western interior decoration," she historicizes the ubiquity of palms in 1970s cafés and waiting rooms by way of nineteenth-century mass popular spectacle.[17]

Thus, while Broodthaers's palms define the site specificity of his installation practice, they further conceptualize and importantly dramatize the historical fact of exhibition. Haidu writes, "From the 1850s, the era of the Crystal Palace . . . to the 1920s, that of silent film and winter gardens, the models of experience developed in sites of exhibition, including eventually cinemas, reinvented the notion of public very much as Broodthaers describes, 'as a question of space and conquest.' "[18] *Conquest* is, of course, the key term here. Noting Saussure's famous example of a tree, Kristen Ross points out that structural linguistics arose alongside the "needs of Western colonialism" in the late nineteenth century to link space with nature as itself a "natural or arbitrary fact, much like the sign itself."[19] The arbitrariness of Broodthaers's label "Fig." quietly speaks to the spatial violence of conquest harbored in structural linguistics, just as his palms unspectacularly, and *non*arbitrarily, figure the structural violence of colonial racism and conquest.

Borrowed from nineteenth-century decorative style, Broodthaers's potted palms operate as an insidious emblem for the importation and domestication of "exotic," natural specimens, thereby extending the structural collapse between that which is spatial and natural. As a figure, his palms capably refer to private, interior spaces and to public space and spectacle. For example, Broodthaers's historical "set" in *Décor: A Conquest* (1975) openly refers to film décor, lighting, and cinematic props. In Haidu's words, his sets "shift the terms of art's reception onto a specific historical stage—the genealogy of the cinematic and the cinema, with their roots in public spectacles such as the Crystal Palace and the development of cinemas themselves."[20]

In contrast to Eric de Bruyn, for whom "signature, money, flag," and arguably palm "stan[d] for the totality of a symbolic order as such," Broodthaers's interest in the public space of the winter garden routes the palm's signifying power toward a more figural logic attached to nineteenth-century historical violence expressed not as art but as, precisely, wild nature domesticated as décor.[21] To figure the violence of colonial expeditions, the collecting of natural specimens for Western display, and the movement of conquest stilled within the space of leisure and entertainment belonging to nineteenth-century public spaces, Broodthaers soberly places a potted palm.

Racisme végétal: La séance (1974), a limited-edition artist's book, distills the banal sobriety of the palms into an image. On the book's cover, two swaying palm trees loom against a tropical horizon in postcard-like form. In tension with the linguistic antinomy of the title "vegetal racism," the cover offers an ostensibly simple image of Belgian colonialism and its conquest of the tropics. But there is density in the palm as a figure of leisure here. It offers its "model of experience" of nature as something seemingly neutral, but nevertheless hard at work sublimating the violence of human and geographical conquests into postcard wishes, interior decoration, or, for Broodthaers, even art.

Broodthaers expressed as much in the catalog for *L'Angelus de Daumier*, mentioned at the beginning of this essay. With an attention to the sober grandeur of the aristocratic milieu, he installed a series of colored rooms corresponding to particular periods of his oeuvre. In these rooms, he "attempted to articulate differently objects and paintings realized at various times between 1964 and this year, in order to form the rooms in a 'décor' spirit."[22] In the exhibition catalog, he described the green room in the following way:

> Contains a winter garden overlooking the public garden of the Salomon de Rothschild Foundation: rows of garden chairs, red carpet and exotic engravings adorning the walls. This room has already been exhibited elsewhere, but in a different form, it happens to be the beginnings of the idea of DÉCOR which can be characterized by the idea of the object restored to its real use, that is to say that the object is not in itself considered as a work of art here (see also PINK room and BLUE room). Let us add that this use of the object as a decorative object is also found in the first version of the Museum (see also WHITE room). New tricks, new scams.[23]

Noting the "real use" of objects, Broodthaers restores the "historical material of objects" to the site-specific "beyond" of the green and other colored rooms. Evoking the historical dimension to the palms' figural function (as well as that of other items), Broodthaers openly rejects the status of "art" in these spaces, preferring instead to elicit an encounter with the real. And this "real," he suggests, exists in décor that is historically covered by the tarnish of Belgium's colonial past. His "objects" or figures, as I later discuss, do not merely critique artistic autonomy, institutional market shares, or medium specificity. As with melodramatic figures that proffer an unforeseen reversal in the expected order of things, they prompt a critical recognition of colonial history and in its historical perception from the inside of the museum.

~

> A world of secret affinities opens up within: *palm tree* and feather duster, hairdryer and Venus de Milo, prostheses and letter-writing manuals.
>
> —Walter Benjamin, "R [Mirrors]," emphasis added

In the space of Benjamin's Parisian arcade, conceptual time-travel and dialectical, historical analysis by way of objects and their capacity to figure historical charge and change abound.[24] Comparing the fossilized remnants found in the geography of the Miocene to the "walls of these caverns"—the arcades—Benjamin finds that the palm tree shares with the household implement a "leafy" morphology. But more important is how they register historical transformation from their common position in the evolving habitus of modern life that in the nineteenth century was also marked by a new urban site where photographers could first monetize mechanically reproduced representation as remembrance: "This was the period of those studios—with their draperies and *palm trees*, their tapestries and easels which occupied so ambiguous a place between execution and representation, between torture chamber and throne room, and to which an early portrait of Kafka bears pathetic witness."[25]

In this famous passage from Benjamin's "Little History of Photography," the author registers his visual perception of the young writer whose expression unites the radically disparate acts and functional spaces housed in the nineteenth-century photography studio. Within the studio's imposed "greenhouse" décor of palm fronds, and where the "upholstered tropics" are made "even stuffier and more oppressive" by the props given no doubt to the child by the studio photographer, the boy's gaze becomes an aperture for perceiving historical time in which the contradictory drives of execution and torture and representational, honorific staging confront each other. The photograph of Kafka reminds Benjamin that the ostensibly democratic technology of photography was also equally a form of violence, as many photography historians have also pointed out. For these historians, the technological imperative of stasis in early photography amounts to nothing short of enslavement: photographs become a visual expression of structural power systems.[26] Violence also manifests itself when the photographic image "produc[es] for the first time a picture plane where all surfaces are equal." On such a plane, a palm frond signifies as powerfully as the human being—in this case the child called Kafka.

Multimedia installation art tempts us to think along similar lines, wherein a palm tree, a rifle, and a television monitor signify on a level playing field, so to speak. How, then, do Broodthaers's palms perform the work of being both the "plastic givens," as he called them, of his site-specific practice *and* an apparatus for distinctly historical perception of violence and the great "peripeties of our history"? How, then, do Godard's palms operate in a site-specific landscape whose original premise promised the museum curators not a mere history but an "archaeology" of the cinema?

Seeing that critics have often described Godard's *Travel(s) in Utopia* as nothing short of a monumental institutional critique, it seems important to observe that "being invited means being a participant in official life." These are Broodthaers's words, penned in 1974:

> It all depends on its definition (that of Art)
> And this definition is fragile, what
> Becomes of it indeed when
> The artist who paints or who speaks
> Is wearing ceremonial dress? Being invited
> Means being a participant in official life.[27]

What is at stake here is not the definition of art but the modes whereby site-specific works and their objects generate a recognition of history and, even more, of the repression of that history. It is imperative to ask these questions of Godard, and of his palms.

As I explained at the beginning of this chapter, not unlike Broodthaers, whose *L'Angelus de Daumier* was commissioned as an installation cum retrospective, Godard was invited by the Pompidou to design a large-scale installation that would examine his oeuvre across decades. The filmmaker began this process by constructing a series of miniatures or maquettes bearing the design of his "archaeological vision" across the gallery spaces. These were intended to display or "exhibit" Godard's "cinematic thought" as object-driven spaces. The curator Dominique Païni explains:

> In the beginning the project, then called *Collage(s) de France, archéologie du cinéma d'après JLG* (Collage(s) of France, archaeology of cinema according to JLG), comprised nine rooms designed to be traversed by the visitor in a specific order. Thanks to an overarching logic of juxtaposition—a montage of images

> borrowed from art history, cinema history and the present—close in principle to that of a rebus, each room invited the visitor to engage in a process of poetic and philosophical reflection.[28]

I will return to the ruinous legacy or "failure" of Godard's vision for *Voyage(s) in Utopia*, but for now, it's important to note how the exhibition situates its nine model-rooms within both history and the history of art. Incidentally, the room's maquettes have since gone on to be the subject of a standalone exhibition at the Miguel Abreu Gallery in New York City (January 14–March 18, 2018). They were also the subject of Godard's and Anne-Marie Miéville's 2005 video *Reportage amateur (maquette expo)*.

Godard's original design of nine rooms was a crucial feature of his initial approach to an archaeology, which, as one form of historical recovery among others, derives its historical knowledge from the position and condition of objects once they are exposed by a vertical or horizontal archaeological cut. In the final version of the Pompidou's Godardian "utopia," however, a large-scale archaeology began to look more like last year's weekly planner, insofar as the three resulting rooms traversed a span of days: from the day before yesterday, to yesterday, to today. By contrast, Broodthaers used just two gallery spaces to traverse the nineteenth and twentieth centuries in *Décor: A Conquest*. Palms clustered seemingly innocuously against canons heavy with antiquated militarism populate the first room of Godard's exhibit, while in the second a precisely arranged arsenal of rifles decorate a wall behind tropical outdoor furniture, lit by the false glow of a movie-set arc lamp.

With the Pompidou's reductive gesture, the curators arguably strove to preserve Godard's progressive sense of history while also maintaining what Païni has called Godard's "theoretical environment," wherein the filmmaker asked the visitor to experience the "time of materialization" of a film, or the time between conception, staging, shooting, and that final moment when the film is placed in "the tomb of distribution and communication." A conciliatory gesture, perhaps, Godard's original models were eventually retained and exhibited throughout the three spaces comprising *Voyage(s)*, and as such they became archaeological material shadowing what was supposed to be and contrasting with what came to pass.

Contemplating the differences between the content of the model galleries and the real environments possesses its own temporality, what might be called the "could have been." A simplistic critical tactic at best, it does reveal that palm trees were part of Godard's initial plan, surviving in the maquette that the curators finally placed in "The Day before Yesterday" gallery, while living, potted palms did eventually appear in the gallery called "Yesterday." Using this strategy, we might say that the palms persist as the symbol of both what was and the ever present now of *Voyage(s)*—even as it was situated spatially, historically, in the temporal reserve of "Yesterday." While this reading is far from satisfactory, the emphasis should be placed on the word *symbol*. For the question at hand is how the palms ultimately function in what we are still propelled to call "Godard's installation."

There were in fact botanical specimens displayed throughout the exhibition, such as large potted olive trees that flanked the exhibit's entrance. The common house plants (possibly artificial) are demonstrably set up as elements of "décor" in the "Today" gallery. Together, these may make for an observation that Godard too was commenting on centuries of humans' colonization of environments and this process's arrangement and display as institutional, historical, or cinematic signifiers—the palm tree being an apt sign for the Los Angeles film industry and landscape, it should be noted. The olive trees clearly function to bridge the inner environment of Beaubourg with its exterior, urban domain, where an encampment for the homeless could nevertheless be clearly seen through the glass and steel architecture of the building. This is the present, Godard seems to say, which still looms up clearly between the olives, a significant object throughout Greek mythology and Athens's botanic symbol. Upon entering the exhibition, the visitor was greeted with a placard found in the first room that read: "Democracie et tragégie sont nées à Athènes en même temps" (Democracy and tragedy were born in Athens at the same time).

Quite possibly generating the deep historical matter that scholars today continue to observe throughout the history of the avant-garde, Godard may also allude to Aristotle's categories as defined by the tree of Porphyry. In this classic formulation, the highest form of matter and substance is divided and subdivided and subdivided yet again until the lowest species is reached and division can go no further: enter the houseplant in the third gallery, "Today." Between the botanical poles of the ancient olive tree and the fake philodendron we find the potted palms in the gallery "Yesterday." A dense cluster of cheaply potted palms obscure televisions screens displaying films by the past greats of French cinema—Renoir, Bresson, Cocteau, and others.

Reflecting on Godard's installation-exhibition, Nicole Brenez and Michael Witt posit that, like all of his films, it is "a proposition about art," where "the term 'art' . . . refers to a mode of permanent research . . . into the totality of the beliefs and rules relating to representation—its parameters, tools, forms, functions, and myths."[29] Evoking Kant, but also resisting the idealism therein, cinema scholar Daniel Morgan will call this Godard's "activity of aesthetic judgment."[30] In another mode, Daniel Fairfax's excellent essay about the exhibition goes to great lengths to justify why Godard's relationship with the Pompidou failed, and to understand the "ruinous" aesthetics of the final installation:

> It is nonetheless hard to avoid the conclusion that the collapse of the original exhibition was actively willed by Godard, both to create the type of crisis condition that appears to be the most fertile environment for his aesthetic output and to fit his metanarrative of the oppressive institution stifling his artistic intentions. In fact, it was only through the self-martyrization Godard created that the institutional critique present in the ensuing installation could gain substance. . . . As pliant as Beaubourg's administration may have been . . . it was necessary for Godard's project that the limits of the institution's cooperativeness be breached, and doing so in such a provocatively fractious fashion was the only way an atmosphere of genuine conflict could be generated.[31]

Whether we consider Godard a perpetual genius or a "spiteful" artist of institutional critique, what counts here is how to locate his historical apparatus and the claims that are made by the selection and placement of objects. I pose the question again: how do Godard's palms generate a recognition of history, and even more a recognition of historical repression?

And in posing these questions, I continue to wonder what Godard wants us to recognize with his strident refusal to accept institutional "repressions, the toning-down, the half-articulations, the accommodations, and the disappointments of the real," words that Peter Brooks used to describe the theatrical genre of melodrama.[32] Are we simply to bask in the "warm nostalgia" (for "Yesterday"? for classical French cinema?) that Fairfax observes in Godard's palm-filled gallery space? What does either nostalgia or an artist's recalcitrant stance toward an institution generate as historical recognition, or as the sign of it should we adopt the language of melodrama or, in another vein, the language of Romanticism's "historical travesty"?[33] From the latter point of view, discussed by Dave Beech and John Roberts, only empty signs and symbols (rather than figures) persist in an aesthetic landscape where the original, anti-authoritarian bid for Romantic autonomy—or the "refusal of institutional closure"—is replaced by a concept of modern autonomy in the work of art that is premised on "a defense of cognitive and aesthetic closure."[34]

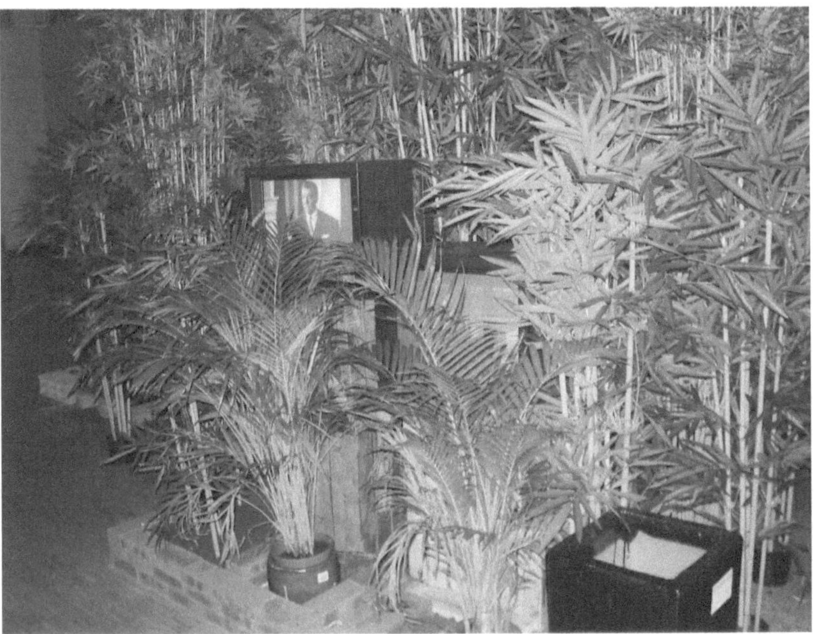

Figure 6.2. Interior view of Jean-Luc Godard's exhibition *Voyage(s) en utopie*, May 11 to August 14, 2006, Le Centre National d'Art et de Culture Georges-Pompidou, Paris, France. Photograph by and courtesy of Michael Witt.

If this is the case with Godard's *Travel(s) in Utopia*, especially insofar as some understand it as an inheritor of institutional critique that arose in the 1970s, then the question is not whether Godard was merely working in a "melodramatic mode." On the contrary. Brooks's own important critical peripety was to reframe our understanding of melodrama without any sense of its pejorative status in the history of theater and literature—a stance that was later taken up in the 1970s and 1980s by feminist (and other) film critics when they recuperated melodrama as an important affective and political mode. Thus, the question concerning Godard becomes whether he in fact *attained* the basic, revolutionary qualities of melodrama. For, if we uphold Brooks's notion, supported by Beech and Roberts, that Romanticism planted the seed of the modern and that the melodramatic is central to the "modern sensibility" governing contemporary art in a post-sacred world devoid of moral or ethical unity, we ought to think seriously about how a contemporary artist such as Godard drew upon, or not, "spectacular signs" to counter or simply address "cosmic," ethical, and also historical imperatives and narratives.[35] To do so would require asking how Godard understands and stages historical recognition by way of his objects, figures, and his "coups de théâtre" within the institution of the museum itself.

~

In 1981, Kristeva observed something similar to Brooks's central thesis in *The Melodramatic Imagination* in her analysis of the effects of twentieth-century economic, moral, and national disasters. In their wake, "*historical* tradition and *linguistic* unity were recast as a broader and deeper determinant: what might be called a *symbolic denominator*, defined as the cultural and religious memory forged by the interweaving of history and geography."[36] Kristeva's central concerns are to map a view of the dissolution of the nation and to account for the rise of "sociocultural ensembles" (such as Europe). Ethical problematics are central to this project, in particular those related to how sociocultural groups "escape from history" in the wake of art, philosophy, and religion's deployment of a unified "symbolic denominator" to account for those groups.[37] Because these ensembles tend to route an understanding of identity groups (women, in this case) by way of "reproduction and its representations," rather than by way of production, economic and otherwise, Kristeva diagnoses an urgent need for a new ethics arising in aesthetic production:

> It seems to me that the role of what is usually called "aesthetic practices" must increase not only to counterbalance the storage and uniformity of information by present-day mass media, data-bank systems, and, in particular, modern communications technology, but also to demystify the identity of the symbolic bond itself, to demystify, therefore, the *community* of language as a universal and unifying tool, one which totalizes and equalizes. . . . At this level of interiorization with its social as well as individual stakes, what I have called "aesthetic practices" are undoubtedly nothing other than the modern reply to the eternal question of morality.[38]

Her later turn to the concept of *figura* revisits these earlier interests, not least in how the figure retains and materializes history, which is made recognizable as such in language and the image.

In *The Severed Head: Capital Visions*, Kristeva follows Erich Auerbach's observation that, historically, the term *figure* was a mode of thinking that actualized the perception of substance within form, such that the figure came to indicate "something real and historical that represents and announces something else just as real and historical."[39] Kristeva's formulation, which she developed in part through a philological method, moves beyond the "rotten brains of allegory," as the avant-garde poet Robert Desnos wrote in a 1929 essay, and toward the perception of the "new" within the "old" such that real bodies may be perceived in historical forms.[40] For her, the figure or figurism "insinuates history without really imposing it . . . but its true power consists of possessing the key to art," insofar as it manifests in "resemblances throughout human history . . . in order to keep open the promise, the prophecy, the action forever to come."[41] In this we should recognize something similar to the *promesse de bonheur* that Krauss located in Broodthaers's embrace of early cinema as also a willful strike against the modernist closure of medium specificity.

Essential to Aristotle's generic category of tragedy, *peripeteia* advances plot progression by way of dramatic reversal, when ignorance, for example, turns into its opposite: knowledge. In 1976, a significant moment for the "neo-avant-garde" and just two years after the publication of Kristeva's *Revolution in Poetic Language*, Peter Brooks took up this ancient concept in his now-classic study of theatrical melodrama in order to register how the genre's modes and devices characterized artistic expression in a secular, postrevolutionary world. For Brooks, peripeteia is essential to melodrama's aesthetic, cultural, and formal operations as a historical theatrical genre: "The peripeties and *coups de théâtre* so characteristic of melodrama frequently turn on the act of nomination or its equivalent, for the moment in which moral identity is established is most often one of dramatic intensity or reversal."[42] Moments of peripety allow characters in melodrama to restore to visibility the moral attributes of their universe that had been effaced by the triumph of secular villainy, or the consequences of historical change. Peripety "make[s] possible a remarkable, public, spectacular homage to virtue, a demonstration of its power and effect; and the language has continual recourse to hyperbole and grandiose antithesis to explicate and clarify the admirableness of this virtue."[43] Crystalized in theatrical action, peripety dramatizes a "moment of ethical evidence and recognition."[44] It is important to underscore that this recognition, forged as it is through a "moment of astonishment," registers the restoration of ethics but also the very history of a fallen or obscured ethical regime.

Crucially, according to Brooks, the effect here is dependent on the play of signs, which, in the theatrical setting, are most often manifested in props, objects—elements of décor or mise-en-scène (Brooks's example comes from Guilbert de Pixerécourt's 1819 *La Fille de l'exilé*). However, on stage, or in the "real" of public spectacle and its modes of experience, the sign becomes a pure signifier that functions as visual spectacle: it is the signifier's visual display and the spectator's sight of it that count the most. Hence, Brooks argues, melodramatic peripety and its corresponding signifiers in fact stage a much larger dramatization of the "trials and eventual victory of [the] sign" itself.[45] In the case of melodrama, the most important sign is that of virtue, especially in its conquest to be legible within a historical world transformed by villainy or vice.

However far Brooks's literary history falls from the crises of the avant-garde discussed in this volume, his scholarly contribution of the 1970s nevertheless provides a helpful framework for thinking about Broodthaers's and Godard's site-specific works and their use of particular objects in institutional space to address the historical and ethical domain. Brooks conceives of early nineteenth-century French melodrama as an explicit response to grand historical change, notably the French Revolution—one of the great historical peripeties or reversals of national fortune. Yet, even as a genre that may be thought of in opposition to the avant-garde, melodrama enacts something similar to the avant-garde, an aesthetic response to significant historical change. Whereas postrevolutionary France may have invented melodrama to reinvigorate the visibility and power of the sign, in a long history of the avant-garde we similarly witness the invention of plastic strategies, tactics, and devices to visibly register the stakes of "art" in a world whose historical arc was irrevocably reversed by World War I, the Shoah, Vietnam, colonial revolt, and, in a more formal or art-historical vein, readymades, minimalism, happenings, and the post-medium condition.

While the recuperation of "virtue" is not at stake in this discussion of Broodthaers or Godard and their site-specific works, I suggest that the ethics of historical recognition—and the signs, signifiers, and figures that reveal this recognition—are. As it responds to historical reversals and change, the avant-garde in the long 1970s encourages us to think about ethics as Brooks thinks about melodrama when "it insists that the ordinary may be the place for the installation of significance. It tells us that in the right mirror, with the right degree of convexity, our lives matter."[46] But the avant-garde also suggests ways of thinking ethically that exceed those of melodrama.

It is helpful to remember that when Kristeva began to publish for the journal *Tel Quel*, acting also as part of its editorial board in the late 1960s, the group considered itself and the journal to be part of the avant-garde. Historical concerns were indeed crucial to this intellectual group, as Toril Moi points out: "Focusing, like structuralism, on *language* as the starting-point for a new kind of thought on politics and the subject, the group based its work on a new understanding of history as *text*; writing (*écriture*) as *production*, not representation."[47] We should focus equally here on the subversion of "representation" for production and "history as text," especially within the space of the "aesthetic" project. Newly recognized as "social or signifying space" capable of producing a "plural history . . . situated in relation to their specific time and space" in conjunction with a "*politics* which would constitute the logical consequence of a non-representational understanding of writing,"[48] Kristeva's avant-garde strived to locate the production of historical recognition as a fact emerging within the space of art. This is a significant charge for the legacy of the avant-garde of the long 1970s, one that every artist or filmmaker may not live up to.

In *Late Godard and the Possibilities of Cinema*, Daniel Morgan suggests that nature and natural beauty are nothing short of an analytical tool for aesthetic, political, and historical investigations in Godard's later works. Morgan places Godard's project alongside that of Adorno, whose critique of Hegelian aesthetics charges that while natural beauty was actively denied, repressed, and replaced in Hegel by a superior form of artistic beauty, it is nevertheless essentially recoverable "by the appropriate techniques of analysis or artistic production."[49] This is where Morgan places Godard's enterprise, arguing that Godard's use of nature and natural beauty is a potent "analytic tool" for how the filmmaker "links the respective iconographies of the sublime and the beautiful to competing conceptions of politics and history."[50] Godard uses the iconography of nature, Morgan argues, because of its "historical association of the experience of the sublime," but the goal here is not to achieve a similarly sublime effect. Rather, Godard's shots of nature are a device "to work with meanings attached to an aesthetic mode."[51]

I don't think we can read the flora or the palms in *Voyage(s)* strictly along these lines, but Morgan does provide the grounds for thinking about Godard's work in failed Romantic rather than avant-garde terms—terms that allow us to approach the "ruinous" design of his installation as decadent "stagecraft" whereby any "systematic effort to dramatize the signs of a cosmic ethical struggle has been muted and diverted" toward the construction of a monument to the failure of art's and the artist's autonomy.[52] And this is where Godard does not lament but wails, "replacing the controls of reason with the transgression of aesthetics . . . revolt(ing) against academicism, classicism . . . in favor of the Protestant virtues of immediacy, self-dependency, anti-authoritarianism and subjective authenticity."[53] These are the words of Beech and Roberts in their critique of a neo-aestheticism in the humanities, or what they otherwise call the "historical travesty of Romanticism" to which I referred earlier.[54]

It should be clear that I am not suggesting that Godard's thesis in *Voyage(s)* pivots on a concept of natural beauty in his chosen flora, or its inherent relationship to the sublime. But if we take his palms as seriously as critics have taken his institutional "critique," in *Voyage(s)'* discursive unfolding, then I suggest they stand as a symbol of, if not a sign for, Godard's own institutional ecology of art and his violent defense of it. Godard's palms are more a prop in the genre of classical tragedy evoked at the exhibition's entrance. He thus exchanges the premise of avant-garde institutional critique, by way of his institutional "rejection," for a defense of an outmoded conception of art's relationship to autonomy—both his own and that of the real social sphere. In brute terms, this instance of Godard's practice is not melodramatic, insofar as it rejects the democratic and melodramatic idea that "our lives matter."

It may be worth mentioning that Adorno's critique of Hegel does bear resemblance to Brooks's terms for melodrama, wherein an occulted or repressed morality—in Adorno's case the "virtue" of natural beauty—can be restored to legibility in the visible domain of signs through artistic technique. However, if we also consider that *Voyage(s)* also presents the unfolding of an *art historical* ecology—one that is built by Ancient Greek tragedy, the cinema, installation art, and television—the palms assure the legibility of Broodthaers's place in a post-medium world—one that Godard may or may not be lamenting, insofar as *Voyage(s)* is largely understood as a meditation on the "death of cinema." As the central character in Krauss's meditation on the post-medium condition, as I mentioned earlier, Broodthaers's part was indeed as an agent of peripety: he was the one who, amid the color field painters, the discourses of modernist and Greenbergian purity, the structural filmmakers—and Godard—turned to the aggregative condition of the cinema as an avant-garde premise for the display of (art) historical crisis. In so doing, Broodthaers seized upon the radical dispatch of historical recognition, insisting that it quietly rise up from the disasters of official culture that are harbored in the figure of the palm tree.

While Godard's palms may indeed signal the impossibility of perceiving modernity, whose magnitude, Morgan argues, shares the sublime qualities of scale, they also denote what has been deemed "natural" for the artist himself: his performance of lava-death and ruin in the name of art as "institutional critique."[55] Godard's scene, as in Benjamin's thought, is spectacular. But Broodthaers's scene is the one that remains visible and recoverable; his palm tree persists as a ubiquitous "natural" figure recognizing the historical peripeties that, before the avant-garde crises of the long 1970s, changed or destroyed human lives under colonialism, and that, after the avant-garde, transformed a perception of the ideals, goals, and *work* of art and its history as anything but unified or autonomous.

Although Broodthaers, unlike Kristeva, eschews recourse to religious philology, the grounding of his conceptual enterprise in poetic language ultimately assists him in wresting his figures' signification from the platitudes of myth, representation, icon, symbol, and official culture. In turn, his figures restore the "historical, material aspect" to the representational "beyond" such that they—in this case his palms—perpetually activate perception between past and future forms and the anticipation of what is to come.[56] Unmoored from their idealist function as a component of his "art" and detached from any stable relationship to the "sublime" of the modern epoch, Broodthaers's palms are both the "flicker" of history in his site-specific installations *and* the material for perceiving the action of historical reversals, or "the peripeties of our (art) history" that allowed the colonial past to be perceived within the institutional space of the museum. In his rather terse, melodramatic, and figural mode, soberly political in nature, Broodthaers conceives of historical recognition within site-specific, institutional critique and its rejection of medium specificity as also a practice of ethics.

Notes

An early version of this essay was presented at the conference Expanding Cinema: Spatial Dimensions of Film Exhibition, Aesthetics, and Theory, held at Yale University in 2012 and organized by Mal Ahern. I am grateful for the wisdom and encouragement of the editors of this volume, Jean-Thomas Tremblay and Andrew Strombeck, whose intellectual generosity helped me see this essay through. My thanks are also due to Kara Keeling, who commented on an early version of this essay.

1. See Maria Stavrinaki, *Dada Presentism*, trans. Daniela Ginsberg (Stanford, CA: Stanford University Press, 2016). This book preceded the monumental exhibition she curated for the Centre Pompidou: *Une énigme moderne* (May 8, 2019–September 16, 2019). See also Maria Stavrinaki, *Saisi par la préhistoire* (Paris: Les Presses du réel, 2019).

2. Rosalind Krauss, *A Voyage on the North Sea: Art in the Age of the Post-Medium Condition* (New York: Thames & Hudson, 1999).

3. Krauss, *Voyage*, 44, 45.

4. Krauss, *Voyage*, 20.

5. See Rosalind Krauss, Annette Michelson, et al., *October: The Second Decade, 1986–1996* (Cambridge, MA: MIT Press, 1997).

6. Douglas Crimp, *On the Museum's Ruins* (Cambridge, MA: MIT Press, 1995), 212.

7. See "Marcel Broodthaers: Writings, Interviews, Photographs," ed. Benjamin Buchloh, special issue, *October* 42 (1987).

8. *Un Jardin d'Hiver II* was first installed at the Palais des Beaux-Arts in Brussels in 1974.

9. Jacques Rancière, *Figures of History*, trans. Julie Rose (Cambridge, UK: Polity, 2012); Julia Kristeva, *The Severed Head: Capital Visions*, trans. Jody Gladding (New York: Columbia University Press, 2011), 59.

10. See Marcel Broodthaers and Stéphane Rona, "The Angelus Is Ringing" (1976), first published as "C'est l'angelus qui sone," in *Marcel Broodthaers Collected Writings*, ed. Gloria Moure (Barcelona: Ediciones Polígrafa, 2012), 473.

11. Alice Jardine, "Introduction to Julia Kristeva's 'Woman's Time,'" *Signs: Journal of Women in Culture and Society* 7, no. 1 (1981): 7. See Julia Kristeva, *Semeiotikè, Recherches pour une sémanalyse, Essais* (Paris: Le Seuil, 1969); Julia Kristeva, "Woman's Time," *Signs: Journal of Women in Culture and Society* 7, no. 1 (1981): 13–35.

12. *Voyage(s) en Utopie, Jean-Luc Godard, 1946–2006: À la recherché d'un théroème Perdu* (Paris: Le Centre Pompidou, May 11–August 14, 2006).

13. Erika Balsom, "From Bad Object to Lost Object: The Desires of Film Theory," supplement, *Spectator* 27 (2007): 13.

14. Roland Barthes, "The Death of the Author," in Roland Barthes, *Image, Music, Text*, ed. and trans. Stephen Heath (London: Fontana Press), 142–148.

15. Peter Brooks, *The Melodramatic Imagination: Balzac, Henry James, Melodrama, and the Mode of Excess* (New Haven, CT: Yale University Press, 1976).

16. Walter Benjamin, "L [Dream House, Museum, Spa]," in *The Arcades Project*, trans. Howard Eiland and Kevin McLaughlin (Cambridge, MA: Harvard University Press, 2002), 405, emphasis added.

17. Rachel Haidu, *The Absence of Work: Marcel Broodthaers, 1964–1976* (Cambridge, MA: MIT Press, 2010), 236.

18. Haidu, *Absence of Work*, 229.

19. Kristen Ross, *The Emergence of Social Space: Rimbaud and the Paris Commune* (Minneapolis: University of Minnesota Press, 1988), 87–88, as quoted in Haidu, *Absence of Work*, 235.

20. Haidu, *Absence of Work*, 233.

21. Eric C. H. de Bruyn, "Bateau/Tableau/Drapeau: On Eran Schaerf's and Eva Meyer's *Pro Testing* and the Contemporary Politics of Allegory," in *Allegorie: DFG-Symposion 2014*, ed. Ulla Haselstein (Berlin: De Gruyter, 2016), 697–727.

22. Marcel Broodthaers, "Notes on the Subject, 1975," in *Marcel Broodthaers Collected Writings*, 489.

23. Marcel Broodthaers, "Catalogue, *L'Angeus de Daumier* vol. I," in *Marcel Broodthaers Collected Writings*, 482.

24. Walter Benjamin, "R [Mirrors]," in *The Arcades Project*, trans. Howard Eiland and Kevin McLaughlin (Cambridge, MA: Belknap Press of Harvard University Press, 1999), 540.

25. Walter Benjamin, "Little History of Photography," in *Walter Benjamin: Selected Writings*, vol. 2, part 2, 1931–1934, ed. Michael W. Jennings et al. (Cambridge, MA: Harvard University Press, 2002), 515, emphasis added.

26. See Marcus Wood, *Black Milk: Imagining Slavery in the Visual Cultures of Brazil and North America* (Oxford, UK: Oxford University Press, 2013).

27. Marcel Broodthaers, "The Eye of the Storm, 1974," in *Marcel Broodthaers Collected Writings*, 447.

28. Dominique Païni, "According to JLG . . . ," *Rouge* (2006): http://www.rouge.com.au/9/according_jlg.html.

29. Nicole Brenez and Michael Witt, "'1750 Percussion Rifles': Work of the Document, Rights and Duties of Cinema," trans. Michael Witt, *Rouge* (2006): http://www.rouge.com.au/9/percussion.html.

30. Daniel Morgan, *Late Godard and the Possibilities of Cinema* (Berkeley: University of California Press, 2013), 18.

31. Daniel Fairfax, "Montage(s) of Disaster: *Voyage(s) en Utopia* by Jean-Luc Godard," *Cinema Journal* 54, no. 2 (2015): 31–32.

32. Brooks, *Melodramatic Imagination*, ix.

33. Dave Beech and John Roberts, *The Philistine Controversy* (New York: Verso, 2002), 39.

34. Beech and Roberts, *Philistine Controversy*, 40.

35. Brooks, *Melodramatic Imagination*, 21, 106.

36. Kristeva, "Women's Time," 13.

37. Kristeva, "Women's Time," 14.

38. Kristeva, "Women's Time," 35.

39. Eric Auerbach, *Figura* (Paris: Belin, 1938), 32, as quoted in Kristeva, *Severed Head*, 58.

40. Robert Desnos, "Pygmalion et le Sphinx," trans. Simon Baker, *Papers of Surrealism* 7 (2007): 2. See Benjamin Buchloh, "Marcel Broodthaers: Allegories of the Avant-Garde," *Art Forum* (May 1980): 52–59. Kristeva, *Severed Head*, 59.

41. Kristeva, *Severed Head*, 59.

42. Brooks, *Melodramatic Imagination*, 39.

43. Brooks, *Melodramatic Imagination*, 25.

44. Brooks, *Melodramatic Imagination*, 26.

45. Brooks, *Melodramatic Imagination*, 28.

46. Brooks, *Melodramatic Imagination*, ix.

47. Toril Moi, introduction to *The Kristeva Reader*, by Julia Kristeva (New York: Columbia University Press, 1986), 4.

48. Moi, introduction to *The Kristeva Reader*, 4.

49. Morgan, *Late Godard and the Possibilities of Cinema*, 72.

50. Morgan, *Late Godard and the Possibilities of Cinema*, 86.

51. Morgan, *Late Godard and the Possibilities of Cinema*, 77.

52. Brooks, *Melodramatic Imagination*, 89.

53. Beech and Roberts, *Philistine Controversy*, 39.

54. Beech and Roberts, *Philistine Controversy*, 39.

55. Morgan, *Late Godard and the Possibilities of Cinema*, 77.

56. Kristeva, *Severed Head*, 59.

Chapter 7

I Felt Like a Machine

Martha Rosler's Aesthetics of Survival

Matt Tierney

What are technology and science to the avant-gardes of the long seventies? Just as new machines are often tasked with solving problems caused by formerly new machines, artists began again in the last third of the twentieth century to chafe within the values and institutions that they had set out to transcend. It is the friction of this chafing and the aesthetic expressions that sparked from it that yet provided some of the most cogent defenses of human life against dehumanization by militarism, industry, and neoimperialist mass media. Toward the beginning of that period, composer George Rochberg called the criticism of technology, as it approached the edge of the avant-garde, an "aesthetics of survival." Toward the end of that period, video and performance artist Martha Rosler called it "person-centered counterpractices." Both index the capacity of art not merely to represent the quantified and datafied capacities of the human brain or body but indeed to criticize those very aestheticizations of quantified and datafied experience. This essay emphasizes the importance of Rosler's written work during these years: her dissertation; her essays in artworld polemic and aesthetic theory; and her "food novels," which were brief serial narratives that opposed newly emergent regimens of commodified art while telling stories of life lived restlessly under mechanized conditions of laboring stuckness. Overall, this writing seeks humane ways to push back against the historical mechanization of laboring bodies, a certain avant-garde's uncritical embrace of science (and of scientific forms like photography and later video), and the techno-fascist turn in what Rosler called "state art."

A Complex Relationship with Technology

For Rosler, as for Rochberg and many others, particularly Peter Bürger, the crisis of the 1970s was simply and clearly expressed: after emerging in opposition to the economy of art, an array of early century experimental techniques and communities had turned into mere commodities in that economy. Avant-gardists, in short, were stuck in a mess of their own making. In her 1986 essay on the topic, "Video: Shedding the Utopian Moment," Rosler explains that artists had "intended on the one hand to replace individualized production with a more collectivized and anonymous practice and on the other to get away from the individualized address and restricted reception of art," but their process of deinstitutionalization and disindividuation had, in spite of itself, built up new institutions and new regimens of individualism: "nothing succeeds like failure, and in this case failure meant that the avant-garde became the academy of the post-war world."[1] Rosler's own work during these years aimed to break with that new academy while not endorsing inherited systems of value. Rosler's work, that is, aimed to proceed toward anti-institutionalist and collectivist ends without accepting the dehumanizing new star system of artists and galleries.

Rosler also leveled her critique at science and technology, because it was these fields whose new inventions had enabled the rise of the new avant-gardes in the first place. The more machinic artforms of the new avant-garde, like photography and film, were too often accepted as having expanded the human sensorium: as having led a process by which human capacities had been augmented, expanded across the globe. Yet for Rosler, writing in 1996, new inventions do not "drive social events"—instead, "technological developments are accomplished within a framework of social and economic imperatives" even when "in practice this is a complex relationship in which technology also organizes experience and functions as a means of social control."[2] Rosler argues that new machines might structure perception (both affording and policing it) but will never themselves be political actors. A familiar critique of technological determinism, to be sure, but one that Rosler finds has gone missing from predominant narratives of art history.

This critique is not missing from all practices of avant-garde art, however, as Rosler explains. Surrealism and Dada saw technological thinking as an impediment to human expression, and so "attempted to counter and destroy the institutionalization of art in machine society, to merge it with everyday life and transform both through liberation of the senses, unfreezing the power of dissent and revolt."[3] This idealistic avant-garde critique, in its early iterations, saw its target in the yoking of new institutions to new machines—and saw its task as the dismantling of both. For Rosler, surrealism and Dada were failed movements in this respect, but neither the critique nor the task had died with them. Instead, critique and task were inherited by experimentalists in video production, most famously Nam Jun Paik, who found ways to make and market video as a kind of anticommodity commodity. "Paik imported TV into art-world culture, identifying it as an element of daily life susceptible to symbolic, anti-aesthetic aestheticism," writes Rosler.[4] Paik's critique of technology should have deformed the market for art, argues Rosler, but his critique instead becomes one more component of the art commodity. His anticapitalist ideas do little aside from adding themselves to the market, paradoxically becoming saleable elements in the commerce of contemporary art. This is how Paik's project, like surrealism and Dada before it, also fails by Rosler's standards.

The videographic critique of technology, however, need not fail. Rather than make a spectacle of breaking the industrial apparatus of television and in the process construct a whole new industrial apparatus (the tendency she locates in Paik), Rosler advises working within televisual technology and discourse while hewing tightly to a radical humanist message. Doing experimental video need not indulge naïve myths of avant-garde transgression through "the destruction of TV as a material object, the deflection of its signal, or other acts of the holy fool," not when there is another option anyway, in "socially invested, socially productive counterpractices, ones making a virtue of their person-centeredness, origination with persons—rather than from industries or institutions."[5] This is how Rosler's essay on video concludes, with a demand, yet without concrete instances of what such socially productive and person-centered counterpractices might look like.

These counterpractices materialize elsewhere in Rosler's writings as well as in her artworks, not only of video but also of print and performance. The writings are, in general, works of theory as well as defenses of theory. Artists may feel that theory is antithetical to finding and keeping an audience, she told the Caucus for Marxism and Art at the College Art Association in 1978, but courting theory is a necessary risk so long as "class struggle is a structural feature of class society, and not a battle that one can choose to take up or put down at will."[6] Because "we are increasingly beguiled by an accordion like succession of mediations between ourselves and the natural and social world . . . [such that] we are led to grant the aura of life to things and to drain them from people," she concludes, "we best comprehend ourselves as social entities in looking at photos of ourselves, assuming the voyeur's role with respect to our own images."[7] The accordion of mediations stands between people and each other, and between people and themselves, so that the commodity is what must be removed. Not demolished, as Paik would demolish the television, but erased—or else, as in Rosler's theory of video, used otherwise than as a commodity.

This is the objective of Rosler's videos, her best-known work of the 1970s. In such moving-image installations as *A Budding Gourmet* (1974) and *Vital Statistics of a Citizen, Simply Obtained* (1977)—or most famously, as *Semiotics of the Kitchen* (1975)—Rosler's project is to facilitate a spectator's voyeurism of her own image. Redirecting the look of an audience into a tautological circuit, the television monitor neither vanishes nor explodes, but it is nonetheless sidelined. Put differently, the monitor is the vehicle of a political and economic self-analysis that is both hostile and indebted to broadcast technology, but broadcast technology is not really what the artwork is about. Instead, it responds to shifts in the structural conditions of alienation and the commodity form through a transformative self-analysis, not the destruction of the machine. This is what Rosler means by person-centered counterpractices. Oriented toward social investment and production, her criticism of technoculture is not the mock-heroic act of a holy fool. Instead this criticism situates television, along with the technoculture that it anchors, as one alienating commodity among many. Rather than smash it or treat it like it is something other than it is, she repositions the monitor in an uneasy relation to exchange, where its cultural role may be dedramatized, or where it may simply and unheroically get switched off.

Parallel to Rosler's argument but written earlier and venturing beyond the specific analysis of video is George Rochberg's essay, "The Avant-Garde and the Aesthetics of Survival." While it may seem strange to connect a relentless conceptualist like Rosler to a composer like Rochberg, best known for his seemingly traditionalist turn to tonal music, these two figures share a critique of the role of telecommunication and computation in emerging artworks. If this technology critique ever becomes something more than an archival curiosity, if it ever coalesces into a sensible formation of politics or art, then it may be due to its capacity to stretch the distance separating Rochberg from Rosler. Like Rosler, Rochberg defends radical humanism against both liberalism and technocentrism. Writing in a special issue of *New*

Literary History on "Modernism and Postmodernism: Inquiries," Rochberg describes atonal serial music composition as an approach by which composers hoped to displace bourgeois standards of music appreciation. Presaging Rosler's arguments about Paik, Rochberg writes that the algorithmic thinking of serial music has displaced not only appreciation but also understanding. For Rochberg, when dissonances proceed in ways too rapid or complex to comprehend, they become useless. They do nothing to facilitate new forms of organization or thought, but just collapse again into the kinds of pure exchange value (prestige, for example) against which they had been counterposed to begin with. All this matters to Rochberg because his questions, like Rosler's, are "basic" to something more like use value: "can art (and presumably the avant-garde) itself be an agent of change? Can it influence or affect its human environment?"[8]

The key word here is *human*. Rochberg's avant-garde, like Rosler's, has little use for either nostalgic or futurist faith: as much as hers, his displaces the pseudo-heroic narratives of technological antihumanism without retreating into the dream of beauty. Yet like her, in place of both, he proposes an appeal to communitarian ethics. What she insists should be a person-centered activity of art, he calls an "aesthetics of survival." Famously, Rochberg had turned away from serial music after the death of his son in 1964. Finding tonality better suited to the lyricism of his grief, Rochberg's third string quartet courted controversy by inviting accusations of conservatism. Borrowing from Hermann Hesse in an essay of 1973, Rochberg called Schoenberg a "genius of suffering," but felt that Schoenberg's twelve-tone technique had lost its force.[9] The technique had expressed what could not be expressed by the music that had come before it. Schoenberg had been "unable to relate any longer to the traditions from which he came, compelled to leave behind whatever security those traditions offered—yet always longing for them."[10] But serialism eventually failed, not only through its repetition by other composers but also through the refined calculation of its effects on cognition.

The failure of Schoenberg's music, on this view, is like the failure that Rosler later notes of visual art. Dada and surrealism, for Rosler, fail when they try to dismantle their institutional housing but end up building new institutions despite themselves. The musical avant-garde, in Rochberg's essay on the aesthetics of survival, fails when it chases the flag of science rather than that of art. Aiming not to make meaning or feeling, but instead to experiment on the human nervous system, such an avant-garde can no longer express much of anything, or at any rate cannot make itself understood:

"when the human nervous system is confronted by music characterized chiefly by perceptual disorder, lack of identity, and avoidance of periodicity, it loses interest, becomes indifferent,—and ends up rejecting what it cannot relate to."[11] The aesthetics of survival is a way of responding to this problem. Obfuscation and overstimulation accomplish nothing, it is said, unlike the regrounding of art in fantasy. Compared to the aesthetics of survival, deliberate obscurity retrenches itself in commerce and reason while claiming to depart from them.

Whereas Rosler criticizes the technological determinism of art history, Rochberg criticizes more broadly the knowledge that is highly valued, particularly in the kinds of expertise that commit only to morally abstracted ideals of progress: "in science today we see the remarkable phenomenon of an unquestioned, world-wide agreement to pursue knowledge to its absolute limits; regardless of its ultimate consequences for human existence."[12] These are in fact versions of the same argument. Rosler contrasts her person-centered counterpractices to the seemingly autonomous growth of technologies and technocratic systems, while Rochberg applies his aesthetics of survival to fending off a related kind of autonomy, that of scientific research. Together, they turn art not against science and technology, but instead against any cultural or intellectual practice that would delegate social responsibility to regimes of specialization that are fundamentally antisocial. The kinds of art that both envision, in short, are those that would refuse to relieve humans of their obligation to each other. Judging anthropocentrism to be a lesser evil than inhumanity, in other words, both Rochberg and Rosler forge ahead toward ethical artmaking.

Rochberg's take on the avant-garde, like Rosler's, might boil down to a simple dictum: art is obliged to participate in social change, and even to instigate it, by subordinating scientific experimentation and technological progress to an ethic of human survival. And like hers, his might be said to offer a kind of codicil: art that merely leverages scientific and technological expertise, rather than making itself felt and understood by human beings, is failed art. Rosler goes even further in her 1974 dissertation from the University of California, San Diego, seeing the latter as complicit in official violence. The antonym of person-centered counterpractices, with their aesthetics of survival, Rosler calls "state art." State art is the art of cultural imperialism and industrial capitalism; and in a moment when telecommunicative and computational advances stem from military research, state art is the art of securitization and control.

This is not a metaphor or anyway it is not only a metaphor, for it has a date and an address. Rosler's dissertation reckoned that "the epitome of state art was the Art and Technology show mounted by curator Maurice Tuchman at the Los Angeles County Museum of Art in 1968."[13] The late sixties saw large-scale receipt of corporate moneys by some of the best-known figures in the avant-garde. Tech-development firms of military research and mass media were especially generous. Perhaps this explains Rochberg's complaint with new technology, and not only Rosler's. Either way, under LACMA's auspices, Claes Oldenburg partnered with Disney, Roy Lichtenstein with Universal, Victor Vasarely with IBM, Robert Irwin and James Turrell with Garrett AiResearch, Robert Rauschenberg with Teledyne, and Larry Bell with the Rand Corporation. At the height of US military incursion into Vietnam, and the crest of US media incursion into globalizing television and film markets, the avant-garde had sold itself to the very forces of incursion. Their alibi, as if they needed one, was that their art was the culmination of an autonomous technological development.

The Trough of Techno-Fascism

In fact, these corporate partnerships were not the passive actions of small-scale cultural actors on the receiving end of massive technological change. They were more insidious than this, as Rosler explains in her dissertation: " 'State' artists now share the 'official secrets' of the rulers—they can understand and manipulate the tools of rulership, industrial processes, mass-communication media, engineering and scientific control systems, which more and more in the massified Western culture elude the comprehension of the increasingly illiterate population."[14] The artists brought together by Tuchman at LACMA do not only gain financially from their corporate collaborations: they learn to work within machine operations and research procedures that can only serve the industries that made them, and whose geopolitical consequences will never fully be explained to an audience ill-equipped to understand them. Like Nam Jun Paik in Rosler's account of his work, or like the descendants of Schoenberg in Rochberg's account of theirs, the artists of the Art and Technology exhibit sought to expand beyond the limited scope of their institutions but merely opened the door of those institutions to the tools and rhetorics of technocultural violence.

Rosler does not call the LACMA project a failure, however: she calls it state art. To her, these are "collaborations" not just in the weak definitional sense of confederation but also in the strong sense of moral and political complicity. Max Kozloff, writing in *Artforum* in 1971, agreed. Adding other neoimperialist agents to the list of corporate partners (General Electric,

Hewlett-Packard, Jet Propulsion Lab, Litton Industries, Lockheed Norris, and North American Rockwell), Kozloff's indictment is severe:

> In short, it is a rogue's gallery of the violence industries. Subsidized decisively by the American government, they had grown to their present bulk through the business of slaying. The show epitomizes the fact that our most prominent visual artists had been offered an extremely direct contract to be of service to the prestige of these industries (in return for various hard and software) and had accepted. During the term of the project, there occurred the My Lai massacre, the Chicago Democratic Convention riots, the assassinations of Martin Luther King and Robert Kennedy, the invasion of Cambodia, and the student killings at Kent and Jackson State. While these convulsions were taking place, inflaming the radicalism of our youth and polarizing the country, the American artists did not hesitate to freeload at the trough of that techno-fascism that had inspired them.[15]

Techno-fascist state art versus person-centered survival aesthetics: her stakes could not be higher or clearer. Departing or transforming the avant-garde is not about originality or autonomy but about facing oneself in the morning.

Starting in 1974, Martha Rosler wrote and sent four works of mail art, her so-called "food novels." Three of these works, narratives composed entirely of postcards, were later photo-reproduced and printed under the title *Service: A Trilogy on Colonization* in 1978: *A Budding Gourmet* (1974), *McTowersMaid* (1974), and *Tijuana Maid* (1975–1976). Because their inception coincides with Rosler's dissertation, it makes sense to seek in them a pragmatic refutation of state art. There, she gives the clearest sense of what a person-centered survival aesthetics might actually look like. As first-person stories, the food novels present intimate accounts of lives lived in both a creative and a destructive tension with machines that are both literal and figurative. And as mail art, a genre frequently mobilized by feminist conceptualists (from Carol Bergé and Alison Knowles to Yoko Ono and Cosey Fanni Tutti), they disturb the temporal acceleration of technologically enabled communication.

Each of the volumes is only a few dozen pages, and together they perform three critiques at once: one, a feminist critique of the racist presumptions that surround domestic life and care; two, a Marxist critique of women's labor both in and out of the home; and three, a ludic speculation about the mail's place among the advancing technologies of message transmission. The co-constitution of these diverse critiques is what resolves into what Judith Barry and Sandy Flitterman-Lewis call a "fissuring effect."[16] Yet the same co-constitution is what binds the critiques together, as they lodge their multivalent and intersectional protest against telecommunication and empire—what Kozloff had identified as techno-fascism. In a decade of emergent global cable and satellite networks, Rosler's perspective is both decolonial and local, exposing a communicative process that "whether welcome or unwelcome . . . thrusts itself upon you, so to speak, and must be dealt with in the context of your own life." In an age when art produces rapid yet often incomprehensible signals, such that the only meaning conveyed is the technical means of transmission, Rosler demands patience, unevenness, and the complication of form by theme, synchrony by diachrony, and (pace McLuhan) medium by message.

At the formal register, through deceleration and sabotage, Rosler's text limns a picture of communication that trades speed and conquest for slowness and play. She describes the project in her "Note on One Aspect of Form," at the very outset of *Service: A Trilogy on Colonization*:

> This is a book of three novels and one translation. In their original form the novels were sent through the mail as postcard series, one card about every five to seven days.
>
> Mail both is and isn't a personal communication. But whether welcome or unwelcome it thrusts itself upon you, so to speak, and must be dealt with in the context of your own life. Its immediacy may allow its message to penetrate the usual bounds of your attention. A serial communication can hook you, engaging your long-term interest (intermittently, at least). There was a lot of time—and mental space—around each installment of these novels, time in which the communication could unfold and reverberate. So they are long novels, and slow ones.[17]

Long novels even though each is only between eleven and fifteen pages. Slow novels even though, aside from their receipt in the original performance, each is rapidly consumed.

As Siona Wilson explains, "In this work [Rosler] demonstrates the interpenetration of the spheres of consumption and production, and indicates the importance of women as the primary mediating principle."[18] Rosler thus promises something that both is and is not personal. As they invoke both consumption and production, the postcards traverse a world in which both private and public have been defeated by an unexamined mass mediation. "How can there be said to be a private sphere when millions are told simultaneously to insert suppositories in order to gain hemorrhoid relief?" Rosler asks an audience at the Dia Art Foundation in 1987; then, invoking Ronald Reagan's widely publicized prostate surgery: "and how can there be said to be a public sphere when . . . schematic diagrams of the operation on the president's penis and lower intestine appear prominently in the mass media?"[19] The postcards are and are not personal because they traverse a world that is neither public nor private. They therefore disrespect the body as a closed space for individuation and emotional interiority, while equally setting aside the romance of art as produced by a secluded artist for common consumption. This dual rejection might explain Rosler's vaguely emetic language of penetration and "thrust." Into the ostensibly nonpublic domain the postcard intrudes as one body may intrude upon another in an act of penetrative sex. More importantly perhaps, beyond this vulgar copulative metaphorics, Rosler sees her project as having enacted a kind of immediacy that has nothing to do with instantaneous transmission, and that is indeed opposed to instantaneity all together.

This immediacy is something else, neither formlessness nor speed but rather reverberation and unfolding, something other than the vehicle of a message or the story it tells. It is perhaps what Benjamin Buchloh means in 1982 when he characterizes Rosler's work as authentic: "The authenticity with which Rosler confronts the viewer is that of the apparent impossibility of political commitment and cultural activism within the framework provided by the cultural apparatus and the necessity of a transformation of practice within that framework."[20] There is a communicative paradigm for thinking about the production of aesthetic meaning, wherein the artwork is seen as a signal that is sent from an artist to spectator. Rosler assails the art institutions that sustain this paradigm, but she does not exactly try to escape it. Instead she commits herself to a marginal position within both institution and communication. She traces the failures of both of these apparatuses to facilitate social change under existing conditions, then she makes another space for art, and another time of sending and receiving. The space-time is women's space-time, not only because the art is sent by a woman to (mostly) women. It is feminist as well because it makes its technology critique through a protest against the claustrophobic space-times of domestic work and of nondomestic (yet no less gender-designated) women's work.

It is from the opening volume of the trilogy that Rosler adapts her contemporaneous video of the same title, *A Budding Gourmet*. In the video, Rosler's first, the artist sits in a kitchen and explains the cultural elevation that accompanies newly popular methods of European cookery and consumption. She mimics the speaking style of rising superstars in food culture, particularly author and TV host Julia Child as well as *New York Times* restaurant critic Craig Claiborne (the pair also featuring in a fictional dialogue by Rosler, entitled *The Art of Cooking*). Made popular by figures like Child and Claiborne, these methods promise class mobility and classed comforts. Near the end of the video, a cut reveals collaged data on global poverty and hunger, before the video at last returns to the image of Rosler's ambitious narrator. According to contemporary critic Nora M. Alter, the video combines critiques of US imperialism and bourgeois femininity with a critique of the televisual form. In these early videos, Alter argues, Rosler has made "satirical essays that expose television's use as a powerful tool that actively participates in creating and reinforcing hegemonic values"; yet instead of destroying television or redirecting its signal, "Rosler has improved on the clever idea of television and moved it out of stagnation."[21] The imperial violence of the nation and the technological norms of television are thereby twisted from their moorings, and in the same gesture, so too is femininity dislodged.

The same transformations occur in all three volumes of *Service: A Trilogy on Colonization*. But in passing through negation the postcard novels also strive to make something more properly affirmative: the symbolic condition for women's space-time that Buchloh calls authenticity. From the wreckage of imperialism, television, and complicity, there emerges an idea of a sliver of a possibility. From the "apparent impossibility of political commitment and cultural activism within the framework provided by the cultural apparatus," there is adumbrated, without optimism, a potentially less complicit and less technicized kind of life. In the first volume (i.e., the print version of *A Budding Gourmet*), this space-time appears only as a negation. Behind the narrator's imperialist account of cookery is another presence. While parody was the guiding figure of the video adaptation, it is from structural irony instead that Rosler here constructs a seamless rhetorical container.

What's in This Stuff?

The narrator of the first volume is not imperialist only by implication of her classed and national identity, that is, because she is a bourgeois American. She is imperialist because she lays claim to whole continents in her quest for cultural value. She takes a class in Brazilian cooking because her peers have not done so. "Everybody goes to Europe these days, and things there seem so *commercial* in a lot of ways. The people hardly seem natural anymore. . . . But South America, not everybody goes there"—with these lines, Rosler indicts both the mass-mediatized consumer culture and the institutions of the sanctioned avant-garde.[22] Of consumer culture, the narrator deems some parts of the world to be more natural than others based on the degree to which they have already been subsumed and exhibited as flavors available in middle-class US homes. Meanwhile, by favoring less "commercial" objects and affects, the narrator does what art institutions do. Like museums and galleries, she appropriates extrinsic worldly conditions in the name of providing her intimates with new and unfamiliar experiences. Yet for Rosler's narrator as for the institutions of art, new experiences serve not to estrange guests from their daily lives, but instead to reassure those guests in their sense of common background and purpose. Spectators have more in common with each other, because they are spectators, than they have with artists. Similarly, bourgeois American diners may find they have much in common with each other when confronted by the textures and flavors of, say, Brazil. Like ostensibly transgressive artworks, foreign food only appears to complicate middle-class existence, when in fact it renders this existence more secure. The less "commercial" value obtains to something, the more it stands apart from accustomed consumption habits, and the more this unfamiliarity imbues it with a supposedly transgressive value.

Brazilian cooking thus appeals to Rosler's narrator because she can turn it into cultural capital, and she does so in two ways. First, she marks it as virtually uncolonized, and therefore more natural, because it is not yet represented in her culinary lexicon. Second, she may include it among any number of commodities from which she benefits not because they are expensive but because they are new to her, and new to the people she knows. As a category of commodity, it is also endlessly expansive, inasmuch as Brazilian food is not the only cuisine over which the narrator may declare mastery and from which she may extract value. She is eager to assimilate any cuisine whose unfamiliar flavors may stand in for vast regimens of unfamiliar social and cultural practices: "I even do Indian cooking, not just your standard curry . . . but real Indian cooking, and the Indians are extremely spiritual. It's a kind of reverence for the food. The Orientals all have it, Chinese and Japanese too."[23] With this, Rosler closes *A Budding Gourmet.* Unlike her subsequent adaptation of the narrative to video, the print version does not contrast the narrator's bourgeois cultural colonialism with images and data on global hunger. Instead, Rosler pushes her narrator to the absurd limit of her ravenous orientalist taste. In the televisual argot of Child's *The French Chef*, she gives voice to the appropriative sins of domestic prestige. But she does so in an ironic narrative voice that has no outside. Whatever may make for a non-imperialist and non-telecommunicative style of femininity, it is nowhere evident in the print version of *A Budding Gourmet*, yet it is everywhere absent.

McTowersMaid is the fourteen-page second volume of *Service: A Trilogy on Colonization*, and it is here, in a comedic release from the claustrophobic irony of *A Budding Gourmet*, that Rosler charts something like an affirmative political vision. This time, our narrator works in a fast-food restaurant. In a version of McDonald's called McTowers, she is eventually promoted to chef, and from there moves to the night shift. Again the topic is food in its effect upon the labor of women, as the narrator realizes: "I felt like a machine, and my feet hurt from standing so much. And I kept thinking, 'what's in this stuff?' "[24] An awareness of the mechanized experience of her own life here meets with an awareness of the risks of others' consumption. Or rather the two nearly meet, separated by the width of several characters between "standing so much" and "And I kept thinking." Between the narrator's alertness to her own exploitation as a worker and her alertness to the exploitation of consumers, there is a small gap. The remainder of the series of postcards is devoted to bridging this gap.

Crucially, the narrator "felt like a machine." This latter phrase is shot through with a feminist critique of technology that predates *McTowersMaid* by many decades, identifying and rejecting the back-breaking routinization of women's labor. When a woman feels like a machine, on this view, it is because she has become one. Her body has been instrumentalized as if it were a protocomputational form of automation. Flesh and blood, yes, but set in motion as if she were a clockwork device designed for cooking. As Katherine Stubbs notes, Taylorist scientific management was intended to increase efficiency by suiting workplace technologies to the capacities of generic and fungible human bodies; but it was paired with a second discourse of productivity:

> Unlike scientific management's effacement of the bodily specificity of the worker, this other discourse was particularly sensitive to the specificity of a worker's physiology and was therefore easily applied to those bodies that deviated from the white male norm: racially marked bodies, ethnic immigrant bodies, and female bodies. It was this last class of bodies that seemed especially susceptible to the discourse of mechanization.[25]

All of Rosler's narrators, and not only the narrator of *McTowersMaid*, are mechanized in this way. Not interchangeable with one another, they are nevertheless all equally susceptible to becoming automatic machines.

Indeed, by retaining a sense of bodily specificity, the capitalist political economy may instrumentalize different women differently, whether through the patriarchal form of home cooking or through the masculinist industry of food service. But the mechanization is incomplete; a woman is not a machine, and Rosler makes space for other kinds of action than those that have been programmed. As Stubbs notes, this alternative to Taylorism must backfire. By making use of human bodies without erasing their specificity, the mechanization of women fails: "Rather than becoming an abstracted, disembodied citizen, the mechanical female became hyper-embodied as she became mechanized—became, in another operation of duality, more corporeal as she became more artificial . . . [as] the very artificiality of this version of embodiment nonetheless presented some women with a rich construct that could become the means of staging a resistance."[26] Stubbs is describing the turn-of-the-century social thought of Gertrude Barnum, but her argument could just as well describe Rosler's protagonist.

Upon reckoning with the fact that mechanization of her body is concomitant with undernourishment of her customers, the narrator begins to add flavor to her the McTowers burgers. She begins by adding herbs and spices to the burgers, "just oregano, basil, thyme or rosemary or a little lemon peel," before trying out "Japanese miso or Mexican chili sauce if I thought the person could dig it," and finally adding marijuana and "special mushrooms."[27] Her customers are happy, her coworkers learn to like it, but their manager is unhappy; so together "the group decided to take the big step": "We kidnapped the manager and told him we weren't going along any more with the company's miserable policies. . . . We raided his files and finally found out the name of the company that owns McTowers: the giant agriglomerate Corporate Foods. We are preparing to fight! Workers' power!"[28] The narrator's culinary trajectory resembles, in some ways, the trajectory of the narrator of *A Budding Gourmet*. But whereas that narrator had replicated the embrace of individualism and the expansion of US imperialism in her assimilation of "uncommercial" global cuisines, the narrator of *McTowersMaid* instead jumps the gap between her own exploitation and the exploitation of consumers. The expansion from domestic to foreign flavorings, and finally to drugs, leads to a radical collectivism.

Here there is no irony. There are only jokes. But these jokes, a pranksterism that leads to modest revolution, commandeer the basic infrastructure of food provision. In a way that the narrator of *A Budding Gourmet* cannot imagine, the narrator of *McTowersMaid* employs the technologies of humor and food service to open up the possibility, if only the possibility ("we are *preparing* to fight") of "workers' power." She does not contribute to a practice of sabotage that can be replicated in another time and place. But in her own time and place, she effects what Lauren Berlant, in her own writing about infrastructure, has called a "pedagogy of unlearning." In Rosler's postcard novel, what is unlearned is the proper conduct of capitalism: in order to "absorb the blows of our aggressive need for the world to accommodate us *and* our resistance to adaptation and that, at the same time," the narrator's story holds out "the prospect of a world worth attaching to that's something other than an old hope's bitter echo."[29]

Tijuana Maid, the final volume of *Service: A Trilogy on Colonization*, contains neither irony nor humor. But in its own way, it likewise seeks "something other than old hope's bitter echo." It does so in painful earnest, in eleven postcards that tell a story of a migrant woman who travels from a village to Tijuana and from there to California. The migrant woman leaves her children with her sister and gains passage to San Diego by entering into indentured servitude, promising half her first months of salary to the men who help her across. When she gains employment as a home cook, she is handed "a book to study called *Home Maid Spanish Cook Book*. The book said 'Our aim is not to teach the Mexican or Spanish speaking maid how to make her own native dishes. . . . We want to have her help Y O U in the kitchen. To do things Y O U R way.' The book has drawings of an American kitchen with everything named in Spanish. This book also gives recipes for typical American foods, like Hamburger Sandwiches, Hot Dogs, Tuna Casserole, Steak, Meat Loaf, and Apple Pie."[30] The protagonist is assaulted by her employer in San Diego, then after fleeing, by a new employer in La Jolla. She wants safety, and to bring her children, and to retain her mica—her Green Card. She wants to cook Mexican food, and Rosler includes a recipe for "Stuffed Chili Peppers with Sauce for a Party."

This final volume is presented twice: once in Spanish and once in English. It draws together, around a single life, a perspective to technology and to feminine mechanization that is neither fully ideological (as is the narration of *A Budding Gourmet*) or bacchanalian in its resistance (like *McTowersMaid*). Instead, this final narrator is stuck. The technologies of border and kitchen, of abuse by immigration officials and patriarchs, leave both models behind. This final narrator must simply survive. She wants neither cultural capital nor revolution but instead "a job with a family that will let me bring my kids."[31] It is with this final image that Rosler confronts state art. Aside from the appropriations of non-US culture by US chefs, there is the forced application of US cuisine as a technology of control through which to grind non-US chefs. Apart from the naive acceptance or the idyllic transgression of complicit art institutions, there are the lives of those human beings who must simply and pragmatically build their lives otherwise than toward-death. Rosler's person-centered counterpractice lies in the progression from the first narrator to the second to the third—and in the invitation to a spectator neither to love nor to hate the techno-fascist machines of art or war, but simply to understand that dehumanization is their only purpose, and to move beyond them.

Conclusion

When George Rochberg coins the phrase "aesthetics of survival," he is talking mostly about the survival of art that embraces the role of fantasy and takes its distance from both institutional acceptance and dehumanizing technocentrism. Survival, in Rosler, includes this sense. But it also includes the survival of political movements and of human collectives, as these are threatened by techno-fascism. This techno-fascism can take the form of collaboration, as that sponsored by LACMA, between major avant-gardists and the industrial apparatuses of geopolitical control (especially air power) and cultural imperialism. Yet it can also take the form of a less sanguine technocentrism, like Nam Jun Paik's. Against both, the person-centered counterpractices of *Service: A Trilogy on Colonization* insist on cultivating human survival in a very immediate sense: a literal and authentic (in Buchloh's limited use of that word) sense that has no use for state art.

Notes

1. Martha Rosler, "Video: Shedding the Utopian Moment," in *Illuminating Video: An Essential Guide to Video Art*, ed. Sally Jo Fifer and Doug Hall (New York: Aperture, 1990), 39.

2. Martha Rosler, "Post-Documentary?," in *Samuel P. Harn Eminent Scholars Lecture Series in the Visual Arts, 1996–1997* (Gainesville: College of Fine Arts and Harn Museum, University of Florida, 1999), 48.

3. Rosler, "Video: Shedding the Utopian Moment," 46.

4. Rosler, "Video: Shedding the Utopian Moment," 45.

5. Rosler, "Video: Shedding the Utopian Moment," 50.

6. Martha Rosler, "Radical Practice," in *Proceedings of the Caucus for Marxism and Art, 1978* (n.p.: Caucus for Marxism and Art, 1978), 6.

7. Rosler, "Radical Practice," 6.

8. George Rochberg, "The Avant-Garde and the Aesthetics of Survival," *New Literary History* 3, no. 1 (1971): 73.

9. George Rochberg, "Reflections on Schoenberg," *Perspectives of New Music* 11, no. 2 (1973): 57.

10. Rochberg, "Reflections on Schoenberg," 57.

11. Rochberg, "The Avant-Garde and the Aesthetics of Survival," 90.

12. Rochberg, "The Avant-Garde and the Aesthetics of Survival," 77.

13. Martha Rosler, "The Formalist Heritage and Socially Committed Art," PhD dissertation, University of California at San Diego, 1974, 65.

14. Rosler, "Formalist Heritage and Socially Committed Art," 65.

15. Max Kozloff, "The Multi-Million Dollar Art Boondoggle," *Artforum* 10, no. 2 (1971): 76.

16. Judith Barry and Sandy Flitterman-Lewis, "Textual Strategies: The Politics of Art-Making," *Screen* 21 no. 2 (1980): 46.

17. Martha Rosler, *Service: A Trilogy on Colonization* (New York: Printed Matter, 1978), unnumbered first page.

18. Siona Wilson, "The Filmic Mode: Feminist Art Practices and the Avant Garde in America and Britain during the 1970s," PhD dissertation, Columbia University, 2005, 348.

19. Martha Rosler, "On the Public Function of Art," in *Discussions in Contemporary Art, Number One*, ed. Hal Foster (Seattle, WA: Bay Press, 1987), 15.

20. Benjamin H. D. Buchloh, "Documenta 7: A Dictionary of Received Ideas," *October* 22 (1982): 123.

21. Nora M. Alter, *The Essay Film after Fact and Fiction* (New York: Columbia University Press, 2018), 226, 231.

22. Rosler, *Service*, 5–6.

23. Rosler, *Service*, 11.

24. Rosler, *Service*, 6.

25. Katherine Stubbs, "Mechanizing the Female: Discourse and Control in the Industrial Economy," *differences* 7, no. 3 (1995): 141.

26. Stubbs, "Mechanizing the Female," 160.

27. Rosler, *Service*, 8, 9, 10.

28. Rosler, *Service*, 14.

29. Lauren Berlant, "The Commons: Infrastructures for Troubling Times," *Environment and Planning D: Society and Space* 34, no. 3 (2016): 414.

30. Rosler, *Service*, 3.

31. Rosler, *Service*, 11.

Chapter 8

Yayoi Kusama's Immaterial Drive

SHANNON FINCK

Between 1967 and 1971, Yayoi Kusama repeatedly performed, recorded, and altered a piece called *Self-Obliteration*. Opening at the Black Gate Theater, a Lower East Side establishment supporting experimental performance and independent film, and culminating in an outdoor event at SUNY Buffalo's festival for the media arts, Eyeconosphear, this work was among Kusama's last contributions to the New York avant-garde scene. Because several of these performances were documented and featured in her film collaboration with video artist Jud Yalkut, *Self-Obliteration* endures as a unique representative of the sort of work Kusama produced during this time—her period of erotic happenings, anatomic explosions, and stylized antiwar protests.[1] Kusama and Yalkut's film, *Kusama's Self-Obliteration* (1967), is not a conventional documentary on the artist, her process, or this piece as it evolved. It is, rather, an intoxicating romp in 16 millimeter through sexy factory parties that dissolve into the idyllic fields of Woodstock, where Kusama rides a polka-dotted horse. It is grainy, graphic, and utterly utopian. This work captivates, too, for the way it dovetails the gritty, improvisational bent of Kusama's street performances and the polished intricacy of her art environments.

In its initial three-show run, *Self-Obliteration* combined public lecture with live body painting, interpretive dance, a light show, and an amplified chorus of frogs, prodded gently to croak at varying intervals to produce a distorted, atonal score. Each evening's performance was different, amorphous, and abstract, held together by a unified call to action: "Obliterate your personality with polka dots. . . . Self-destruction is the only way to peace."[2] By the time Kusama staged this production on the lawn of Buffalo

State Teacher's College, the show, then in its final run, had morphed into a psychedelic panorama featuring asynchronous projections of Yalkut's film and accompanied, not by frog song, but by the highly accomplished University of Buffalo Percussion Ensemble.[3] Less relies on happenstance in this later iteration, and far less even relies on the artist's direct or immediate participation. The cinematic compilation of serial *Self-Obliterations* and this final performance—live, but largely filmic—signal Kusama's foray into digital media and image-based environments. Where before, her art was a product of intense physical labor, bodily exposure, and Situationist spectacle, the mixed-media works she began creating in the 1970s offered her the opportunity to experiment with dematerialization—a long-standing conceptual interest of hers—in practice as well as theory. Over the next four decades, Kusama embraced emergent technologies in pursuit of further obliterations of self, adapting visual and interactive media in ways that evoked embodied experience without centering the experience of her own body. But these later works—specifically the wildly popular Infinity Mirror Rooms—are, I contend, haunted by a spectral Kusama, a mod ghost in the mirrored machine.

Spanning the 1960s, Kusama's New York period has largely defined her reputation. During these years, she produced career-making works of visual art, such as the Net paintings and Accumulation sculptures. In 1965, she debuted her first Mirror Room, *Phalli's Field*, and her endeavors grew more interactive. Assuming the title of "High Priestess of the Polka Dot," she took her radical message of infinite connectedness from the art gallery to the streets. But by 1973, she had receded from the avant-garde scene altogether, moving herself and her studio to a long-term mental health care facility in Tokyo. There, her work shifted direction from the participatory to the voyeuristic. Before reviving the Mirror Room project, she made a number of whimsical peep-in mirror boxes—small-scale replicas of no longer extant, full-sized mirrored chambers that permit viewers to look inside but forbid entry to the infinity in miniature they contain.[4] This period of subdued reflection hardly marks the end of her career—Kusama remains prolific today—but it does mark the end of an era in which corporeality and tactility dominate accounts of her work. This chapter reexamines the prevailing assumption that Kusama left corporeality and tactility behind in light of encounters with her art environments in the contemporary context of the major-museum retrospective.

In such chronicles of Kusama's career, the period of protest art in the late 1960s and early 1970s functions as both break and hinge. In some ways, her performance work frustrates expectations, disrupting what might otherwise seem to be an orderly evolution of her style, from brush strokes repeated ad infinitum to mirror images reflected ad infinitum. In other ways, it affirms familiar associations between avant-garde aesthetics and twentieth-century political and cultural movements. I return to this work and revisit its history as a means of exploring tensions between Kusama's countercultural legacy and the singular popularity of today's Infinity Mirror Rooms—tensions that recent museum exhibitions tend to minimize as they recast her career in the transfixing light of the Mirror Room installations. Dwelling on these tensions proves integral to understanding a shift in Kusama's interests from the spectacular to the specular—a formal adaptation of the scale and scope of her work addressing the artist's complex negotiation of her own increasingly public figure. Contemporary audiences lured into whitewashed galleries to wait in long lines for the "immersive" experience promised by the Infinity Mirror Rooms find themselves, instead, swept up in a narrative about Kusama's art that is tethered to time, place, and politics, even as it projects infinity. I argue that the present-day fetishization of the Mirror Rooms taps into a common nostalgia for a moment when attending to Kusama's productions involved a more transparent and assertive body politics. The Mirror Rooms offer sites of mourning, in which we remember and preserve the body's function as the seat of experience and a vital medium for protest. In the Mirror Rooms, we discover that we are not quite freed, by distancing or networking technologies, from the desire to exist *in the moment*, or from the body's ways of feeling out and feeling through a fraught moment in history, nor are we ready to part with the promise of inhabiting such a moment.

Bodies That Matter

We may not think of Kusama primarily as a body artist, but she has long been a storyteller of the body's fragility and resiliency. Her first US solo exhibition at the Zoë Dusanne Gallery in Seattle showcased about twenty abstract pieces in watercolor and pastel—a vibrant constellation of speckles, spots, and skeins in which inklings of the magnitude and scope of her later work are visible. These early compositions, described by critics as "intimate" and "organic," play with light, depth, reflection, and repetition, and they establish her signature dot motif, though they do not yet spy the infinite in the infinitesimal. Instead, their province is particulate matter: minute eggs, buds, pores, follicles, the walls of cells, fingerprints rendered as under a microscope. In *Flower QQ2* (1954), a work of pastel, tempera, and ink on paper not much bigger than a standard letter, what looks like an engorged, red thumbprint bleeds into the foreground out of solid, black environs. Serpentine papillary ridges in loops and whorls take shape near the center of the image. If you look at it long enough, the thumbprint appears to recede and then resurface, almost to breathe.[5] The deep, blue expanse of *Inward Vision No. 4* (1954) enfolds delicate shapes that could be roe at the edges of a pond, the disembodied wings of insects, or the foamy bubbles of an amphibious creature surfacing for air—the surface itself not quite like water, but something veined and membranous, like skin.[6] More physical than metaphysical, these pieces reflect the artist's longtime preoccupation with the body's irrepressible tactility.

Kusama's work is keenly attuned to the ways a body can open or close itself off to experience, the ways that a body can say emphatically *yes* or solemnly *no*. On display as part of early exhibitions, too, was a single oil painting called *Accumulation of Corpses* (1950). In it, swirling, golden shapes (the titular corpses) form a vast, ominous, and oddly animate tunnel that threatens to constrict a central, bright white clearing where two leafless trees stand gravely in contrast.[7] These illuminated concrete forms fend off the dark abstractions together, their bare branches intertwined. Often interpreted as a battlefield scene or mass burial site, a visionary depiction of World War II trauma, this strangely corporeal landscape may, in fact, be Kusama's first piece of antiwar art.

Kusama was conscripted to sew parachutes for the Japanese military in her teens. She credits this repetitive, physical labor for the development of both her resistance to biopower and her therapeutic process.[8] At first, she practiced soothing activities, like drawing and painting, to grapple with "the protracted gloom of the never-ending war."[9] Later, these activities became strategies for managing a chronic dissociative condition. In her autobiography, she describes her psychosomatic symptoms in terms of a separation of the soul from the body that renders the senses indiscriminately numb to joy and pain. "Once that happens," she explains:

> I can take hold of a flower . . . without being able to feel it. . . . I have no sense of my body as something real. . . . I am told that when reality is too agonizing, human biology has ways to turn it off, and that this innate defense system is what triggers the condition. But the horrible suffering of depersonalization is

> much greater than the pain of any reality. . . . At least in reality you get a solid sense of the self that is suffering.[10]

To combat this feeling of disembodiment and its accompanying psychic wounding, she recorded the material facts of the world around her over and over, "churning out one sketch after another" of the unfelt flower, the pumpkins in the garden, the Japanese Alps in the distance, the stars in the night sky.[11] This habit gave rise to her obsessional art: the wide nets, macaroni coats, piles of penises, and polka dots—art objects she made and made again, returning to her body in the process. Her work continues to hold space for such triumphant returns.

Perhaps it was painful to her, then, when Sidney Tillim, reviewing the debut of her Net paintings at the Brata Gallery in 1959, wrote up all five immense, belabored pieces collectively as an "art of withdrawal" or "self-effacement."[12] Though it was a glowing review, Tillim appears to have missed Kusama's intent, one that Mika Yoshitake, curator of the 2017 *Infinity Mirrors* exhibition at the Hirshhorn Museum in Washington, DC, would later capture by noting the work's environmental, "wholly corporeal effect," achieved "through the body's relation to the sheer magnitude of the canvas."[13] Where Yoshitake finds gravity and presence, Tillim reads pregnant absence: "What comes through is . . . something like a memory of the place where things used to be rather than a void in which anything can happen."[14] Tempting as it is to interpret these rival criticisms as a case of Tillim getting the wrong answer and Yoshitake coming up with the right one half a century later, it is more likely that the influence of retrospective is at work here. We have come to expect embodiment from Kusama—if not hers then certainly our own.

The Interminable or Infinity Net paintings and their predecessors, large-scale watercolor works like *Pacific Ocean* (1958, 1959), express a nascent inclination toward a classic Kusama maneuver, in which the artist, using the visible labors and machinations of her body, creates an intimate space. In this space, the viewer becomes a participant whose bodily experience is required to coproduce the artwork. In the tradition of feminist body artists like Carolee Schneemann and Hannah Wilke, Kusama "enacts her body in a reversibility of inside and out, the work of art/environment is an enactment of Kusama."[15] Of course, Tillim couldn't possibly have known this in 1959 because there was not, at that point, a pattern to discern beyond the vaguely "sculptural quality" of the five white canvases of the Infinity Nets.[16] We should know it by now: Kusama went on to employ this tactic to much fanfare in her art environments in the mid-1960s, in works like *Phalli's Field* and *One Thousand Boats Show* (1963), and to perfect it, to significantly less fanfare, in her happenings of the late 1960s and early 1970s.

Bodies That Move

Though she would perform *Walking Piece* and *Narcissus Garden* around the same time, the first performance piece that Kusama identified as a "Happening" was *14th Street Happening*, in 1966.[17] The happening repurposed polka-dotted phalli from *Phalli's Field* to construct a soft barrier in the middle of a major thoroughfare, where Kusama lay quietly, disrupting the flow of traffic and commerce. Part excursion beyond the relative safety of in-crowd galleries and part anticapitalist intervention, *14th Street Happening* has the feel, given what follows, of a test of her capacity to make a scene.

The happening for which she gained recognition as a protest artist was an impromptu affair she called *Body Paint Festival* (1967), for which she enlisted a ragtag troupe of hippies to disrupt Sunday Mass at St. Patrick's Cathedral. Her performers were instructed to remove their clothing, so she could paint their bodies, and then to burn American flags in front of the church.[18] As they danced and kissed before a rapt congregation, Kusama stood in the smoke—an antiestablishment apparition dropping draft cards onto the small pyre.[19] There is no official count of precisely how many performances Kusama organized, in the late 1960s, around the themes of free love and peace in New York and later across Europe and Japan; Alexandra Munroe estimates "at least seventy five."[20] Many were photographed, including *Antiwar Happening*, on the Brooklyn Bridge, as well as *Anatomic Explosions*, staged variously at the New York Stock Exchange, the offices of the *Wall Street Journal*, the New York Board of Elections, and in front of the statue of George Washington at Federal Hall (all in 1968). Those photos are now iconic.

These happenings were all as free as the love on display. Kusama's politics were (and remain), by all accounts, somewhat opaque, but they were not for sale. For each performance, she used found objects, volunteer performers, and public space. Neither she nor her troupes defaced public property or incited riots; these were noisy but peaceful protests. "It is true that at each of my Happenings, we broke ten or fifteen different laws," she recalls, "but those laws only represented the ideology of the Establishment, which was essentially irrelevant to my art."[21] Kusama notified the city and the press in advance of the performances via hand-delivered fliers. Anyone was welcome, and anything could happen in the short span of time before the assembly was shut down by the police. Some performances, however, were exclusive scene parties, held at Kusama's Studio or booked at small theaters. Those events were truly evanescent. Their focus was the sexual liberation of the American people—a project Kusama considered integral to the antiwar movement. Again, anyone could come, but participants had a right not to be captured in the act: the media were locked out.[22] The *Self-Obliteration* film contains the only extensive visual record of the love-ins.[23] Discreet though they were, these closed-door or ticketed events were not secretive, serving to promote forms of healing touch, connection, and release that could be practiced individually and in private to, then, radiate out toward a greater public good in the affects of participants, changing the culture.

But the liberatory ethos of Kusama's happenings conceals a thornier relation to embodiment on the artist's part. Public or group nudity proved a tried-and-true method for drawing a crowd, and a certain degree of vulnerability was crucial to retaining one, but, contrary to general misconception, Kusama has never been inordinately forthcoming with her own body. Although she was photographed nude a handful of occasions, she rarely engaged in any of the naked revelry, orgies, or protests she staged.[24] Where and when she chose to appear nude as part of the spectacle, she did so cannily, offering herself less as an object than as a model for the body's interaction with the art environment. Rather than demonstrating having or being a body herself, Kusama studied embodiment and pushed its limits. Her autobiography is frank in its account of her asexuality: "I am a person who has no sex."[25] Instead, she posed and framed bodies. She constructed elaborate theaters for bodies to perform in and made bodies new and strange unto themselves by bathing them in paint and light. Unlike many other body artists at the time, she saw her creative role as that of a "stage-maker" who made fantasy and forms of open-minded expression possible for other people.[26] And while the happenings may stand out for their coincidence with the quirk and kink of the hippie movement, they operate much like any other installation she created, with Kusama an absent presence. The happenings bear her name, her brand—her signature polka dots—and her antiauthoritarian spirit, but they resist baring all.

The twinned histories of nude activism and feminist art that currently situate Kusama's protest work are histories of tactical exposure. Stacy Keltner and Ashley McFarland outline a diverse genealogy of civil disrobings, dressing down a wide array of social justice issues from inequality to climate change.

Women's protest art in the 1960s and 1970s, likewise, used nudity as a way of revealing "culturally produced links" between bodies and their material historical categorization and subjugation.[27] Kusama's democratizing focus on other bodies—for instance, in her queer orgies or mass weddings—aligns her protest work, albeit tenuously, with artists such as Cindy Sherman, Mary Duffy, and Jennifer Miller. Yet, while those artists consider bodies in various conceptual spaces, Kusama performs her body *as* space. This is how Amelia Jones understands Kusama's work: as a series of "scenes to both stage her particularized body/self and express it externally—to spread it over the surrounding environment" until "everything becomes a kind of extended flesh."[28] "These scenes," she notes, "never fully contain Kusama, who performs herself well beyond the mechanisms of art historical and critical analysis."[29] Mignon Nixon theorizes Kusama's physical presence in her work somewhat differently, using a concept called "object-drives." Nixon defines object-drives in art as "objects in which the body is registered rather than represented," delivered instead as a "fragment, effluence, or field."[30] The collapse of the visual frame, a common feature of such works, invites what Nixon describes as "bodily dissolution and excess."[31] Kusama's soft sculptures register the body in this way, as do orgies. In later work, mirrors construct the field, followed by the documentation and distribution of images over the internet. Nixon contends that "the juxtaposition of the serial multiple and the obsessional multiple, the photograph [or the mirror image, or the digital image] and the part object," communicates with viewers at the primal level of the drives.[32] For Nixon, Kusama never fully shows up in her work not because she somehow transcends appearances, but because she's been playfully and pleasurably deconstructed in the process.

Weaponizing pleasure against the ever-present peril of bodily harm or dissolution is a powerful gesture of resistance, especially if one supplies the training ground for others to do so. In Nixon's work, object-drives in women's antiwar art raise the stakes of these pleasurable deconstructions from exploratory performance to uncivil disobedience, shunting the threat of the shattered body back at the opposition, like a cannister of tear gas. In a lecture on Nancy Spero, whose *War Series* (1966–1970) depicted mushroom clouds with sex and digestive organs, covered in their own filth, fluids, and viscera (literal "dirty" bombs), Nixon parses a critical distinction between withdrawing or withholding the body in order to resist the violence of the state and returning to the body with the same objective. Nixon argues that acts of protest wherein persons merely restrict the state's access to their bodies as tools of war (such as draft dodging or combat refusal) can all too conveniently erase the peaceful subject from the social body. For this reason, such tactics have been co-opted to justify some of the most horrifying remote military technologies, many of which are routinely optimized. Drone strikes, chemical agents, and other antipersonnel tactics operate at a remove from military personnel, even as they kill anonymous, often civilian bodies. By minimizing the need for infantry, then, these tactics cunningly oblige protesters who withdraw their bodies.[33]

In contrast, Spero, in her *War Series*, and Kusama, in her happenings, offer visible, viable alternatives to war by "employ[ing] libidinal rather than militant gestures of resistance."[34] In other words, their strategy rests on the simple willingness to *appear* differently. According to Nixon:

> [Kusama's] nude performers claimed their freedom in democratic space but also embodied the vulnerability that public self-exposure exacts. If putting the body "on the line" was a precept of antiwar protesters determined to display the physical courage of soldiers in defying state authority, Kusama and her performers . . . all but mocked the bravado of militancy. Risking ridicule over violence, they exposed themselves to derision . . . [using] ludic tactics to dramatize the absurdity of war.[35]

Nixon's defense of Kusama's protest performances—that they were, indeed, revolutionary acts that "opened antiwar politics to questions of desire" tied, not just to the war in Vietnam, or to any particular war, but to the root cause for war—is the most serious account of the events I've seen. Despite having clear ties to the sexual revolution, the LGBTQ rights movements, and such historic demonstrations of pacificism as the sit-in, the love-in, and John Lennon and Yoko Ono's Bed-In for Peace, Kusama's guerilla performances were, by and large, not taken seriously as art or activism. As a result, as they grew more political, more revolutionary, riskier and more *risqué*, they began to take a significant toll on Kusama's career and health. In her autobiography, Kusama reflects: "The things I did or created were invariably met with misunderstanding and insinuations of scandal. The more serious I was about my work, the worse the friction with the world outside became."[36] Initially, she doubled down on her message of freedom and peace, retaining a lawyer to handle the legal fees she and her nude dancers incurred by taking their clothes off at the United Nations and the New York Stock Exchange, and hiring protection for herself in the wake of physical threats.[37] She got angry. She got arrested. Eventually, she began to lose faith in the political efficacy of carnivalesque explosions, where bodies lit their own erotic charges and deployed their libidinal excess against state-sanctioned violence.

In an essay published in *October* on the cusp of the recent Kusama renaissance, Nixon points out how the coverage of Kusama's happenings, which often appeared alongside news of Vietnam almost as farce, began to "shadow the war news."[38] Her attempts to amplify the antiwar message of these performances through film and television were dismissed by the press as attention-seeking, or evidence that she had sold out. When, after an arrest in Japan and a series of clashes with authorities in Europe, she was hospitalized in Tokyo for exhaustion, the press wrote that the artist had become a victim of her own hippie pandering—her manic quest for mainstream cultural relevance. Nixon is highly critical of this narrative, proposing the more logical alternative that "this artist—born in Japan in 1929, who witnessed the ravages of economic depression, totalitarian militarism, and all-out war (starvation, deprivation, forced labor, aerial bombardment, atomic apocalypse, and military occupation)—actually did feel compelled to voice a moral objection to the relentless carpet bombing of Vietnam."[39] But the headlines minimized this history, foregrounded the anatomic while neglecting the atomic explosivity of the happenings.

Recent interest in Kusama seeks to disentangle this specific moment in the artist's career from its initial reception, but for motives unclear. It could be that, in the twenty-first century, we are beginning to evaluate protest art differently. Jonathan P. Eburne, Amy Elias, and Melissa Karmen Lee, for example, stress the importance of distancing our judgments about protest art from measures of apparent or instantaneous "effectiveness."[40] It takes time to discern the cultural significance of an artistic or political movement, they argue, even if certain acts or actions can be said to be effective in obvious or predictable ways right away (such as unseating a leader, changing a law, or ending a violent campaign). Perhaps recent retrospectives, neatly packaged in what little positive press there was surrounding Kusama's performance art, entail the artworld's public apology. Or, from a cynical standpoint, perhaps museums sponsored by Big Oil and Coca-Cola have merely found a new way to stifle or caricature political art as they profit from art history's sneering and neglect. Whatever the case, contemporary audiences asked to consider Kusama's body of work cannot stand in line inside these institutions, preparing to split their atoms on the polka dot—that symbol of the energy that is in all things, through which we "obliterate nature and our bodies"—without also reflecting on the institutionalized violence of the atomic age.[41] If we take a long view, we notice that Kusama has given as much thought to the body that labors, suffers, and gets blown to smithereens as she has the body that consumes endless macaroni or dissolves in a sea of phalli.

Bodies That Meme

When asked in a 1999 interview what she thought about retrospectives that sought to "reassert her place in the history of art in the 1960s," Kusama dodged the question: "I suppose," she countered, "I would not be able to know how people will evaluate my art until after I die."[42] Museums, however, have not shown a willingness to wait that long. North American exhibitions held in five major cities (Seattle, Los Angeles, Toronto, Cleveland, and Atlanta) between 2017 and 2019, like others before them, were all nominally organized around the 1960s. It seems all but inevitable that the radical possibilities of Kusama's early work would reach us muzzled in the context of contemporary exhibits at museums with corporate donors. But *Yayoi Kusama: Infinity Mirrors*, curated by Yoshitake and premiered at the Hirshhorn, is notable for the way it mines and mourns an embellished history of the Mirror Rooms as fully immersive, experimental art spaces. Moving beyond a melancholic revisitation of the specter of 1960s counterculture, this exhibition's remixing of Kusama's early and late work forms around its own kernel of rebellion.

In the exhibition's catalog, Yoshitake sums up the guiding concept for her presentation of works with the phrase "body memories." The Mirror Rooms, she claims, "demonstrate how the body mediates the world when subject and object are in parity" at "the edge of awareness."[43] The idea seems to be that the rooms would achieve this effect by situating finite experience—twenty or thirty seconds per room allotted to each museum guest—within the Rooms' visually infinite expanses.[44] Once guests stepped outside each room, however, the destabilizing juxtaposition that Yoshitake associates with boundless, atemporal movement was promptly superseded by a fairly linear timeline of Kusama's work. Lines of people moved through the gallery and toward the telos of seeing, photographing, and sharing it all online.

Though the Mirror Rooms have been closely associated with Kusama's 1960s oeuvre, this connection is somewhat mythological. In truth, she created and/or reinvented all of the Infinity Mirror Rooms much later. She is still making them. In *Yayoi Kusama: Infinity Mirrors*, the Mirror Rooms were scattered throughout the gallery, disrupting the chronology presented by the timeline. The paintings, soft sculptures, footage, and media exhibits that surrounded visitors grounded them squarely in a psychedelic setting. Full-color photographs of the anatomic explosions and antiwar happenings adorned the gallery walls where guests milled about on their way to the next hall of mirrors. Among assorted mimeographed and offset-printed fliers for gallery shows and street performances, there was a typescript of her notorious letter to Richard Nixon, inviting him to "calm [his] manly fighting spirit" at an orgy for peace.[45] *Kusama's Self-Obliteration* played on a loop in an adjacent room. Everywhere, Kusama's visage appeared with the heavy eyeliner and it-girl haircut that were fashionable in the late 1960s. Ticketholders were called back to this bygone past, then encouraged to move strictly forward in time through the gallery space, stepping out of time now and then by entering one of the Mirror Rooms.

The exhibition, then, was sequential, but the Rooms ruptured the sequence. In *Time Binds*, Elizabeth Freeman argues that nonsequential temporal arrangements can put the past in dialogue with the present in new and unexpected ways.[46] By incorporating Kusama's contemporary Mirror Rooms into the story told by the greater collection, Yoshitake strove for something like this effect. Brief dalliances in infinity hinted at the pleasures of embodied experience that occurs out of sync with the exhibit's capitalist management of bodies. I read this staging as a slight variation on the theme of Kusama's guerilla love bombs on the Brooklyn Bridge and on Wall Street. Guests exiting the Mirror Rooms, blinking back into an ordinary temporality, carried with them the sense that they had witnessed something they would have liked more freedom to explore. The rest of the exhibition showed them precisely what they felt they were missing—what a body is, in the present, not permitted to do in infinite space. The 1965 installation of *Phalli's Field*, for example, was an open chamber, designed for people to "walk barefoot through the phallus meadow," touching and feeling the stuffed tubers as they "experience[d] their own figures and movements as part of the sculpture."[47] Eikoh Hosoe's photographs of pieces from *Floor Show*, Kusama's first solo exhibition at the Castellane Gallery, capture this aspect of the work, depicting the artist sitting, standing, and rolling around in the plush enclosure, as well as the photographer himself beside his camera, the field of his vision expanded by the mirrors. *Love Forever*, a scaled-down replica of the hexagonal chamber Kusama built in 1966 for *Kusama's Peep Show*, or *Endless Love Show*, was originally envisioned as a room large enough to host an orgy.[48] Moreover, Kusama's own careful management of her image instructs us to search for *her* across the boundless plateau, as though she, the quintessential body performing the ecstasy of infinite space, were an anchor to a place and time we can no longer access within the Mirror Rooms. Pictured frequently with and as part of her art throughout her career, she haunts the environmental pieces especially.[49] It is hard to picture *Phalli's Field* or *Endless Love Show* without her red-jumpsuited form among the phalli or the colored lights.

Today's installations are tightly run little time machines, surveilled and regulated by museum staff. They appear primed, conversely, for conspicuous consumption. Lingering is impossible, contact forbidden. Hardly anything

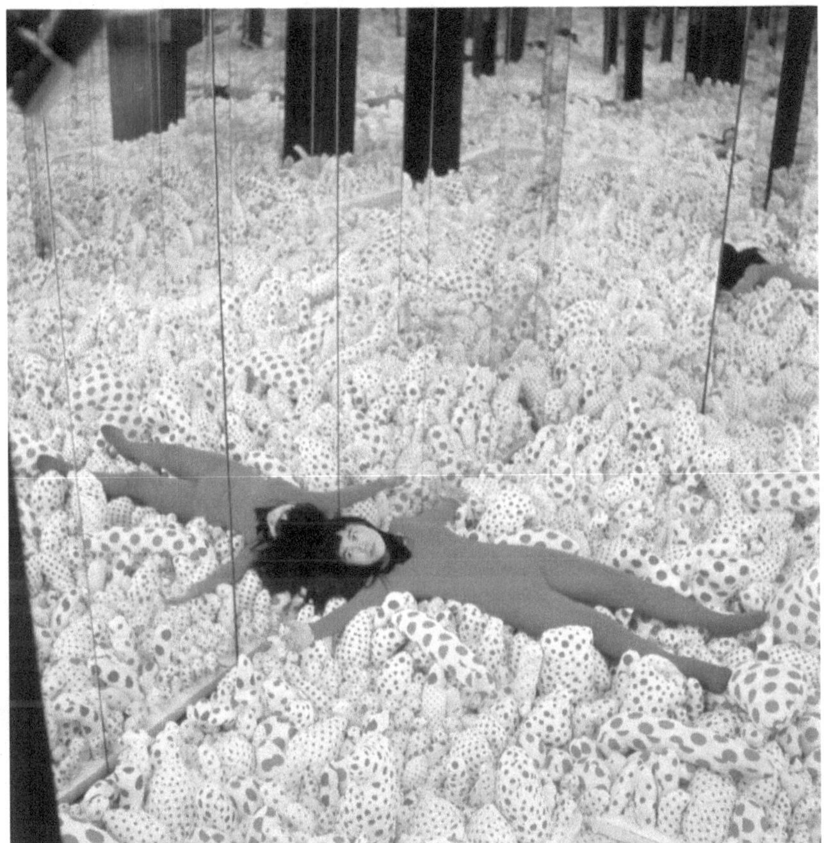

Figure 8.1. Yayoi Kusama poses as part of her 1965 installation, *Infinity Mirror Room—Phalli's Field*, at New York City's Castellane Gallery. Courtesy of Yayoi Kusama, Inc.

can be heard above the din of the crowds. It occurs to most visitors to try and capture the moment by taking a photograph or ten, though this activity has been much maligned in the popular press.[50] Many argue that the latest exhibitions are victims of their own success. Reviewing Kusama's most recent US exhibition, *Every Day I Pray for Love*, open for just one month in 2019 at the David Zwirner Gallery, Jason Farago writes, for instance:

> You needn't be Dr. Freud to diagnose that the narcissism of a new selfie-devoted public has canceled, utterly, the goals of self-obliteration that Ms. Kusama intends her infinite installations to achieve. The self cannot dissolve when the selfie is the goal.
>
> And the erotic or psychedelic excesses of Ms. Kusama's early art are long gone, too. In her orgiastic "body festivals" of the 1960s, she encouraged audiences to slather one another with paint; now others must be cropped out of the cameraphone frame. Sex and drugs are nothing compared with the thrill of "likes."[51]

An obvious problem arises when so much renewed interest in Kusama's work insists that "the body's phenomenological encounter with space is central" while most of the contemporary exhibitions offer structured spectacles, the body struck dumb and then brusquely ushered along.[52] No wonder the confused responses that these exhibitions have garnered are less about the way the body remembers than the way we remember the body's role in the cultural and artistic movements of the late twentieth century.

Denied access to a conventional "erotohistoriography," Freeman's term for "the conscious use of the body as a channel for and means of understanding the past," bodies move through these ethereal spaces governed by what appears to be a shallow drive toward photographic reproduction and digital redistribution via social media, a compulsive *I was there*-ism.[53] The accusations of narcissism—ours, Kusama's—are the same as they have always been. But what if there isn't really that much difference between extended flesh and expanded cinema? What if the selfie is the pleasure we take? Freeman reminds us that "erotics . . . [traffic] less in belief than in encounter, less in damaged wholes than in intersections of body parts."[54] On the one hand, a seconds-long dip into each art environment expressly prohibits a "deep dive" and, thus, produces longing for a mostly fictive past when Kusama's work was made for plumbing such depths. On the other hand, the unruly proliferation of amateur images across social media adds a layer to the work.

The infiltration of the museum as capitalist space by the digital commons so resonates with Kusama's bust-out movements on Wall Street and at other centers of commerce that the negative press feels pat. "How does a gathering become a 'happening?'" Anna Tsing asks; "One answer is contamination."[55] Tsing contends that, in many contexts, contamination evinces life, art, movement beyond capitalist regimes. In this particular context, Gloria Sutton proposes we understand the "replication of forms or structures through digital techniques" as akin "to the way that Kusama uses analog techniques of repetition and patterning to construct a . . . representation of subjective experience."[56] Sutton points out that the arc of Kusama's career reveals a migrating interest from "the modernist viewing subject" and firsthand experience toward "communication networks" and virtual extensions of empirical knowledge.[57] In other words, the promise of human connection underwriting Kusama's work in the 1960s resurfaces in the newer installations and reinstallations via the gradual accumulation of images that both fragment the work in isolated acts of "selfie-obliteration" and compose it, using the internet as a kind of infinity net to gather them all.[58]

The digital age changed Kusama's process indelibly. She has been vocal in her belief that "avant-garde artists should use mass communication as traditional painters use paints and brushes," as an experimental medium in which to create as well as circulate cutting-edge work.[59] Moreover, she insists that online platforms offer "new forms of being-in-common" that are no less

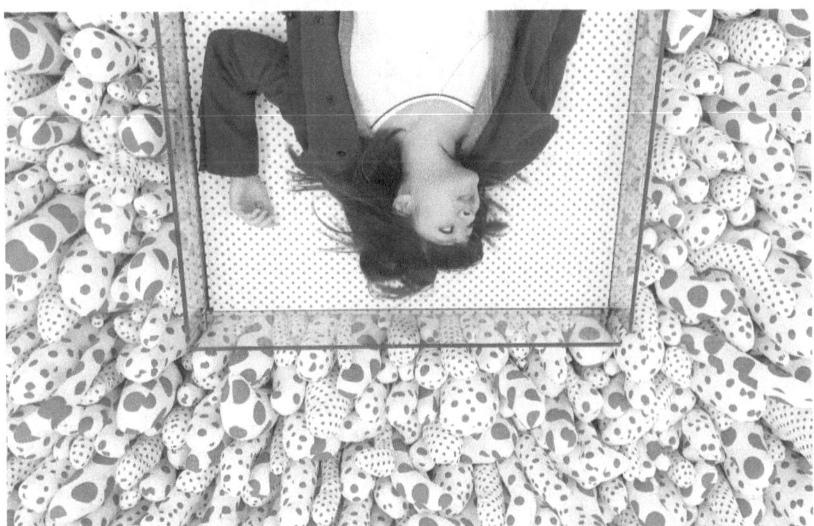

Figure 8.2. Doan Phan poses in a 2017 installation of *Phalli's Field* at the Hirshhorn Museum and Sculpture Garden, Washington, DC. Photo by and courtesy of Kevin Cruz Padilla.

transformative for their being ubiquitous and user friendly.[60] It makes sense that Kusama, obsessed with the elegant simplicity of the polka dot, would turn her attention to the pixel. But is this gesture political? Is it even personal? Is it original? Is It Art?[61] Eyal Amiran, critical of Kusama's strategic use of "the influencing machine" to publicize her work, argues that "in the networked age, the exhibition of the exceptional body is almost an empty gesture" when compared to infinite reproducibility of the image.[62] Amiran's cautious "almost" strikes me as precisely the province and the promise of Kusama's work. Because, if something is *almost* empty, then it isn't empty. A trace lingers—a reminder of the exuberant worlds within and between bodies: the minute eggs, buds, pores, follicles, the walls of cells, fingerprints rendered as under a microscope, speckles, spots, and skeins, and now data. The smithereens.

Kusama has lately returned to painting this exquisite matter. *Infinity Mirrors* collected a number of these recent paintings in an anteroom where visitors waited to enter the exhibition, as an opening overture to the work within. Juxtaposed with the liminal space they occupy, the paintings, massive and arresting, offer yet another example of the way recent exhibitions dramatize, despite themselves, a kind of recalcitrant corporeality. Visitors are made aware of their movement's regimentation right away, as they are already cordoned in line, headed elsewhere, when they realize that they have only just begun to take in the works before them. Kusama's latest work, which so clearly looks back on her earliest representations of vast and vibrant worlds unseen, loops time in a way that reveals the contrivances of the retrospective tasked with contextualizing infinity. Perhaps the cleverest feature of *Infinity Mirrors* is the way that Kusama, a living, working artist who has been fiercely critical of the deathliness of US museums, has managed to stage a spectacularly immaterial resistance to her own memorialization therein. She calls upon the public once again to appear, awaken, assemble, and thereby determine her legacy.

Notes

1. Jud Yalkut, *Kusama's Self-Obliteration*, dir. and perf. Jud Yalkut and Yayoi Kusama (New York: Film-Makers' Cooperative/New American Cinema Group, 1967), 16 millimeter.

2. Yayoi Kusama, quoted in Al Van Starrex, "Naked Happenings," *Man* (October 1968): 45.

3. This performance is described at length in Gloria Sutton, "Between Enactment and Depiction: Yayoi Kusama's Spatialized Image Structures," in *Yayoi Kusama:*

Infinity Mirrors, ed. Mika Yoshitake (Munich: DelMonico Books, 2017), 148–149.

4. See Yayoi Kusama, *Mirrored Room—Love Forever No. 2* and *Mirrored Room—Love Forever No. 3*, in *Yayoi Kusama: Infinity Mirrors*, figures 4 and 5.

5. Yayoi Kusama, *Flower QQ2*, in *Yayoi Kusama*, color plate 3.

6. Yayoi Kusama, *Inward Vision No. 4*, in *Yayoi Kusama*, color plate 5.

7. Yayoi Kusama, *Accumulation of Corpses (Prisoner Surrounded by the Curtain of Depersonalization)*, in *Yayoi Kusama*, figure 3.

8. Midori Yoshimoto, *Into Performance: Japanese Women Artists in New York* (Piscataway, NJ: Rutgers University Press, 2005), 46.

9. Yayoi Kusama, *Infinity Net: The Autobiography of Yayoi Kusama*, trans. Ralph McCarthy (Chicago: University of Chicago Press, 2012), 70.

10. Kusama, *Infinity Net*, 87.

11. Kusama, *Infinity Net*, 62.

12. Sidney Tillim, "In the Galleries: Yayoi Kusama," *Arts* 34, no. 1 (1959): 56.

13. Mika Yoshitake, "Infinity Mirrors: Doors of Perception," in *Yayoi Kusama*, 21.

14. Tillim, "In the Galleries," 56.

15. Amelia Jones, *Body Art/Performing the Subject* (Minneapolis: University of Minnesota Press, 1998), 8.

16. Yoshitake, "Infinity Mirrors," 20.

17. Kusama, *Infinity Net*, 100.

18. It remains unclear how much, if any, body paint this performance actually included. Official records kept by Kusama Inc. confirm the use of body paint at theaters and at *Body Paint Festivals* at Tompkins Square and Washington Square that year.

19. Resonances between this early happening and ACT UP (AIDS Coalition to Unleash Power) and WHAM's (Women's Health Action and Mobilization) cosponsored, nonviolent direct action "Stop the Church" warrant mentioning. "Stop the Church," which took place at St. Patrick's Cathedral in 1989, paired a "die-in"—challenging the archdiocese's general position on sex education and more pointed silence on the rising number of AIDS victims—with an exuberant celebration of the life of the body in the form of a ticker tape parade of condoms and literature on safe sex and reproductive health. Binding these protests across time is the underlying message that the answer to senseless death is persistent, vibrant living.

20. Alexandra Munroe, "Obsession, Fantasy and Outrage: The Art of Yayoi Kusama," in *Yayoi Kusama: A Retrospective*, ed. Bhupendra Karia (New York: Center for International Contemporary Arts, 1989), 29.

21. Kusama, *Infinity Net*, 109.

22. In her autobiography, Kusama clarifies that "prominent professional men" and sometimes their wives attended her orgies. See Kusama, *Infinity Net*, 135.

23. In addition to Kusama's accounts of the sex happenings, collected in her autobiography, scholarship that pieces some of these events together includes Laura Hoptman's and Alexandra Munroe's essays in *Love Forever: Yayoi Kusama, 1958–1968*

(Los Angeles: Los Angeles County Museum of Art, 1998); Mignon Nixon, "Anatomic Explosion on Wall Street," *October* 142 (2012): 3–25; Laura Hoptman, Akira Tatehata, and Udo Kultermann, eds., *Yayoi Kusama* (London: Phaidon, 2000); Frances Morris, ed., *Yayoi Kusama* (London: Tate, 2012).

24. A notable relaxation of what evidence suggests was a firm boundary regarding her own public nudity took place at a *Bust-Out Happening* in Central Park in 1969, where Kusama stripped with artist Louis Abolafia to kick off his mayoral campaign. Her choice to do so on this occasion was overtly political. See Kusama, *Infinity Net*, 139.

25. Kusama, *Infinity Net*, 109.

26. Chris Rainone, "The New Nudism: A Skin Freak Testifies," *Rogue*, August 1969, 59.

27. Stacy Keltner and Ashley McFarland, "Women, Party Politics, and the Power of the Naked Body," *Counterpunch*, August 31, 2016, https://www.counterpunch.org/2016/08/31/women-party-politics-and-the-power-of-the-naked-body/.

28. Jones, *Body Art/Performing the Subject*, 8.

29. Jones, *Body Art/Performing the Subject*, 8.

30. Mignon Nixon, "After Images," *October* 83 (1998): 120.

31. Nixon, "After Images," 120.

32. Nixon, "After Images," 129.

33. Mignon Nixon, "Sperm Bomb: Art, Feminism, and the American War in Vietnam," Public Lecture, The Courtauld Institute of Art, London, United Kingdom, April 17, 2012.

34. Mignon Nixon, "Anatomic Explosion on Wall Street," *October* 142 (2012): 15.

35. Nixon, "Anatomic Explosion," 15.

36. Kusama, *Infinity Net*, 192.

37. Yoshimoto, *Into Performance*, 32–33.

38. Nixon, "Anatomic Explosion," 10.

39. Nixon, "Anatomic Explosion," 13.

40. Jonathan P. Eburne, Amy Elias, and Melissa Karmen Lee, introduction to "Rules of Engagement: Art, Process, Protest," special issue, *ASAP Journal* 3, no. 2 (2018): 173–185.

41. Yayoi Kusama, quoted in Melissa Ho, "Chronology and Plates," in *Artists Respond: American Art and the Vietnam War, 1965–1975*, ed. Melissa Ho (Princeton, NJ: Princeton University Press, 2019), 121.

42. Grady Turner and Yayoi Kusama, "Yayoi Kusama," *BOMB* 66 (1999): 62–69. An earlier version of this section was previously published in *ASAP/J* under the title " 'We Will Never Meet Again / Nor Part Ways': Dematerializing Yayoi Kusama," May 9, 2019, http://asapjournal.com/we-will-never-meet-again-nor-part-ways-dematerializing-yayoi-kusama-shannon-finck/.

43. Yoshitake, "Infinity Mirrors," 32.

44. Time limits in the Mirror Rooms varied some from museum to museum, but they were invariably brief. I saw the exhibition at the High Museum in Atlanta, Georgia, where this was the range.

45. Yayoi Kusama, "Open Letter to Richard Nixon," November 11, 1968, in *Yayoi Kusama*, ed. Laura Hoptman, Akira Tatehata, and Udo Kultermann (London: Phaidon, 2017), 106.

46. Elizabeth Freeman, *Time Binds: Queer Temporalities, Queer Histories* (Durham, NC: Duke University Press, 2010), 3–4.

47. Kusama, *Infinity Net*, 51.

48. This room did, in fact, hold an orgy that was televised in Germany. See Kusama, *Infinity Net*, 100.

49. Kusama was known to collage herself into photographs of her work and her studio in which she did not originally appear as well. See Yoshimoto, *Into Performance*, 65–66.

50. The most infamous account of selfie-taking in the exhibits as poor form involves an "influencer" who dropped a smartphone onto a glass pumpkin and smashed it to bits, temporarily closing *All the Eternal Love I Have for Pumpkins* to other guests and leading to a wholesale ban on photography in that room. This story has been repeated so often that the details vary significantly. It is hard to say now whether it happened at all.

51. Jason Farago, "Kusama Arrives. Is It Worth Your Time to Wait in Line?," *New York Times*, November 9, 2019, https://www.nytimes.com/2019/11/08/arts/design/yayoi-kusama-review-david-zwirner.html.

52. Yoshitake, "Infinity Mirrors," 14.

53. Freeman, *Time Binds*, 95.

54. Freeman, *Time Binds*, 13.

55. Anna Lowenhaupt Tsing, *The Mushroom at the End of The World* (Princeton, NJ: Princeton University Press, 2015), 28.

56. Sutton, "Between Enactment and Depiction," 140.

57. Sutton, "Between Enactment and Depiction," 140.

58. The first use of the term *selfie-obliteration* to describe the synthesis of Kusama's art with social media appears to be Priscilla Frank's "Selfie Obliteration: How Yayoi Kusama Invented the Photo-Friendly Art Show," *Guardian*, October 21, 2015, https://www.huffingtonpost.com/entry/yayoi-kusama-selfies_us_562687ede4b08589ef493823.

59. Munroe, "Obsession, Fantasy and Outrage," 30.

60. Jo Applin, "'I'm Here But Nothing': Yayoi Kusama's Environments," in *Yayoi Kusama*, ed. Frances Morris (London: Tate, 2012), 191.

61. "But Is It Art?" was the title of a brief news article on one of Kusama's biggest and most well-attended happenings, *Wake the Dead*, held at the Museum of

Modern Art. *Wake the Dead* challenged the institution of the American museum to include more work by living artists, though the article merely reports on "nudies" at the museum. See Kusama, *Infinity Net*, 140.

62. Eyal Amiran, "The Pornocratic Body in the Age of Networked Paranoia," *Cultural Critique* 100 (2018): 151.

PART III

COMMITMENTS

Chapter 9

Sandinista!

The US Avant-Garde's Response to Central American Upheavals in the Long 1970s

Javier Padilla

I.

I start this meditation on avant-garde United States poetry and "Third World" politics with an apology. The wording of the apology is from Lewis Mumford, and its occasion was the beginning of World War II, but I think it summarizes a general malaise in our post-Trump contemporary world. "There have been times during the past few months when I felt that I must apologize to myself, if not to this audience," Mumford writes, "for undertaking to divert their thoughts, even for a brief hour, from the disasters which now impend over the entire world: disasters whose scope is so vast and whose ultimate results may be so tragic to the human race at large, that few of us, even the most far-sighted, even the most vigilant, have fully taken them in."[1]

By recuperating Mumford's words, I am evoking not only Anthropogenic climate change, global pandemics, and habitat collapse but also the resurgence of what Walter Benjamin understood as the aestheticization of politics, though we must not blush from calling it what it is: fascism, pure and simple. Of course, this has long been in the offing in US politics. Already in 1987, Jerome McGann, in "Contemporary Poetry, Alternate

Routes," would speak of postwar US poetry as existing within an arena marked by the "collision of imperialist demands with the isolationist politics and revolutionary nationalism of American ideology."[2] Echoing McGann, I address, in what follows, the problem of US poetic subjectivity vis-à-vis the Marxist-inspired Central American struggles of liberation, which took place roughly from the late 1970s to the late 1980s, in countries like Guatemala, El Salvador, and Nicaragua. My aim is to limn what is valuable in both the personal poetry of witness and the poetics of the avant-garde.

II.

This initial apology is colored by the fact that the main subject of this essay is situated within the realm of aesthetics, specifically those areas of discourse that, as W. H. Auden has said, make nothing happen. I am referring of course to poetry and poetics. In order to foreground what concerns us here I would like to offer a series of questions:

1. What, if any, was the response of US avant-garde poets to the series of revolutions and wars that took place in Central America during the late 1970s and early 1980s? In other words, what was US poets' response to the insurrections in what has pejoratively been called "America's backyard"?
2. What political relations link the detached experimentalism of the Language school to the "poetry of witness" exemplified by the work of Carolyn Forché and her direct involvement in Central America?
3. Is the avant-garde a kind of aesthetic luxury not available to countries ravaged by neocolonial wars in the periphery of capital?

And finally:

4. What can these areas of exploration teach us about the politics of contemporary poetry?

III.

But first I would like to step back and offer some remarks, which I hope will illuminate the title of my intervention.

My title, of course, evokes the title of The Clash's 1980 album *Sandinista!* I also chose this title out of a fascination with the way this word—which comes from the Nicaraguan guerrilla group's adoption of Augusto C. Sandino's anti-imperialist politics—has morphed into a suffix in the English language. We often hear terms like *fashionistas* and, more recently, *Trumpistas*. It is worth pausing here to provide some historical background. For the majority of the twentieth century, countries like Nicaragua were basically ruled by dictators who served at the pleasure of the US. In the case of Nicaragua, this meant a dynastic dictatorship led by the Somoza family. By the 1970s, the Sandinista guerrilla became sufficiently organized to topple the Somoza regime, so that in July 1979 a socialist coalition could take over the country. The US responded by initiating a low-level war of sabotage against the Sandinistas, which culminated in their funding of the Contras in late 1980s. In some sense, the suffix *-ista* is the only linguistic sediment that Nicaragua's 1979 revolution has left on the English language. It seems odd to find what for many Nicaraguans is a central historical experience turned into an ornamental linguistic frisson. This should start signaling major themes in the reflection that follows, namely, the way this suffix signals the fraught nature of political witness in transnational poetry, as well as how signifiers become unmoored from their matrices of political signification—concerns very much at the heart of the Language poets' endeavor.

IV.

While the US avant-gardes were concerned with matters of form and post-structural experimentation, the bulk of Latin American poets were engaged in what became known as *poesia comprometida*, which can be loosely translated as "poetry of commitment." There are complex genealogical questions embedded in this statement, however, since Hispanic poetry took a different route than its Anglo-European equivalent. Indeed, what in Spanish-speaking countries is referred to as *modernismo* is actually known in Anglo-European circles as symbolist poetry or art nouveau. Vanguardismo, on the other hand, is equivalent to modernism in Europe and the US.

These genealogical differences aside, it is not surprising that Latin American poets found themselves writing poetry of witness or social justice. Simply put, their lived circumstances foreclosed what was imagined elsewhere as a pure focus on avant-garde experimentation. Indeed, throughout the twentieth century, as the US consolidated its role as imperial hegemon, it proceeded to install favorable dictators and topple leftist governments. For instance, in Chile, the US toppled the democratically elected government of Salvador Allende on September 11, 1973. The US also toppled the democratically elected government of Jacobo Arbenz in El Salvador and installed a dynastic dictatorship in Nicaragua. Consequently, the 1970s and 1980s were "long" in this region because they were marked by horrible violence, war, famine, and imperial abuse. How could poets like Claribel Alegría in El Salvador or Ernesto Cardenal in Nicaragua turn to so-called experimental poetics when their countries were being burned to the ground? Put another way, is the avant-garde as conceptualized by the Language poets and other schools the luxury of metropolitan centers?

I don't believe that this distinction—between poetic experimentation and political commitment—is apposite, and while one would not call the aesthetically formalist poetry of US writer Carolyn Forché "avant-garde" in the strict sense, it was certainly innovative and strategic in the military sense: she used her visits to El Salvador and her engagement with Alegría as a platform on which to write politically informed poetry on a subject about which the majority of US poets remained completely silent.

Perhaps this can begin to sketch the uneven, relational cultural politics between Central America's convulsive history and US poetry. On the one hand, in a North to South direction as it were, appears the influence of Thomas Merton and Ezra Pound on the poetry of Ernesto Cardenal, the Nicaraguan Catholic monk turned revolutionary intellectual. And on the other, and from South to North, appears American poets' response to the Sandinista revolution of 1979 and the Salvadoran civil war, which raged from 1979 to 1992. Beyond Forché's 1981 poetry collection *The Country Between Us*, about her time in El Salvador, the response from the US avant-garde, particularly the Language poets, has been mostly muted. The silence from the Language poets is particularly ironic, given that their antinarrative concerns with Marxist form and the politics of meaning structures in late capitalism would seem to be a fruitful site from which to elaborate an anti-imperialist poetics. An important exception to the Language coterie's silence can be found in the poetry of the late Hannah Weiner, specifically her experimental poetry *Weeks*, about which I will have more to say shortly.[3]

V.

An anecdote in Robert Pinsky's 1984 lecture "Responsibilities of the Poet" can help us draw the contours of this irony. "A critic, a passionate writer on poetry culture and politics," Pinsky writes, "once said to me, 'When I ask American poets if they are concerned about US foreign policy in Latin America, they all say yes, they are. But practically none of them write about it: why not?' "[4] Pinsky offers an evasive answer:

> The desire to see, and the desire to feel obliged to answer, are valuable, perhaps indispensable parts of the poet's feelings about the art. But in themselves they are not enough. In some way, before an artist can see a subject—foreign policy or any other subject—the artist must transform it: answer the received cultural imagination or the subject with something utterly different. This need to answer by transforming is primary; it comes before everything.[5]

Put another way, a poet does not go about and say, *I will write about the American-backed dictator Somoza in Nicaragua and the 1979 revolution that toppled his regime*, because, Pinsky suggests, the poet must first find an aesthetic mode that transforms this historical occurrence. Although the author's language is obfuscating and evasive, Pinsky's emphasis on transformation strikes me as the right one: the poet must indeed respond from a place of difference. A less charitable way of putting it would be that, for Pinsky, a poet must first be *inspired* to write about this event—a conception that brings to mind a thoroughly conservative notion of poetry and poetics.

Pinsky is well aware of this incipient conservatism. As he notes elsewhere, "This is one answer, the great conservative answer, to the question of what responsibility the poet bears to society. By practicing an art learned from the dead."[6] Pinsky makes a clear allusion to what concerns us here in a subsequent paragraph that veers into the paradoxical dialectic of writing poetry in contemporary society:

> To put it simply . . . we have in our care and for our use and pleasure a valuable gift, and we must answer both for preserving it, and for changing it. . . . Since there is no way to say what evidence will seem pressing to a given artist—Central America, the human body taking care of one's paraplegic sister, theology,

> farming, American electoral politics, the art of domestic design—no subject is ever forgiven. Society depends on the poet to witness something, and yet the poet can discover that thing only by looking away from what society has learned to see poetically.

It is felicitous that Pinsky mentions Central America, insofar as it suggests that the subject was very much in the political atmosphere of 1984. Central America is wedged into a list of possible poetic subjects—"no subject is ever forgiven." But poets are constrained by tradition, and their mediation, Pinsky believes, should not sacrifice innovation in the name of a political, documentary impulse. Both impulses are important and intertwined, or as Pinksy himself puts it later, "What poets must answer for is the unpoetic."[7] Beyond this paradoxical concept of the poet's task, I am attracted to a single phrase in Pinsky's meditation, namely, "to witness." Pinsky's vision for the poet's task is indebted to Forché "poetry of witness"; "We must use the art," Pinsky claims, "to behold the actual evidence before us. We must answer for what we see."[8] It is to Forché's poetry that I turn next.

VI.

There are a number of issues with Forché's poetic endeavor. Indeed, her project—what she calls a "poetry of witness"—has been attacked as politically naïve at best and manipulative at worst. In an original and critical reading of Forché's endeavor, Patrick F. Durgin argues that as a paradigm, poetry of witness "reinscribes conventional humanist subjectivity."[9] Durgin frames such a concern for the human and the discourse of humanism as aesthetically conservative, and the drive toward a posthuman poetic idiom has been understood as progressive. For Durgin, modernists like Gertrude Stein and other forebears like Allen Ginsberg, George Oppen, and John Cage "employ the very formal modes Forché cites in opposition to the subjectivity with which she identifies literary witness."[10] In other words, for Durgin, while Forché's political impulse to "witness" might be laudatory, her formal poetic strategies and poetics are nonetheless regressive—they ignore the aesthetic developments brought about by poets like Stein, Ginsberg, and Oppen—since they do not problematize the idea of personhood, which is key to a poetry that seeks to witness the suffering of others. This is an altogether reductive understanding of Forché's poetry, however, and in what follows I offer a more nuanced understanding of her politico-aesthetic project.

Let us consider one of Forché's poems about her travels in El Salvador, during that country's civil war. The poem is titled "The Visitor," and it is dated 1979, a key year in the Salvadoran conflict, one that marked the beginning of the civil war. Forché begins:

> In Spanish he whispers there is no time left.
> It is the sound of scythes arcing in wheat,
> the ache of some field song in Salvador.[11]

The poem is altogether formal—the shadow of the sonnet haunts it—and its scansion is almost iambic. But what is most important here is the complex negotiation of voices. The figure who "whispers," we are led to assume, is a Salvadoran man held prisoner. What complicates the poem is the presence of his "wife's breath" outside the prison, which seems to erase the limits of personhood between the prisoner and the visitor. In other words, while the poem is formal, its conclusion destabilizes not only the line between prisoner and visitor but, more poignantly, the line between "Third world subject" and "Western observer." "Where does the jail end in a generalized conflict?" the poem seems to be asking, though it offers no resolution, with the last line—"There is nothing one man will not do to another"—a lament for the extent to which human beings are capable of mutual destruction.

Other philological issues structure the way we read the poem. The poem appears in the first section, "In Salvador, 1979–1980," of a poetry collection titled *The Country Between Us*. This section of Forché's book is marketed as "a series of poems about El Salvador, where Forché worked as a journalist and was closely involved with the political struggle in that tortured country in the late 1970s."[12] The description reinforces the idea of Forché as a Western observer of a "Third World" conflict. In other words, it highlights the thorny politics of witness during the long 1970s, wherein Western journalists and intellectuals traveled South to "witness" the atrocities that Western countries themselves were sponsoring. Yet Forché's case is exemplary, since she not only traveled to El Salvador but also forged close connections with the Salvadoran poet Claribel Alegría.

VII.

Which brings us to the question of political tourism, always a danger for metropolitan poets visiting so-called "Third World" countries.[13] It is a hazard that also plagues the project of the Language poets. Oren Izenberg highlights this vulnerability in his critique of the Language poets and their collaboration with Soviet (or "Second World") writers through the poem *Leningrad*. As Izenberg writes, the Language poets' "attempt to theorize and to practice this poetics of community may be compelling as desires, but their analyses and poems are hobbled by simultaneous and contradictory commitments to absolute constraint and absolute freedom."[14] Put another way, and in a manner that echoes Pinsky's conclusions, there is a disjunctive moment here between the Language coterie's formal allegiances to community and their incapacity to see beyond a constrained idea of radical individualism. In a sense, they remained locked in a Cold War logic that relegates former colonies to the "Third World."

Izenberg's critique brings us to the case of Nicaragua. Ernesto Cardenal has boasted that US poets by and large supported Nicaragua's sovereignty and socialist political aspirations. Yet, of all the poets contained in the influential 1960 anthology *The New American Poetry*, only one, Lawrence Ferlinghetti, would go on to speak on behalf of the Sandinista revolution.[15] As Ferlinghetti writes in his travelogue *Seven Days in Nicaragua Libre* (1984), when an American journalist questions him about the purpose of his visit, he answered:[16] "I see it as a voyage of discovery, hoping to discover the Sandinistas are in the right and that I might take some public stand on their favor rather than the political silence maintained by many US writers today."[17] Elsewhere in the same travelogue Ferlinghetti is more eloquent about the Nicaraguan situation:

> What has happened here, rather, is the overthrow of a tyrant (Somoza) supported by the US, and the attempt to overthrow the economic tyrant of colonialism in which Latin America has been for centuries the cheap labor market for North American and multinational business. It is not so much a revolution as it is a crisis of decolonization in a poor country the size of the San Francisco Bay Area in population, devastated by U.S. financed war, desperately short of supplies, attempting to set up some kind of "democratic government."[18]

Ferlinghetti's emphasis on decolonization is particularly apt: before the 1979 uprising, Nicaragua was a de facto colony of the US.[19] Importantly, Ferlinghetti is guided through Sandinista Nicaragua by Ernesto Cardenal, and while his memoir is interesting in several ways, I believe it ultimately fails as a political intervention. This is partly because Ferlinghetti's prose is haunted by the specter of the travelogue—it infantilizes the Nicaraguan uprising, making him what I would call a mere Western *political tourist* of the war-torn Central American countries. Yet, what is interesting is that in the long 1970s *all* transnational projects and modes of cultural exchange between metropolitan and peripheral poets are marked by this political imbalance.

VIII.

It is interesting to note as well that while the Sandinista revolution led to triumph in 1979, it was by no means the end of an internecine conflict that stretched from 1979 to 1989. Here, again, we get an inkling into why the 1970s were "long" for Central Americans. The US-sponsored Contras and the Sandinista government battled a bloody civil war that left thousands dead and many more displaced. Ironically, we see here another reason why US audiences might be somewhat familiar with Nicaragua: the Iran-Contra affair, in which the Reagan administration was involved from 1985 to 1987. This conflict offers further context for Ferlinghetti's engagement with the region as well as for *Weeks*, a defiantly experimental poetry collection written by Language poet Hannah Weiner in 1986 and published in 1990.

Before delving into Weiner's groundbreaking project, we should consider the politics of witness vis-à-vis the aesthetics of Language poetry. In "Post-Language Poetries and Post-Ableist Poetics," Durgin offers an elucidating summary:

> Language poetry involved a generalized politics of constructivist insights that we might think of as logical corollaries to coterminous civil rights movements concerning race, gender, ethnicity, and, yes, disability rights, among others. It is in this revised, formal sense of "witness" that I hope to disclose the relevance of newer practices that take these tenets as their point of departure.[20]

It is beyond the scope of this essay to consider the "newer practices" (namely, the poetry of Laura Moriarty) to which Durgin alludes, and yet his sense of the relation between Language poetry and the politics of witness opens up new ways to consider the supposed division between the more "formalist and humanist" endeavor of the poetry of witness, and the "inhuman" poetry of the avant-garde. *Weeks*, I will contend, shatters this dividing line.

Echoing Durgin's definition of "witnessing as 'participatory engagement with the present triggered by mutual witnessing of a textual event,'" Daniel Morris describes the genesis and ars poetica of Weiner's *Weeks*:[21]

> In *Weeks*, Weiner anchors her fifty-week diary based on her experience of sitting in front of the TV set in her Manhattan apartment in 1986 while transcribing a cacophony of pithy, if disturbing tidbits gleaned from local and national news programs. . . . An inchoate zone of consciousness, Weiner shapes (and is, reciprocally, shaped by) a mesmerizing onslaught of transmissions announcing what news anchors and reporters have framed as notable happenings going on outside the poet's apartment.[22]

Whereas Forché and Ferlinghetti visit the so-called Third World to "see for themselves" and to serve as US witnesses to the Nicaraguan and Salvadoran conflicts, Weiner does not presume such ambassadorial aspirations. Her poetry stays behind, ensconced in the metropole, immersed in the white noise of her television set. In so doing, Weiner's project suggests that the politics of witness, insofar as it tends to fetishize presence, ends up reifying its subjects. As Morris argues, *Weeks* "recollects local mayhem and global disaster by upsetting the binary distinction between public and private space."[23]

In "Week 8" of *Weeks*, Weiner transcribes the following:

> Charges both men with racketeering and conspiracy   Free of the clubhouse types   As the days fold into weeks   We assume that everyone is a darn crook   Russell Means got shrapnel wounds in his belly in Nicaragua   Bill Means is going to Geneva   Conditions of life for Spanish women prior to 1936 were oppressive and repressive in the extreme   Flooding has long been a problem   It denied shooting down a passenger plane   I like you to come down hard on caution   Did you know that some foreign wines could be hazardous to your health[24]

The excerpt exemplifies the reading experience afforded by *Weeks*. It is a deluge of the dialect (or jargon) of the news, with its sense of the urgent and infotainment, as well as half-heard phrases of weather reports and advertisements—the supposedly tragic with the ridiculous and the comic. And in the midst of it all, Nicaragua glimmers like an aberrant presence in the poet's reference to Russell Means (the libertarian Native American activist), injured in combat with the Sandinistas.

Towards the beginning of "Week 11," Nicaragua returns to Weiner's television set, twice. First:

> For several years, the press printed only the official story
> of army-URNG confrontations under the threat of government
> censorship Today, the URNG actions are too big for the press
> to ignore despite continuing government threats they also
> threatened Nicaraguan President Daniel Ortega if he visited
> Guatemala for the inauguration Don't you know, black is
> beautiful An alleged co-ed sex ring in a carriage house
> Obviously those weapons are weapons of intimidation One
> policeman on drugs is one too many[25]

And a couple of lines after:

> One
> suitable phrase leaves no hope Why are there places where
> some thing is not happening The president was taking his own
> shots at the Nicaraguan government The Soviets dismissed
> the invitation as propaganda Neither of us is satisfied
> A grieving widow says a final goodbye All the good things
> that he did for Queen's County We have a system that boasts
> of presuming innocence[26]

Embedded in the news—serious and whimsical—is Central America, both Nicaragua, and, in the reference to URNG, Guatemala. Like other countries in the region, Guatemala was convulsed in a protracted civil war between a US-supported right-wing government and the left-wing Guatemalan National Revolutionary Unit (URNG). The president in question here is Reagan, whose administration fueled the conflicts in the Central American region. The Nicaraguan Sandinista leader—Daniel Ortega—also makes an appearance in the midst of refrains redolent of the 1980s: "black is beautiful," the war on drugs. Weiner leaves all of these tidbits untranslated, which creates the feeling of being awash in a deluge of information and visual stimulation that leaves both speaker and reader unmoored. A question without a question mark stands out: "Why are there places where some thing is not happening."[27]

Nicaragua—Guatemala—Ortega—URNG—they are empty signifiers, mere geographical husks that do not "mean" and become decontextualized, unmoored in Weiner's television. Perhaps here we have a truly horrifying, yet honest, form of political witness, which goes a long way toward showing how the US anesthetizes its own citizens to the chaos it provokes as the world's hegemon. Unlike Ferlinghetti and the authors of *Leningrad*, who get lost in the supposed immediacy of the Anglo-European traveler, Weiner's project foregrounds instead the filter through which she sees the "Third World"; her poetics is shot through by its own inadequacies. In Morris's capacious formulation, "*WEEKS* troubles conceptions of personhood. [Weiner] mashes up, without erasing, inner and outer realms in a text that is paradoxically lyrical and post-humanist."[28]

IX.

I close this meditation on the response of US poets to the Central American revolutions of the 1970s by considering how US poetry's isolationism continues to be present in contemporary cultural production. Indeed, it seems to me, especially in the Trump era, that US poetry is stuck in the Scylla and Charybdis of its role as a global hegemon and the isolationism of an insular and individualistic culture. Or, in more broadly aesthetic terms, between the lure of the personal and the experimental.

That is, I read the debate between writers of color like Cathy Park Hong and Language poets like Charles Bernstein as a not-so-productive way to move beyond this tension between the American "home" and the larger world on which it has an outsized effect. I need not rehash Hong's argument, as it is discussed at great length in the introduction to the present collection, but a 2018 essay by Bernstein in defense of the avant-garde has its own limitations. Bernstein seeks to redeem the avant-garde in ways redolent of Weiner's project: "Judging as 'elitist' poetry that challenges the status quo of anhedonic rationalization and expressive normalization is a right-wing stink bomb in Leftish clothing."[29] And yet, the words "right-wing stink bomb in Leftish clothing" are, in the end, as reductive as Hong's argument, and Bernstein's later claim that "the relation of poem to autobiography is metonymic rather than representational" and that "it is indexical, not iconic, to use Charles Sanders Peirce's terms," does not clarify matters.[30]

My aim in this regard is to limn what is valuable in both the personal and the experimental. There is much to recommend in Forché and Ferlinghetti's strategies, insofar as they used their outsized role as US poets to call attention to the conflicts in Central America, the bulk of which were financed by the US. Their strategies are not without their problems, to be sure, since as political tourists they sometimes use or reify the conflicts themselves. Weiner's strategy, while on the surface diametrically opposed to Forché's poetry of witness, nonetheless foregrounds how "news about the world" is mediated by US media: how a poet watching television in her Manhattan apartment in New York city receives news about conflicts in Central America. Although it might seem to impose an unnecessary distance between the poem and its political subject matter, such mediation nonetheless describes the relation between the US poet with the outside world with unflinching honesty.

To conclude, I deem it necessary to go back to the very roots of the avant-garde, namely, its military etymological provenance, as the vanguard force of an invading army. Simply put, exciting experimental poetry like Weiner's *Weeks* should be both tactical *and* strategic, and I believe that Northern poets like Weiner, Carolyn Forché, or Lawrence Ferlinghetti, who learn from the Global South, and a Southern poet like Ernesto Cardenal, who turns the troubled modernist poetics of Ezra Pound into the service of revolution and social justice, can serve as beacons descrying new horizons for poetry and culture in this convulsive early twenty-first century. In the words of Amiri Baraka, a US poet who knew how to engage with the broader world, and who embraced both the personal and experimental: "Save all that comrades, we need it."[31]

Notes

1. Lewis Mumford, *The South in Architecture: The Dancy Lectures, Alabama College 1941* (New York, NY: Harcourt Brace, 1941), 4.

2. Jerome McGann, "Contemporary Poetry, Alternate Routes," *Critical Inquiry* 13, no. 3 (1987): 624.

3. I am indebted to Juliana Spahr for calling my attention to Weiner's oeuvre.

4. Robert Pinsky, "Responsibilities of the Poet," *Critical Inquiry* 13, no. 13 (1987): 423.

5. Pinsky, "Responsibilities of the Poet," 423.

6. Pinsky, "Responsibilities of the Poet," 424.

7. Pinsky, "Responsibilities of the Poet," 426.

8. Pinsky, "Responsibilities of the Poet," 425.

9. Patrick F. Durgin, "Post-Language Poetries and Post-Ableist Poetics," *Journal of Modern Literature* 32, no. 2 (2009): 162.

10. Durgin, "Post-Language," 162.

11. Carolyn Forché, *The Country Between Us* (New York: Perennial Library, 1981), 15.

12. Forché, *Country Between Us*, 60.

13. I am indebted to Leonel Delgado Aburto for this felicitous phrase.

14. Oren Izenberg, *Being Numerous: Poetry and the Grounds of Social Life* (Princeton, NJ: Princeton University Press, 2011), 38.

15. Donald Allen, *The New American Poetry, 1945–1960* (New York: Grove Press, 1960).

16. The essay is anthologized in Lawrence Ferlinghetti, *Writing Across the Landscape: Travel Journals 1960–2013* (New York: W. W. Norton, 2015).

17. Ferlinghetti, *Writing Across the Landscape*, 293–294.

18. Ferlinghetti, *Writing Across the Landscape*, 291–292.

19. For the history of US involvement in the region, specifically in Nicaragua, see *Michel Gobat, Confronting the American Dream: Nicaragua Under Imperial Rule* (Durham, NC: Duke University Press, 2005).

20. Durgin, "Post-Language," 163.

21. Durgin, "Post-Language," 159, quoted in Daniel Morris, *Not Born Digital: Poetics, Print Literacy, New Media* (New York: Bloomsbury, 2016), 23.

22. Morris, *Not Born Digital*, 23.

23. Morris, *Not Born Digital*, 26.

24. Hannah Weiner, *Weeks* (West Lima, WI: xexodial editions), 14.

25. Weiner, *Weeks*, 14.

26. Weiner, *Weeks*, 19.

27. Weiner, *Weeks*, 19.

28. Morris, *Not Born Digital*, 27.

29. Charles Bernstein, "The Body of the Poem," *Critical Inquiry* 44, no. 3 (2018): 582.

30. Bernstein, "Body of the Poem," 582–583.

31. Amiri Baraka, "Pres Spoke in a Language," in *SOS: Poems, 1961–2013* (New York: Grove Press, 2014), 179.

Chapter 10

The Making of New Narrative

Gay Liberation and the Poetics of Revolutionary Agency

David W. Pritchard

New Narrative writing emerged in the San Francisco Bay Area in the late 1970s. This emergence is typically understood as a response to the work of another Bay Area avant-garde: the Language poets. But the seeds for New Narrative were sown at least a decade before Steve Abbott coined the term "New Narrative" in a 1981 issue of *Soup* magazine. In this essay I will explore how New Narrative's poetics in the later 1970s are shaped by the radical uprisings of the New Left and the onset of a global economic crisis in the late 1960s. In particular, I will show how the founding writers of New Narrative carry forward a vision of revolution as a large-scale transition out of capitalism from the heroic period of Gay Liberation during these years—a vision that registers in their various poetic experiments. By "transition out of capitalism," I mean a simultaneous struggle against alienation and construction, in and through that struggle, of a dis-alienated, postcapitalist—that is, communist—lifeworld. A central part of this struggle is the creation of what Alberto Toscano has called a "totalizing temporal imaginary" capable of grasping the linkages between various constituents of an overall transitional process as it expands and unfolds in space and time.[1] My contention is twofold: first, New Narrative unfolds around the project of creating such a transitional imaginary; and second, we can see this project more clearly when we approach New Narrative's work in light of the politics of the early 1970s.

To make my case I will examine "Karate Flower," a long poem by Bruce Boone from 1973 that anticipates the aesthetic and political concerns of New Narrative proper. It does so through its aggressive use of parataxis: the juxtaposition of disparate particulars through the removal of subordinating conjunctions. In "Karate Flower," parataxis is a means for Boone to speculate about revolutionary agency—that is, the potential or capacity of a collective actant to set itself specific tasks and achieve them as part of a broader revolutionary process.[2] I will approach this device through the lens of Boone's critical work on the pre-Stonewall poetics of Frank O'Hara. In an essay from the early years of New Narrative, Boone argues that O'Hara uses parataxis to construct an oppositional gay language; this language both registers the contradictions of gay life in the years leading up to the Stonewall uprising and anticipates that uprising, out of which arose an explicit form of gay collectivity. Drawing on this argument by way of analogy, I will read Boone the same way he reads O'Hara. Thus, "Karate Flower" is to New Narrative what O'Hara's poetry is to Stonewall—but where O'Hara seeks to hide or encode antagonism in order to survive, Boone articulates it openly. In a word, Boone uses parataxis to think historically from within a revolutionary process: to periodize the emergence of Gay Liberation, to link that emergence to the flowering of other anticapitalist struggles around the world in this same conjuncture, and to look ahead to the consolidation of different struggles into a unified revolutionary front capable of overturning capitalism once and for all.

"Karate Flower," then, concerns revolutionary consciousness in a situation of economic crisis. By studying this pre- or proto–New Narrative work from this vantage, I aim to establish the relevance, if not the centrality, of political commitment to the collective project of New Narrative. And I hope to model a reading practice that is sensitive to the interplay of literary experiment and political militancy, with which we can read the major works of New Narrative's first wave afresh.

The Making of New Narrative

My immediate aim in this essay is to contribute to an emerging scholarly conversation about New Narrative. But I also want to ask a broader question about avant-garde poetics in North America the late twentieth century. How does New Narrative change the way we see this poetics? How does their work fit (or not) into existing critical accounts of the avant-garde? Critics of New Narrative have tended to answer these questions in terms of the group's relationship to Language poetry. This has yielded a series of remarkable insights into the debates about aesthetics, politics, and the avant-garde that shaped North American poetics in that period. But most of these insights have been insights into Language poetry. For instance, Kaplan Harris has shown how New Narrative's ideological critiques of formalism influenced Language poets such as Bob Perelman and Ron Silliman to rethink their blanket denunciations of narrative and other forms of more conventional representation throughout the 1980s.[3] From another angle, Rob Halpern contends that New Narrative and Language poetry actually pursue the same end via different means. Both groups, that is, share a critique of the "transparency of the word [and] self-evidence of the voice."[4] They simply diverge on the question of what literary mode or genre is best suited to advancing this critique. In both these cases, studying New Narrative doesn't change much about how we understand this moment's avant-garde poetics. If anything, it reaffirms our critical common sense about the centrality of Language poetry and reiterates the very approach to the avant-garde that excluded New Narrative in the first place. We read New Narrative to broaden and deepen our account of Language poetry's "politics of form"; we incorporate New Narrative's critique of Language poetry into that account; but we do not undertake the same kind of substantive exploration of New Narrative—either in light of Language or more generally.

Why this critical imbalance? One reason is that critics tend to rely on the opposition between aesthetics and politics in order to distinguish between Language poetry and New Narrative. This opposition is drawn from debates within Marxist theory in the first half of the twentieth century about the historical avant-garde—debates that both the Language poets and New Narrativists took up in the course of formulating their respective poetics in the late 1970s and early 1980s.[5] But critics have tended to ossify the distinction between aesthetics and politics, hardening this contradiction into a binary opposition that we can use to classify interventions. Thus we have Language's avant-garde aesthetics on one side, and New Narrative's identity politics on the other; or, in a variation on this theme, Language poetry carries on the tradition of aesthetic modernism, and New Narrative champions a revival of social realism. Vexed to begin with, this distinction between aesthetics and politics borders on preposterous when applied so reductively to writers like these, whose aesthetic and political commitments are so deeply intertwined.

Examining the relationship between Gay Liberation and New Narrative moves us beyond this ideological impasse, by locating the question of aesthetics and politics within the context of a revolutionary situation. This requires us to think about radical culture in a completely different way. Rather than categorize artworks, we study the way writers involved in a revolutionary process sought to construct an oppositional cultural bloc. When we read New Narrative in this light, we see how questions about form and representation—that is, questions about aesthetics—arise in the midst of a broader anticapitalist struggle. Poetry and poetics can make themselves useful to revolution by taking up these questions; writing becomes a weapon in the fight for the future, rather than a decorative garnish of a more authentic politics. This is the view offered by Chicago Gay Liberation's 1970 manifesto, "Working Paper for the Revolutionary People's Constitutional Convention," which, in succinct terms, introduces us to some of the major questions and problems that New Narrative addresses in attempting to construct such a cultural bloc:

> We see culture not as the output of a few great men and women, but as a possession of all people and as activities (whether sports, hobbies or arts) which all people can participate in. In spite of the restrictions homosexuals have, in fact, become artists, athletes, writers, but the masses of homosexuals have had no benefit from this fact. We have had to depend on the ruling elites who have taken over our talents and used them for their own profit, like the Kennedys who decorated their court with Gore Vidal. This is an expropriation of our cultural resources. We refuse to entertain them any longer with "camp" for their profit.[6]

Nothing here suggests a concern either with the politics of form or with an identity-based political call for gay representation, let alone asks us to choose between aesthetics and politics. Instead, we find a totalizing demand for sexual self-determination in and through culture, with non- or trans-identitarian motivations: the participation of all people in activities that all people possess. If the immediate purview of that demand is identity, its horizon is solidarity among different identities. This way of seeing culture is a direct result of a revolutionary situation of the sort in which Gay Liberation appeared and developed, and which, later in the 1970s, would give rise to the poetics of New Narrative.

Gay Liberation and New Narrative

"Gay Liberation" refers to a diverse constellation of movements, institutions, and organizations that emerged in the wake of the Stonewall riots in New York City in 1969.[7] The point of consistency among these groups is the central place they accorded to demands for sexual self-determination. But consistency and unity are not the same thing. Like many other mass movements in the 1960s and 1970s, Gay Liberation was internally contradictory. It was contoured by capitalism's uneven geographical developments—which were exacerbated by the onset of a global economic crisis during these same years. The poetics we associate with New Narrative grew out of the most militant strains of Gay Liberation: those which sought to connect their struggles around sexuality with other struggles for liberation, such as those involving race, gender, and colonialism. Third World Gay Revolution's manifesto, entitled "What We Want, What We Believe" and modeled explicitly on the famous "Ten Point Program" of the Black Panther Party, is a striking example of this kind of commitment: "We each organize our people about different issues," write the authors, "but our struggles are against the same oppression, and we will defeat it together."[8] What makes these strains "militant" is not their affinity with one current of radical thought or another but their commitment to the basic principle of anticapitalist solidarity among oppressed groups. Thus, the most potent expression of the era's militancy in the United States was the massive antiwar movement that railed against imperialist adventures in Vietnam. Again we can cite Third World Gay Revolution: "We want all Third World and gay men to be exempt from compulsory military service in the imperialist army. We want an end to military oppression both at home and abroad."[9]

What is the connection between New Narrative and these communist currents of the New Left? For one thing, the three writers who founded New Narrative—Steve Abbott, Bruce Boone, and Robert Glück—all participated in a variety of demonstrations, protests, and events associated with Gay Liberation between 1968 and 1973. Steve Abbott even helped to found a chapter of the Gay Liberation Front (GLF) in Atlanta in 1970.[10] Later in the decade, Boone and Glück joined or corresponded with radical organizations that grew out of the ashes of the GLF in the Bay Area, such as the Lavender and Red Union (an avowedly Marxist-Leninist organization) and Bay Area Gay Liberation.[11] All the while, the future New Narrativists wrote and published extensively. Bruce Boone in particular wrote dozens of poems that appeared in movement-related publications like *Gay Sunshine* and *Sebastian Quill*. These are mostly empirical observations. But they gesture to a vast amount of reading, writing, and discussion among the future New Narrativists and their many comrades. What's more, they also locate this flurry of activity in the midst of a broader revolutionary process.

"Karate Flower" is a crucial piece of this pre–New Narrative writing. It was published as a standalone chapbook by James Mitchell's Hoddypoll Press in 1973.[12] I focus on this poem for two reasons. First, it is a clear anticipation of New Narrative writing later in the 1970s; second, it stands to teach us something new about New Narrative proper's theoretical and aesthetic investments, in the way that it takes up and interrogates the problem of historical transition. Why transition? The year the poem was published holds a key to this question: 1973, after all, is frequently identified as the beginning of the global economic crisis often referred to as the long downturn.[13] This moment is also the high water mark of the New Left and Boone's involvement in it. Indeed, while he was writing "Karate Flower," Boone was reading Lenin and attending the meetings of the Progressive Labor Party, a Marxist-Leninist organization.[14] Meanwhile, the revolutionary enthusiasm that marked the early years of Gay Liberation was undergoing a series of transformations as militants sought to work through the contradictions within their ranks and continue their struggles for self-determination—a process that ultimately gave way to a period of uncertainty and disorganization, which was ended only with the appearance of an organized political response to AIDS in the middle of the 1980s.

"Karate Flower," then, sums up the militant experiences of Gay Liberation and the New Left more broadly at the very incipience of the long downturn, and it orients itself toward the possibility of renewing revolutionary struggles against capitalism during the crisis-ridden mid-1970s. Boone records this dialectic of past and future struggles through his aggressive use of parataxis in the poem. Parataxis refers to the removal of subordinating conjunctions and connective tissue between disparate particulars in a text. This device enables Boone to metabolize a historical transition from the standpoint of revolutionary agency. In other words, Boone employs parataxis to formalize a model of revolutionary consciousness in "Karate Flower." This, in turn, aligns his work with a broader genealogy of avant-garde poetics, in which, as critics have shown, parataxis plays a key role in the articulation of political commitments in literary form.[15]

On the other hand, there is a more specific avant-garde sequence at stake for Boone in the years of Gay Liberation. This sequence is represented by some of the gay poets featured in Donald Allen's pathbreaking 1960 anthology *The New American Poetry*: Frank O'Hara, Jack Spicer, Robert Duncan, and Robin Blaser. In the heyday of New Narrative in the later 1970s and early 1980s, Boone writes a series of critical essays about these poets, examining their work for its registrations of the pre-Stonewall contradictions of gay identity. The longest and most systematic of these essays is about the politics of parataxis in the work of Frank O'Hara. Entitled "Gay Language as a Political Praxis: The Poems of Frank O'Hara" and published in *Social Text* in 1979, this essay offers an account of how nonnarrative compositional strategies function in subaltern communities in what Boone, following Frantz Fanon, calls "pre-revolutionary" situations. For Boone, gay life in pre-Stonewall New York is just such a situation, and O'Hara's paratactic poetics is an example of an oppositional language: the kind of language practice that springs up among the oppressed in the lead-up to an open confrontation with the oppressor.

Boone's essay on O'Hara can help us understand how Boone himself uses parataxis in "Karate Flower." It also models a reading practice for us, embodied by the concept of oppositional language, that looks at the articulation of poetic form and historical transition: a reading practice, in other words, that can help us see how New Narrative grew out of the contradictions of Gay Liberation—just as Gay Liberation emerged out of the contradictions of gay life prior to the Stonewall rebellion.

What is an oppositional language? In the most basic sense, it is a language that masks or codes its content in some way so that it can address multiple audiences simultaneously. Boone draws on the work of Valentin Voloshinov and Frantz Fanon (and, more indirectly, that of Antonio Gramsci) to describe this process of coding in terms of the way that a subaltern intellectual, "speaking not only his or her own language but the language of the imperialist oppressor also, . . . produces a kind of text in which the oppressor's language represses his or her own by rewriting it."[16] This creates a "dilemma" for the intellectual that is "both personal and existential," whose "solution calls for a violence experienced as both literal and figurative."[17] In O'Hara's case, the group is gay men; the "dilemma" is the contradictory situation that prevailed in the 1950s and 1960s, in which, as John D'Emilio succinctly puts it, "the danger involved in being gay rose even as the possibilities of being gay were enhanced."[18] This contradiction, of course, eventually sharpened into a riot at the Stonewall Inn. But in O'Hara's poetry it is always mediated in a way that gives us the impression that something is being hidden from us—which leads Boone to speak of a "gay subtext" in O'Hara's work.

In Boone's reading, oppositional language never appears in a "pure" form. It takes shape through clashes between different sociolects and levels of discourse, where a given utterance clandestinely "calls up and relates, or narrates, a community."[19] Oppositional language, then, is always reflexive about its own disjunctions. It invites the reader to make the connections it doesn't. Which is where parataxis comes in. Parataxis effects the "displacement of connectives" that creates the possibility for a subaltern group to attain self-consciousness—that is, to see itself as an oppressed group with an antagonistic relationship to the social totality—while remaining hidden from people outside of that group. These displacements do not exist in some fixed quantifiable form; they are historically mutable and change with the situations that give rise to them. Boone summarizes:

> The gay community of O'Hara's period is gone. We have construed it from its artifacts—and among these the poems of O'Hara himself. And we have read in the texts produced by that community (or more accurately, "pre-community formation") a meaning of opposition that stems from a more politicized, later period. To be sure history itself has polarized these texts and, whether we like it or not, given them a partisan sense.[20]

Oppositional language is thoroughly historical. Thinking through O'Hara's parataxis allows Boone to periodize the development of revolutionary consciousness in the years before its open articulation in Stonewall and the formation of Gay Liberation. The concept of oppositional language, then, allows Boone to grasp the historical transformation of a subaltern *subculture* into an antagonistic *counterculture*—a transformation that registers the emergence of revolutionary consciousness in a particular group—as it registers in O'Hara's poetry.

This brings us back to "Karate Flower." Boone wrote and published this poem in the midst of the counterculture that O'Hara anticipated, so we cannot expect to find the same kind of linguistic displacements in "Karate Flower" that we do in O'Hara's work. On the other hand, both Boone and O'Hara register a process of historical transition in their writing. The concept of oppositional language can thus serve as a guide to how Boone uses parataxis to think about transition, in a threefold sense. First, Boone traces the historical transition that gave rise to something like a "gay community" itself—the transition away from family-centered petty production to industrial capitalism. Second, he responds to the transition within capitalism represented by the crisis of the long 1970s, which entails, among other things, the shift from the pre-Stonewall moment of O'Hara's poetry to the openly revolutionary situation of Gay Liberation. And finally, Boone raises the question of a possible transition out of capitalism altogether, from the standpoint of the potential agent of that transition.

Sincerity, Militancy, Crisis

The title of "Karate Flower" is a good place to start thinking about the parataxis that the poem will unfurl across its nine restless pages. The construction "karate flower" has no clear referent. It juxtaposes karate—a disciplined practice of self-defense that can entail a whole habitus or way of living—with a flower, a common, even clichéd poetical subject, possibly connoting nature or beauty. How do we understand this juxtaposition? On the one hand it could symbolize reification, the reduction of "karate" into a thing: a "flower." This brings to mind a host of Orientalist commodities that threaded their way through the radical movements of the 1960s in the United States, leading in some cases to the affirmation of racist "New Age" spiritualisms among (primarily white) New Left radicals.[21] On the other hand, the phrase "Karate Flower" could allude to the adoption of the language of "faggotry" by revolutionary gay men's organizations in the Bay Area beginning in 1973. Self-defined faggots sought to distance themselves from the more reformist strains of Gay Liberation; according to Emily Hobson, they held that "normative constructions of masculinity underlay violence and imperialism and that gender must be transformed to allow nonoppressive self-expression."[22] If "karate" signifies this militant queer stance, the name of the poem might also signal a radically antiracist and anti-imperialist commitment and highlight the relationship between struggles against normative masculinity and the struggles of Third World revolutionaries.

Boone begins "Karate Flower" by furnishing this dialectic of global capitalism and revolutionary agency with specific historical coordinates. The first stanza prepares us to read the rest of the poem; it teaches us to "notice" the lineaments of radical agency encoded in paratactic constructions. Boone deploys the same paratactic devices here that he will later identify in Frank O'Hara's poetry. But where O'Hara hides sexuality in plain sight, suppressing the referents of activities like cruising and sex in public in the name of queer survival, Boone repurposes O'Hara's formal strategies in order to align the desire for queer survival with anticapitalist politics. In this way he registers a transition away from O'Hara's pre-Stonewall moment into a situation of open queer revolt. He also raises a classical Marxist question: what kind of revolutionary agency might emerge from within the fully alienated lifeworld of capitalism? The scrambled narrative devices that open "Karate Flower" articulate this question and give us a sense of what kind of reading practice might help us puzzle out its answer.

> Oil, that's what I admire, to run the machines.
> And gasoline with a cleanliness like war.
> But there is another part of me, the grandfather
> who made chocolates. When I was young I plucked
> bonbons like roses or anything ridiculous
> you choose to admire. And I admired the beautiful.
> Then the shot rang out. It was the archduke
> or it was a president I hated. There were wars
> and I kept quiet and waited a very long time.
> Sincerity does not necessarily go unnoticed.
> Now I wear a gun.[23]

In the penultimate line here, Boone announces (if you could call it that) his commitment to the historical trope of oppositional language. He does so by using parataxis to highlight the role of readerly agency in the cultivation of revolutionary consciousness. The line renders a way of seeing ("noticing") that requires us to supply the referent that Boone has displaced for "sincerity." It does so by calling attention to the materiality of individual words on the page through the use of internal rhymes across grammatical negatives (sincerity/necessarily; go/un*no*ticed). The grammar itself is surprisingly difficult, as well: the phrase untangles into something like "sincerity can be noticed." We are made to wonder: *Whose* sincerity does not necessarily go unnoticed *by whom*? The answer is that we, Boone's readers, notice sincerity, through our close reading of this line of his poem. We notice the curious placement of the line in the stanza, just before the deictic "now" places us in the present; we notice the curious abstraction of the noun "sincerity," as well as its formal link with "necessarily" via rhyme; we notice the double negative of the grammatical arrangement of the line, as well as the arrangement of the words on the page. What's more, in doing all this noticing we begin to notice our own attentiveness to language as a kind of agency that the poem's form convokes.

Which leaves us with sincerity itself. How do we understand this vexing concept? How can we pinpoint its ideological content? Here, the splitting function of oppositional language comes into play, asking us to choose between two possible readings of sincerity. In the first, more familiar, reading, sincerity is a fundamental component of the ideology of bourgeois lyric poetry. In that context, it refers to a solitary speaker's feelings and insights: the richness, texture, and above all authenticity of their interior responses to and interpretations of some external stimulus or experience. We could certainly try to read "Karate Flower" along these lines, but I suspect we would end up disappointed. Boone is quite arch about the raw materials he brings together in "Karate Flower"; he seems to flaunt the whole question of "sincerity" as a tone, theme, or content. Moreover, lyric sincerity tends to presuppose a narrative arc: the speaker has an experience, then reflects on that experience. No such progression takes place in "Karate Flower." In this stanza we notice an insuperable gap between Boone's speaker and the events spoken about, even as those events appear to affect the speaker and carry him along a developmental trajectory. Boone empties narrative form of its temporal contents; he negates narrative agency through the use of passive constructions (it *was* the archduke; it *was* a president; there *were* wars). This all culminates suddenly in the "now" of the final line, which suggests the terminus of a subjective transformation from a bourgeois child into a "militant" subject (and not, I hasten to add, in a necessarily revolutionary way: reactionaries and revolutionaries alike can carry guns, and this could as easily refer to being drafted—another passive construction!—as it could to joining a revolutionary organization). So much for a lyric reading, then.

What about the second reading of sincerity? If we approach it as a collective rather than an individual comportment, we begin to see how this poem addresses itself to people who are already committed to revolutionary transformation. From this perspective, the whole penultimate line formally encodes a question about the capacities of the revolutionary subject. Once the conditions for a "sincere" revolutionary struggle exist, we can notice them, in the same way we notice the rhyme between "sincerity" and "necessarily." This doesn't translate immediately into revolutionary subjectivity; some form of organization is required to activate the potential embodied by a historical situation. The literary labors of the poet, scored by his arrangement of words on the page, figure the political activity of organizing. Sincerity, then, takes its place alongside the other kinds of subjective judgments made by the speaker in these lines—admiration, hatred, the verdict that the admired things are "ridiculous"; it transforms the activity of judgment into a figurative placeholder for the political consciousness necessary to overcome the gap between the speaker and the events spoken about. This doesn't mean it explains or resolves the gap but simply that it points us toward it. In other words, this gap between speaker and event demands redress by a collective agent. Boone's poem prepares us to align ourselves with that agent.

With this second sincerity in mind, we can see how political consciousness takes shape in this stanza. It is embedded within two overlapping formations: global war in the twentieth century, in its mechanized, systematized, in short, capitalist form, and the social form of the nuclear family. Each of these, in turn, corresponds to a specific kind of revolutionary agency: the historical avant-gardes and gay identity, respectively. In the first two lines, we hear a distant allusion to the avant-gardist enthusiasm for machines and technology in the link between admiration and fixed capital (that is, machines and technology). Importantly, Boone does not affirm the avant-gardes; he merely conjures them in the service of thinking about revolutionary possibility, which does not automatically translate into anti-capitalism. Whence the simile here, with "war" as the vehicle that describes gasoline's "cleanliness." This brings to mind the Italian Futurists: a fascist avant-garde who celebrated war as a means for cleansing or purifying the world. The figuration here sounds a cautionary note; it reminds us that we are dealing with revolutionary *consciousness*—the orientation and intention of a subject toward the social totality—rather than with a revolutionary *subject*, separated out from its object and considered in itself.[24] Thus Boone invites us to be suspicious of figuration—and to doubt the capacity of any representation to render the entirety of what it depicts.

Next, we turn from global capitalist warfare and its radical opponents to "another part of" the speaker, located in the nuclear family. Here Boone relates a condensed history of the emergence of gay identity during the transition from petty, family-centered production to industrial capitalism. John D'Emilio has described this process as a lengthy "transition away from the household family-based economy to a fully capitalist free labor economy," in the course of which masses of laborers were "freed" from the land (and therefore from their means of subsistence) and forced to migrate from the countryside to urban centers, where they were "freed" to sell their labor-power on the market as a commodity.[25] This resulted in the simultaneous immiseration of these laborers and their collective organization in factories and cities.[26] As D'Emilio argues, these circumstances facilitated the emergence of gay identity: "As wage labor spread and production became socialized, it became possible to release sexuality from the 'imperative' to procreate," and thus to make sexuality the locus and quilting point of an entire identity. This resulted in the ad hoc constitution of a "gay subculture" that was "rudimentary, unstable, and difficult to find" up into the 1930s, but which "grew and stabilized" in the decades following World War II—until, of course, the Stonewall riots in 1969 catalyzed the formation of a gay counterculture, embodied by the Gay Liberation Front and other revolutionary queer organizations.[27]

In this light, the image of artisanal, handicraft labor—"the grandfather / who made chocolates"—locates us in a precapitalist mode of production and consumption: our speaker "pluck[s]" the very "bonbons" his grandfather makes. But the activity of making things with one's hands quickly becomes a series of trivial cultural games linked to aesthetic judgment; Boone shifts labor toward a more specifically capitalist ideology of the beautiful, which the speaker indulges more fully with his admiration. The activity that goes along with this admiration—you *choose* "anything ridiculous . . . to admire"—seems to move consumption outside of the family and into the capitalist world market. Boone's line, then, condenses, albeit elliptically, the relative autonomization of social reproduction from the family form that attended the full-scale emergence of capitalism in the nineteenth century: the process that made gay identity possible in the first place.

Thus Boone superimposes two modes of production—precapitalist petty production and capitalism—and two forms of revolutionary agency—the historical avant-gardes and gay identity. He invites us not only to "notice" the agency embedded in his figures of judgment but to compare these different historical conjunctures with one another. Somewhat paradoxically, then, historical thinking in "Karate Flower" develops through the nonlinear calculus of parataxis: the arrangement of details, events, and other particulars without respect to any narrative sequence or chronology. Boone periodizes rather than narrates. This is how I would interpret the placement of the assassination of Archduke Ferdinand after the convocation of the avant-gardes—which emerged during and after the world war that the archduke's assassination allegedly caused—in this stanza. The scrambling makes a kind of militant sense. It tells us: first think of the present, "then" about the lead-up to World War I. The "then" becomes an "and"; the poem invites us to parse this adjacency in terms of the continuities and breaks between the historical periods it juxtaposes. One key similarity immediately jumps out: both World War I and the Vietnam War created the conditions for broad-based antiwar movements that sought to underscore the relationship between war and capitalism, clearing the way for revolutionary organizations to emerge. We can also note an important difference: the apparent absence, in the early 1970s, of a corollary formation to the historical avant-gardes from the first part of the century.

This brings us to an important contradiction in Boone's speculations about agency: that between the end of the historical avant-garde and the persistence of their utopian wager beyond that ending. On the one hand, Boone consistently presents the avant-gardes as historical; their interventions took place in the past, and their polemics belong to that past, and cannot simply be revived in this new period of struggle. This is why all the references to the avant-garde throughout "Karate Flower" are indexed to prior moments of crisis and revolution. On the other hand, Boone aligns himself with the historical avant-gardes and adopts their basic aspiration as his own: to transform the lifeworld by inserting the work of art into it (to borrow Peter Bürger's formulation). "Karate Flower" essentially affirms both the end of the avant-garde and their continuing relevance in this new period of capitalist crisis and revolutionary struggle. This is why the avant-garde's absence is only "apparent" in "Karate Flower," and why poetic form here feels so closely linked to questions of political form, via the activity of organization we've been discussing. Boone attempts to imagine an oppositional cultural front that could actually accomplish the insertion of art into life by making poetry (and other forms of artistic production) useful for militants.

Workers and Queers of the World, Unite!

These speculations on revolutionary agency continue throughout the rest of "Karate Flower." A little more than halfway through the poem, Boone returns to the figure of the family we've been discussing from the first stanza. He doubles back in order to revise its presentation of "the grandfather / who made chocolates." This earlier figure, Boone notes, contains "a misconstruction" that obscures the relation of his grandfather to capitalist property relations. He presents us with a different image of the same basic material, one that situates the family form fully within the processes of capitalist production, where it serves as a fulcrum for the hereditary transfer of wealth from one capitalist to another. The following lines come in the wake of an extended metaphor comparing the 1927 film *Metropolis* to the biography of Vladimir Lenin, with which Boone reminds us that Lenin, like Freder, the film's protagonist, became a revolutionary by betraying his class: by turning away from his immediate interests as the child of wealthy petty bourgeois functionaries.[28] Of particular note here are the "caresses" that lead Boone to love the factory despite its "unsuccessful theft," which elliptically recall the historical link between gay identity and industrial capitalism. This time around, Boone more explicitly encodes a solidaristic link between labor militancy and queer militancy:

> It was grandfather,
> we were told, who made the chocolates. A
> misconstruction—for a German-Swiss arrived
> in Milwaukee that day. It was simple enough.
> The people made the money, and the people made the
> chocolate. It was the German-Swiss who kept
> the money, it was the German-Swiss who ate
> the chocolates.
> . . .
> What is the point,
> if you do not understand that we have no parents
> and we have no country, we have only Russia
> to go back to. The money was in vain.
> And the guilt had no purpose. I have known
> this personally as I have known that the factory
> in Milwaukee was an unsuccessful theft and
> loved it still for its caresses, like a
> can of yellow plums on a dusty shelf.[29]

These lines do not tell us what about the previous passage was inaccurate. They simply offer an alternative construction for us to compare to the first one. In order to make this comparison, we have to hold both the misconstruction and its replacement in our minds simultaneously: we have to superimpose the two moments in the poem onto one another, in the same way that Boone superimposed two historical conjunctures onto one another in the opening stanza. When we do this, we discover that the first stanza doesn't address the question of who owns the means of producing the bonbons our speaker plucked and admired. On the other hand, this later stanza doesn't tell us whether Boone's grandfather is the laborer who makes the chocolates, or if he is one of the capitalists who exploits those laborers. Nor do I think it particularly matters. I'd say Boone adds a new question to his figuration of the family, one about political commitment.

He invites us to side explicitly with labor over capital, with comrades over the family. This, in turn, suggests that the "misconstruction" he laments was an oversight rather than a mistake—an omission of the matter of conscious alignment rather than some inaccuracy in the depiction of the family the first time around.

The lines about lacking parents and country underscore this. The reference is to the famous declaration in *The Communist Manifesto*: "the working men have no country." To this Boone adds a queer palimpsest: *and queers have no nation and no family.*[30] He indexes this proposition to the Russian Revolution, suggesting that proletarians and homosexuals both share a need for revolutionary transformation on the basis that neither group has any "home" within the social totality of capitalism. Queer and labor militants share a common cause: the negation of capitalism. On the other hand, Russia *is* a nation. And the Stalinist deformation of the transition to communism notoriously cloaked itself in the name of Lenin, however disingenuously. We have to take up this constellation of references with great care, as we did with the avant-gardes in the first stanza. By juxtaposing an allusion to Marx with the state capitalism of the Soviet Union, Boone once again invites his readers to compare and contrast disparate elements. He trusts that we will do so in good faith, delinking the fate of the October Revolution from the revolutionary possibility that the names of Marx and Lenin (and even Russia) continue to signify. The question that introduces these lines ("What is the point, if you do not understand") emplaces us in the midst of a flurry of debates about socialism, communism, and national liberation that raged among comrades in various Gay Liberation organizations.

"Karate Flower" continues to develop this combined queer/labor militant perspective on the Russian Revolution and the politics of internationalism for its last few pages. Space prevents me from offering a granular account of these pages or indulging a fuller discussion of Boone's invocations of Lenin and the theory of political consciousness in *What Is to Be Done?* But we have already seen something of the latter book's influence on "Karate Flower." Indeed, the formal arc of this poem is classically Leninist. For one thing, Boone consistently discovers radical agency in the points of contact between different struggles, such as labor and queer militancies. These points of contact become visible during periods of protracted historical unrest, like the one inaugurated by the long downturn in the late 1960s. Finally, transitions within capitalism—that is, crises—always present the opportunity for a different kind of transition: one out of capitalism altogether. Boone uses parataxis to formalize this kind of historical consciousness in a way that invites us to "notice" it, and to align ourselves with it on the page—and presumably in the streets, too.

Conclusion

In this essay I have offered an account of New Narrative's emergence that focuses on its ties to the revolutionary movements of the early 1970s, rather than its encounter with Language poetry at the end of that decade. In doing so, I have tried to show that we can see New Narrative writing in a new light if we begin from the question of its political commitments. Gay Liberation motivated Boone, Robert Glück, and Steve Abbott to come together under the banner of New Narrative. Which doesn't mean that Gay Liberation and only Gay Liberation is the basis for all of New Narrative writing. Rather, I hope the reading I've done here can serve as a model for studying the interactions of New Narrativists with other strains of New Left politics; this in turn might help correct some of the asymmetries that attend the current critical conversation about New Narrative. For instance, the criminally undervisited work of the feminist and labor organizer F. S. Rosa cries out for a reading in light of labor's "rebellion from below" between 1965 and 1981, which she superimposes onto the gentrification of San Francisco in the 1980s (and later onto Israel's settler-colonial occupation of Palestine) in a similar way that we saw Boone superimpose two historical transitions onto one another in "Karate Flower." We can also, perhaps, "notice" new things about Language poetry. Does Ron Silliman's work as a tenant organizer bear any relation to his dizzying mathematical formalism? How does Steve Benson register some of the limits of Gay Liberation's approach to sexuality and anticipate a more porous, anarchic conception of desire like the one that is familiar to us from queer theory? Finally and most importantly, we can start to think about how the resurgent interest in New Narrative has been a response to the 2008 fiscal crisis: an attempt to periodize the present by juxtaposing it with the moment of the long downturn. We can shed new light on the contributions of New Narrative's fellow travelers, like Renee Gladman, as well as on writing done by younger poets like Marie Buck, Diana Hamilton, Shiv Kotecha, and Ted Rees—to name just a few of the newer writers who align themselves with New Narrative.

Ultimately, when we revise our assumptions about New Narrative, we begin to see the primacy of place that poetry occupies in the movement's attempts to construct an oppositional culture. And we begin to see the continued relevance—not to say urgency—of imagining an alternative to the baleful strictures of capitalism. This alternative is communism, which, as Boone writes elsewhere, means nothing but "a human future in love."[31]

Notes

1. Alberto Toscano helpfully characterizes transition as a program of "attack and expansion" as against the "subtraction and interruption" of insurrectionary ultra-leftism. Alberto Toscano, "Logistics and Opposition," *Mute* 3, no. 2 (2011): https://www.metamute.org/editorial/articles/logistics-and-opposition.

2. For an overview of theories of revolutionary agency, as well as a contribution to debates surrounding this concept, see Mike Davis, *Old Gods, New Enigmas* (New York: Verso, 2018).

3. Kaplan Harris, "New Narrative and the Making of Language Poetry," *American Literature* 84, no. 4 (2009): 805–832. See also Kaplan Harris, "The Small Press Traffic School of Dissimulation: New Narrative, New Sentence, New Left," *jacket2*, 2011, https://jacket2.org/article/small-press-traffic-school-dissimulation, which focuses on the curious interstitial figure of Steve Benson.

4. Rob Halpern, "Realism and Utopia: Sex, Writing, and Activism in New Narrative," *Journal of Narrative Theory* 41, no. 1 (2011): 82–104. Elsewhere, in a dazzling critique of Fredric Jameson's "Postmodernism" essay, Halpern argues that New Narrative's omission from the critical record has made it possible to downplay the significance of Language poetry's critical interventions. Rob Halpern, "Recovering 'China,' " *Jacket* 39, 2009, http://jacketmagazine.com/39/perelman-halpern.shtml.

5. See Theodor Adorno, Walter Benjamin, Ernst Bloch, Bertolt Brecht, and Georg Lukács, *Aesthetics and Politics* (New York: Verso, 1979); Peter Bürger, *Theory of the Avant-Garde*, trans. Michael Shaw (Minneapolis: University of Minnesota Press, 1984). See also the debates about this work in the pages of the journal *October*.

6. Chicago Gay Liberation, "Working Paper for the Revolutionary People's Convention," in *Out of the Closets: Voices of Gay Liberation*, ed. Karla Jay and Allen Young (New York: New York University Press, 1992), 346–351.

7. The bibliography of historical work on the Stonewall uprising—its pre-history, its proximate causes, and its far-reaching effects—is too vast to recapitulate here. A very accessible account of this history (and thorough bibliography for further reading) can be found in Martin Duberman, *Stonewall* (New York: Dutton, 1993). See also George Chauncey, *Gay New York: Gender, Urban Culture, and the Making of the Gay Male World, 1890–1940* (New York: Basic Books, 1995).

8. Third World Gay Revolution, "What We Want, What We Believe," in *Out of the Closets*, 363.

9. Third World Gay Revolution, "What We Want, What We Believe," 366. The authors go on to state that they believe that "the only true army for oppressed

people is the people's army, and Third World, gay people, and women should have full participation in the People's Revolutionary Army." As we'll see, this proposition sounds a conceptual rhyme with the way that Boone takes up antiwar politics in the opening stanza of "Karate Flower."

10. See Alysia Abbott, *Fairyland: A Memoir of My Father* (New York: W. W. Norton, 2014), as well as the editorial introduction to Steve Abbott, *Beautiful Aliens: A Steve Abbott Reader*, ed. Jamie Townsend (Callicoon, NY: Nightboat, 2019).

11. For Boone, see *Dismembered: A Bruce Boone Reader*, ed. Rob Halpern (Callicoon, NY: Nightboat, 2020); for Glück, see Robert Glück, "Earlier Selves, Strangers: A Conversation with Robert Glück," interview by Eric Sneathen, *Open Space*, June 21, 2018, https://openspace.sfmoma.org/2018/06/earlier-selves-strangers-a-conversation-with-robert-gluck/. For a timeline of all the different Gay Liberation organizations, see Emily Hobson, *Lavender and Red: Liberation and Solidarity in the Gay and Lesbian Left* (Berkeley: University of California Press, 2016).

12. Hoddypoll is the same press that would go on to publish Boone's canonical New Narrative work, *Century of Clouds*, in 1980. For more on Mitchell, Hoddypoll, *Sebastian Quill*, and early New Narrative, see Mitchell's introduction to the recent edited volume of poetry, *Gay Sunrise*, ed. James Mitchell (San Francisco: Ithuriel's Spear, 2018).

13. For the "long downturn," see Robert Brenner, *The Economics of Global Turbulence* (New York: Verso, 2006). Brenner dates the onset of the long downturn to the mid-1960s; however, he is in agreement with the various accounts that focus on 1973 as the year in which the crisis matriculated from latent to manifest—the year when it became a *global* crisis.

14. Rob Halpern, introduction to *Dismembered*, v.

15. The two best treatments of parataxis in radical poetics are Kristin Ross, *The Emergence of Social Space: Rimbaud and the Paris Commune* (New York: Verso, 1988); and Ruth Jennison, *The Zukofsky Era: Margins, Modernity, Avant-Gardes* (Baltimore: Johns Hopkins University Press, 2012). Ross sees parataxis as an instance of a (pre) figurative "militancy" in Rimbaud's poetry; Jennison treats it as a literary formalization of a "radical agency" that prepares the reader's revolutionary consciousness.

16. Bruce Boone, "Gay Language as a Political Praxis: The Poems of Frank O'Hara," *Social Text* 1 (1979): 59–92.

17. Boone, "Gay Language as a Political Praxis," 84.

18. John D'Emilio, "Capitalism and Gay Identity," in *Making Trouble: Essays on Gay History, Politics, and the University* (New York: Routledge, 1992), 11.

19. Boone, "Gay Language as a Political Praxis," 84.

20. Boone, "Gay Language as a Political Praxis," 86.

21. For more on this jargon of authenticity, see the brilliant analysis in Timothy Yu, *Race and the Avant-Garde: Experimental and Asian American Poetry Since 1965* (Stanford, CA: Stanford University Press, 2009).

22. Emily Hobson, *Lavender and Red*, 75.

23. Bruce Boone, *Karate Flower* (San Francisco: Hoddypoll Press, 1973), n.p. In what follows I assume that Boone himself is the speaker of "Karate Flower," just as Boone and many other critics assume that O'Hara is the speaker of his poems. Although it's not the main focus of my reading, I think that this assumption is part and parcel of the overall hypothesis of oppositional language—and a key anticipation of New Narrative proper's signature interrogations of autobiographical writing that will begin in earnest later in the 1970s.

24. For more on how this distinction—between consciousness as intention versus consciousness as an a priori attribute of the subject—fits into a broader theory of revolutionary consciousness, see Georg Lukács, *History and Class Consciousness: Studies in Marxist Dialectics*, trans. Rodney Livingstone (Cambridge, MA: MIT Press, 1971).

25. John D'Emilio, "Capitalism and Gay Identity," 6–7.

26. The double "freeing" here is a reference to Marx's ironic account of the "freeing" of labor in the chapter about "so-called primitive accumulation" in the first volume of *Capital*: see Karl Marx, *Capital*, vol. 1, trans. Ben Fowkes (New York: Penguin, 1976), 873–876.

27. John D'Emilio, "Capitalism and Gay Identity," 7.

28. This is not to say that Freder and Lenin are identical. Freder's father is not, as Lenin's was, a petty bourgeois functionary; he is a fully bourgeois factory owner. This raises an interesting question about Boone's aesthetic theorization of "class" in "Karate Flower." In a larger version of the present essay, I go into this matter in some detail. For now, suffice it to note that, in keeping with the formal strategy of superimposing disparate elements paratactically I've been discussing, Boone overlays Lenin and aesthetic modernism. Furthermore, he casts modernism as both the culture of bourgeois revolution and a utopian fellow traveler of the proletarian revolutions of the twentieth century. He thus invites speculation about the relationship between revolutions and aesthetic forms.

29. Boone, "Karate Flower."

30. Karl Marx and Friedrich Engels, *Manifesto of the Communist Party*, in Karl Marx, *The Revolutions of 1848*, ed. David Fernbach (New York: Penguin, 1973), 84.

31. Bruce Boone, *My Walk with Bob* (San Francisco: Ithuriel's Spear, 2005).

Afterword

On Theresa Hak Kyung Cha's Untitled

Jean-Thomas Tremblay

Theresa Hak Kyung Cha's *Untitled* (1980) is a tiny, mixed-media sculpture: about four inches long, four inches wide, and four inches tall.[1] The sculpture's core component is a clear, carafe-shaped glass jar. A lid, also made of glass, covers the jar's narrow opening, letting through only a black string. One end of the string dangles outside. The other, located inside, holds together, though precariously, five rectangular pieces of paper, suspended obliquely. Each of the pieces features a different typewritten French word: *eau* (water), *feu* (fire), *terre* (earth), *ether* (ether), and *air* (air). The piece of paper displaying the term *air* is concealed by the other four. As a whole, the sculpture approximates a conceptual vivarium, one that trades actual dirt, water, plants, and animals for labels of the classical elements. *Untitled* also resembles an artisanal bomb, the black string standing in for a wick that, if lit up, might cause the device to detonate.

We close *Avant-Gardes in Crisis: Art and Politics in the Long 1970s* just as we opened it: in Cha's company. In this collection's introduction, Andrew Strombeck and I linked Cha's politically inflected avant-garde innovations to the downtown New York scene, where writers as well as visual and performance artists lured by cheap rents congregated en masse during and after the fiscal crisis, therefore enabling cross-media contamination. Whereas in the introduction we brought up Cha's best-known work, *Dictee*, in this afterword I ponder the seldom-discussed *Untitled*. The sculpture, I propose, encapsulates—quite literally, as it is a capsule—our collection's argument.

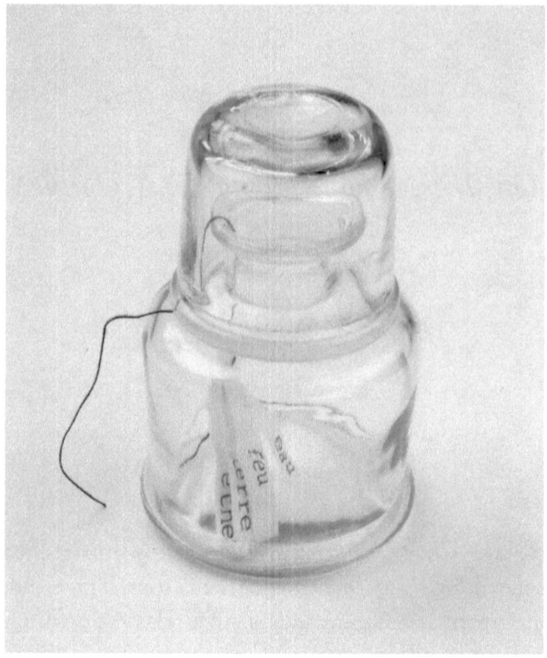

Figure A.1. Theresa Hak Kyung Cha's *Untitled* (Glass Jar), 1980. Gift of the Theresa Hak Kyung Cha Memorial Foundation, 1992.4.31. Courtesy of the University of California, Berkeley Art Museum and Pacific Film Archive.

Avant-Gardes in Crisis has sought to contest a pair of *idées reçues* on the origins and legacies of the avant-garde that have circulated throughout the long 1970s. The first orthodoxy concerns the influence that Peter Bürger's *Theory of the Avant-Garde* has exerted on the reception of the avant-garde. By reducing all that has come after the "historical avant-gardes" of the early twentieth century to "neo-avant-gardes" that repeat a set of formal gestures now detached from their revolutionary contexts, Bürger, as one anonymous reader of this collection judiciously notes, implies that "history stopped being historical a hundred years ago." The second orthodoxy comes from a literary historical project, promoted by a limited but loud cadre of scholars and writers, that boils the avant-garde down to poetic experimentalisms somehow exempt from considerations of identity, especially racial identity. In this scheme, the only history mediated by the avant-garde is a history of forms; the role of today's avant-garde is to carry modernism's legacy by actualizing its techniques.

These dominant views of the avant-garde, we have attempted to show, are united by their shortcomings. Because they are calibrated for the figure of the white male artist, these theories do not register the economic and political tumult of the long 1970s—the effects of which have been especially detrimental to marginalized populations—for what it is: a significant historical crisis marked by increased avant-garde activity. We have contended that a radical *and* minoritarian concept of the avant-garde clarifies the political vernaculars that have arisen through artistic engagements with the unevenly distributed effects of an intensifying crisis in the reproduction of life.

Cha's life and work provide a logical vantage point from which to introduce and summarize a minoritarian avant-garde. Her writing is in no way confined to the codes of modernist experimentation (*Dictee*'s genre is *Dictee*), and her engagement with the historical avant-gardes' visual conventions (such as the readymade) is critical, perhaps even parodic. And yet, no word other than *avant-garde* encompasses her corpus's originality and medial diversity. All on its own, Cha's art calls on us to revisit and renew the avant-garde as a vital descriptor for the innovations of marginalized artists. It is in an effort to be accountable to figures like Cha that we, the artisans of this collection, have set out to retool the avant-garde concept into a heuristic for, rather than an excuse to look away from, experiences of oppression, domination, and inequality.

It is thus no coincidence that, in a collection that sees the 1970s as pivotal to the avant-gardes, I feel an impulse to return to Cha. In a sense, Cha herself is stuck in the 1970s, having been tragically killed shortly after the end of that decade, in 1982. More to the point, Cha reminds us that *we* remain stuck in the 1970s: most radical interventions in the late twentieth and early twenty-first centuries may be seen as attempts to counter the transformations precipitated by the seventies. Across her oeuvre, and perhaps especially in *Untitled*, Cha emerges as an oracle of sorts: a figure who apprehended increased precarization, even if she would not live to see the 1970s get longer and longer.

Cha made *Untitled* the year she moved to New York. There, she worked as an editor for Reese Williams's Tanam Press, which published *Dictee*. Although there is a distinctly "downtown New York" character to *Dictee*'s dazzling amalgam of media (concrete poetry, mythology, collage, photography, and countless others), it is in the San Francisco Bay Area, where she spent most of the 1970s, that Cha familiarized herself with the artistic and intellectual practices she would progressively combine. Cha studied at the University of California, Berkeley from 1969 to 1978, earning no less than four degrees: a BA in comparative literature, a BA in art, and both an MA and an MFA in art. Cha's art, which experiments with translation, mistranslation, and untranslatability, remarkably synthesizes her multidisciplinary training. Cha's decade at Berkeley coincided with the student protests against the United States' involvement in the Vietnam War. And antiwar activism concurred with student-led efforts to amplify minority voices in the school's curriculum. At Berkeley, Cha witnessed the founding of such departments as Ethnic Studies and Women's Studies (now Gender and Women's Studies)—and her own work would go on to achieve canonical status in these departments' corresponding disciplines. In the Bay Area, Cha was surrounded by artists experimenting with performance and video. "In this explosive and heady atmosphere," Constance M. Lewallen sums up, "everything was up for grabs; experimentation was the norm."[2] The explosiveness of Berkeley's activist and artistic cultures is captured by *Untitled*, a Duchampian readymade that looks as though it were about to blow up. If the readymade solidified concerns about mechanization and overproduction during the Second Industrial Revolution, *Untitled* testifies to the acceleration of such processes in the postindustrial age.

The slips of paper labeled *eau*, *feu*, *terre*, *ether*, and *air* in *Untitled* are indicative of Cha's broader reflection on the elemental in the late 1970s. In her 1978 MFA thesis, a short, unpublished document titled "Paths," Cha notes that the Alchemist manipulates commonplace elements with care and precision. In doing so, the Alchemist "enters a covenant with these elements."[3] Instead of transforming them forcibly, the Alchemist lets them "transform his soul."[4] Much like the Alchemist, Cha muses, the artist enters a covenant with her materials. Judiciously employing a medium enables the artist to shift perception, both her own and her audience's. Art, for Cha, demands a surrendering to the elements or materials on the part of artists and spectators. The result, she promises, exceeds the sum of its parts.

I discern in Cha's elemental covenant the signs of an ecological sensibility. Cha's alchemical practice supposes both a material frugality and a withholding of interventions threatening to damage a milieu beyond repair. *Untitled* figures its historical present as a crisis of resources, specifically of energy. As Cara New Daggett recounts, it is in the 1970s, in the context of major oil crises, those gridlocks in the supply of fossil fuel to the Western economy, that energy became consolidated as an object of politics. Energy's emergence "as a political rationality that justifies extractivist and imperial capitalism" hence offers one metric by which to periodize the long 1970s.[5] Economic constructions of energy crises both trigger and conceal a more momentous disaster, namely, climate catastrophe. In *Untitled*, the notion of energy crisis is untethered from the domain of international economic conflicts, where it is used to legitimize petrocapitalism. Cha responds to climate crisis by performing a kind of energy management. For one, her sculpture registers an exhaustion with site-specific monumentalism. Like her contemporary Ana Mendieta, Cha sidestepped the concrete and tar pours of much of the site-specific art of the late 1960s and early 1970s, which transformed not only landscapes but entire ecosystems.[6] Viewed through Strombeck, Jennifer Wild, Matt Tierney, and Shannon Finck's contributions to the present collection, *Untitled* downsizes the infrastructures of avant-garde production. This "minor" sculpture has a negligible environmental footprint. The piece only minimally alters its materials. Glass production already involves sand, fire, and air, and paper trees and water; Cha refrains from generating additional waste. *Untitled* both conserves energy and is *about* conservation. The glass guards the elements, fragile as paper.

Yet, by seeking to protect the elements, *Untitled* also entraps them. The sculpture constitutes, in the idiom of this collection's first section, an enclosure of the elemental commons. Although the sculpture lessens waste, the very way it produces meaning hinges on the imperial logics of environmental violence. The global project of extraction reproduces itself in part by converting resources into symbols.[7] By abstracting the earth into elemental symbols and inscribing them on tiny labels, *Untitled* announces its complicity with a certain minimization, in both senses of the term, of planetary destruction. *Untitled* evokes human beings' power to shape the earth and indeed to destroy it, the sculpture's bomb-like silhouette reminding us that, in the atomic age, the planet is always on the verge of blowing up.

Untitled cultivates what ecocritics call a "sense of the planet" or "planetary consciousness"—that is, a recognition of the (imperiled) interconnection and interdependence of humankind and the earth.[8] Likewise, Cha's "Perte Loss" (1979), a general outline for an unfinished video project, hints at planetary consciousness by tracking the massive repercussions of seemingly trivial gestures. We would be forgiven for mistaking the outline for a poem—and I shall read it as such. The following excerpt is taken from the document's last third:

Change breath sequence to begin when the past is going to
  become present—
change wind it begins to move also. the wind begins to
  move—alchemical process
North
East
West
South

Fingers tied with string pulled out
Changes breath
changes wind.[9]

In "Perte Loss," Cha recycles the language of alchemy to posit the coevalness of breath and wind. Changes to the former change the latter. The white space included in the first two lines gives us room to take a breath, or attune ourselves to the wind. As we do so, we perform the perceptual adjustment that Cha describes, in her MFA thesis, as an outcome of the artist's elemental covenant. In the script, breath and wind lead us to coordinates. Not only does breath flow northward, eastward, westward, and southward, but breathing's phenomenology is *itself* orienting—a compass. Whereas "Perte Loss" moves from the tiny to the planetary, *Untitled* synthesizes the interplay between these scales: the sculpture is a pint-size microcosm of the earth. *Untitled* brings to mind what Wild, in her chapter, calls a "living figure" of history. While the palm tree, in Marcel Broodthaers's installation work, activates a dialectical struggle against the museum as a colonial institution, Cha's elemental enclosure recapitulates a history of environmental destruction driven by imperialism and colonialism. But Cha's elemental rolodex isn't exactly a *living* figure; it is a record of figures on life support. The sculpture conveys a certain morbidity, as if planetary history were only to be told in the past tense, or with no verbs at all, just reified elements.

The elemental phase I identify in Cha's oeuvre—a phase that coincides with accelerated resource concentration and depletion in the 1970s—does not signal a turn away from, or even a momentary bracketing of, her examination of Korean American identity. *Untitled* resembles, in size and color(lessness), *Surplus Novel*, another piece created by Cha in 1980.[10] *Surplus Novel* consists of two small bowls gifted by Cha's sister and brother. The bowls contain strips of paper similar to the ones spelling out the five classical elements in *Untitled*. Here, the typewritten text amounts to a Beatles-esque song that Cha wrote to recount her experience of walking down the street and being hailed as "Yoko." The two sculptures' simultaneous creation as well as their formal and material similarities—their smallness; their assemblage of paper strips, typewritten text, and everyday kitchen objects—suggest a thematic dialogue. Arranged differently, Cha's cautionary tale about a planet in danger becomes a commentary on everyday experiences of sexism and racism, and vice versa. Even on its own, *Untitled* asserts the imbrication of environmental violence and identity-based structures of domination. *Untitled*, like *Dictee*, draws on Cha's Catholic high school training in French, Greek, and Roman classics. With an irony not unlike the irreverent comedy of *Surplus Novel*, Cha lists the classical elements in French, employing the idioms of Western assimilation to critique a planetary destruction orchestrated through imperialism and colonialism.

Untitled marks the emergence of an *aesthetics of commitment* proper to the contemporary crisis in the reproduction of life. This aesthetics, whose genealogies this collection has begun to trace in the long 1970s, refuses to disentangle a critique of resource concentration and attrition from a critique of attendant systems of domination. It is an aesthetics that invests its political energies into scenes of exhaustion. An aesthetics that searches for total revolution in the small, the fragile, and the minor.

Notes

1. Theresa Hak Kyung Cha, *Untitled*, mixed media, 1980, University of California, Berkeley Art Museum and Pacific Film Archive, in *The Dream of an Audience: Theresa Hak Kyung Cha (1951–1982)*, ed. Constance M. Lewallen (Berkeley: University of California Press, 2001), 103.

2. Constance M. Lewallen, introduction, "Theresa Hak Kyung Cha—Her Time and Place," to *Dream of an Audience*, 1.

3. Theresa Hak Kyung Cha, "Paths," 1978, University of California, Berkeley Art Museum and Pacific Film Archive, from the Online Archive of California, https://oac.cdlib.org/ark:/13030/tf296n989f/?order=2&brand=oac4.

4. Cha, "Paths."

5. Cara New Daggett, *The Birth of Energy: Fossil Fuels, Thermodynamics, and the Politics of Work* (Durham, NC: Duke University Press, 2019), 4–5.

6. See Miwon Kwon, *One Place After Another: Site-Specific Art and Locational Identity* (Cambridge, MA: MIT Press, 2002); Christine Redfern, *Who Is Ana Mendieta?* (New York: Feminist Press, 2011), 30.

7. See Macarena Gómez-Barris, *The Extractive Zone: Social Ecologies and Decolonial Perspectives* (Durham, NC: Duke University Press, 2017), 5. Thanks to Michael Dango for conversations on this topic.

8. See Ursula K. Heise, *Sense of Place and Sense of Planet: The Environmental Imagination of the Global* (New York: Oxford University Press, 2008); Timothy Clark, *Ecocriticism on the Edge: The Anthropocene as a Threshold Concept* (New York: Bloomsbury Academic, 2015), 9–10.

9. Theresa Hak Kyung Cha, "Perte Loss," 1979, University of California, Berkeley Art Museum and Pacific Film Archive, from the Online Archive of California, https://oac.cdlib.org/ark:/13030/tf38700290/?brand=oac4.

10. Theresa Hak Kyung Cha, *Surplus Novel*, mixed media, 1980, University of California, Berkeley Art Museum and Pacific Film Archive, in *Dream of an Audience*, 101.

Contributors

Sarah Dowling is the author of *Translingual Poetics: Writing Personhood under Settler Colonialism* (2018) and numerous articles on twentieth- and twenty-first-century poetry. In addition, Sarah is the author three books of poetry, *Security Posture* (2009), *Down* (2014), and *Entering Sappho* (2020). Sarah teaches in the Centre for Comparative Literature and Victoria College at the University of Toronto.

Shannon Finck is a lecturer in the Department of English and Philosophy at the University of West Georgia. She earned her PhD in transatlantic modernism with a secondary emphasis in global postmodern and contemporary literatures from Georgia State University. She also holds an MFA in narrative poetry and nonfiction. Her critical and creative work appears in such journals as *ASAP/J*, *Angelaki*, *Miranda*, *a/b: Autobiography Studies*, *LIT: Literature Interpretation Theory*, *Journal of Modern Literature*, *Lammergeier*, and *Fugue*. Currently, she serves as poetry editor for the independent literary journal *Birdcoat Quarterly*. She is working on a book titled *Thin Skin: Autotheory and Resilience.*

RL Goldberg is a graduate student in English, gender, and sexuality studies, and the Interdisciplinary Doctoral Program in the Humanities at Princeton University. Their work has appeared in *TSQ: Transgender Studies Quarterly*. They are a Bain-Swiggett Fellow with Princeton's Prison Teaching Initiative.

Priscilla Layne is an associate professor of German at the University of North Carolina at Chapel Hill. She received her PhD from the University of California at Berkeley in 2011. Her book, *White Rebels in Black: German*

Appropriation of African American Culture, was published in April 2018 by the University of Michigan Press. Her publications address topics like rebellion in postwar Germany, German hip hop and punk, and German appropriation of Black popular culture. She is currently working on her second book project, *Out of This World: Afro-German Afrofuturism.*

Javier Padilla is an assistant professor of English at Colgate University. His current research project, *Poetics of the Instant*, analyzes the aesthetic, cultural, and sociopolitical role of poetry in times of decolonization, liberation, and exclusion. His articles and translations have appeared in *Capilano Review*, *Literary Imagination*, *Revista Iberoamericana*, *Journal of Modern Literature*, and *Cuadernos Hispanoamericanos.*

David W. Pritchard is a PhD candidate at UMass Amherst. He is currently writing a dissertation on New Narrative, Gay Liberation, and revolutionary poetics. Recent critical writings may be found in *Historical Materialism* and *Mediations.* He is also a poet whose chapbooks, poems, and prose about poetry can be found in, or are forthcoming from, such outlets as *The Tiny*, *Blush Lit*, *jacket2*, and Damask Press.

Samia Rahimtoola is an assistant professor of English at Bowdoin College. Her research focuses on twentieth- and twenty-first-century American literature, particularly where it intersects with critical/queer/decolonial environmentalisms. Her critical writing has appeared in the anthology *Ecopoetics: Essays in the Field* (2018) and *ISLE: Interdisciplinary Studies in Literature and Environment.*

Andrew Strombeck is an associate professor of English at Wright State University. He is the author of *DIY on the Lower East Side: Books, Buildings, and Art after the 1975 Fiscal Crisis* (2020). His scholarship on twentieth- and twenty-first-century art and literature has appeared in journals such as *Post45*, *Los Angeles Review of Books*, *The Millions*, *Contemporary Literature*, *Modern Fiction Studies*, *African American Review*, and *Cultural Critique.*

Matt Tierney is an assistant professor of English at Pennsylvania State University in University Park. He is the author of two books: *What Lies Between: Void Aesthetics and Postwar Post-Politics* (2015) and *Dismantlings: Words against Machines in the American Long Seventies* (2019).

Jean-Thomas Tremblay is an assistant professor of English at New Mexico State University. Their scholarship in literary and cultural studies, gender and sexuality studies, and the environmental humanities has appeared in such journals as *differences*, *Modernism/modernity*, *Criticism*, *Discourse*, *Post45*, and *Women and Performance* as well as in many public venues, including the *Los Angeles Review of Books*, *Full Stop*, and *Public Books*. They have edited a special issue of *New Review of Film and Television Studies* titled "Breath: Image and Sound" and are completing *Breathing Aesthetics*, a monograph on creative responses to the contemporary crisis in breathing.

Jennifer Wild is an associate professor in the Departments of Cinema and Media Studies, and Romance Languages and Literatures at the University of Chicago. Her first book, *The Parisian Avant-Garde in the Age of Cinema* (2015), was shortlisted for the Best Moving Image Book Award by the Kraszna-Krausz Foundation and received Honorary Mention for the Wylie Prize in French Cultural Studies. Having published widely on the European historical avant-gardes and early cinema, she is currently completing a book manuscript about the politics of the image in nineteenth- and twentieth-century French social, cinematic, and artistic history.

Index

www.ingramcontent.com/pod-product-compliance
Lightning Source LLC
LaVergne TN
LVHW050150080826
844660LV00002B/150

* 9 7 8 1 4 3 8 4 8 5 1 5 7 *